MORE PRAISE FOR *A PLACE OUTSIDE THE LAW*
by Peter Jan Honigsberg

"As presented convincingly by the author, the misconduct by the US government is so egregious that readers with a moral compass could fairly conclude that many individuals have been wrongly incarcerated. A well-documented, hard-hitting, necessary exposé."

—*Kirkus Reviews*, starred review

"*A Place Outside the Law* makes an indispensable contribution to accountability for the multiple transgressions of the rule of law that the United States has committed—and continues to commit—in the Global War on Terror. From ignoring the presumption of innocence, to outrageous behavior against defense lawyers, from disappearance and prolonged arbitrary detention to physical and psychological torture, this shameful page of US history still demands truth and justice. Peter Jan Honigsberg's book adds human voices and touching stories to show us why we need to insist on the US government's obligation to investigate, reveal the truth, and prosecute and punish the perpetrators, especially those bearing the greatest responsibility for these crimes. This book brings us closer to that inevitable hour of reckoning."

—JUAN MENDEZ, former United Nations
Special Rapporteur on Torture

"Many Americans have forgotten the horrors of Guantánamo, perhaps unaware that the prison still operates today. Honigsberg interviews not only detainees but generals, interrogators, JAGS, chaplains, and guards. Their compelling, human stories paint a rich and complex picture of a deeply controversial chapter in America's history."

—JENNIFER M. GRANHOLM,
former governor of Michigan

"*A Place Outside the Law* documents a dark time in America's history and serves as an important reminder that the Constitution cannot be set aside for reasons of expediency. Ultimately, if America is to be an example and a force for good in the world, we must recognize that GITMO was a mistake and should never be repeated."

—MAJOR GENERAL MIKE LEHNERT, USMC (ret.),
former Joint Task Force Guantánamo commander

"This is the definitive account of what happened at Guantánamo in all of its chilling and horrifying detail. What makes this book unique and compelling is that it is the story of what it does to people's lives to create 'a place outside the law.' Through his countless interviews, Professor Honigsberg describes the impact of Guantánamo on those who have been part of it: soldiers, medical personnel, lawyers, interrogators, torturers, detainees. It is the story of what happens when a country abandons the rule of law."

—ERWIN CHEMERINSKY, dean and Jesse H.
Choper Distinguished Professor of Law,
University of California, Berkeley, School of Law

"Guantánamo Bay is the symbol for lawlessness, injustice, and an ill-conceived 'war on terror.' In 2006, we, as UN experts, urged its closure. Ten years later, forty Muslim men still remain there. Peter Jan Honigsberg reminds us, on the basis of 158 interviews with former detainees and staff, that Guantánamo Bay shall not be forgotten."

—MANFRED NOWAK, professor of human
rights in Vienna and former UN
Special Rapporteur on Torture

A PLACE OUTSIDE THE LAW

A
PLACE
OUTSIDE
THE LAW

FORGOTTEN VOICES FROM
GUANTÁNAMO

PETER JAN HONIGSBERG

BEACON PRESS
BOSTON

BEACON PRESS
Boston, Massachusetts
www.beacon.org

Beacon Press books
are published under the auspices of
the Unitarian Universalist Association of Congregations.

22 21 20 19   8 7 6 5 4 3 2 1

This book is printed on acid-free paper that meets the uncoated paper
ANSI/NISO specifications for permanence as revised in 1992.

Text design and composition by Kim Arney

Soldiers taking detainee to Camp X-Ray/Soldier observes detainee processing: Shane T.
McCoy; Matt Diaz photo: © Matthew Diaz; Rushan Abbas photo: © Rushan Abbas; Yvonne
Bradley photo: © Yvonne R. Bradley; Mourad Benchellali photo: © Mourad Benchellali;
Carol Rosenberg photo: © Carol Rosenberg; Peter Jan Honigsberg photo: © Witness to
Guantánamo, LLC, and Johnny Symons; Clive Stafford Smith, Brandon Neely, Darrel
Vandeveld, Gitanjali Gutierrez, Jennifer Bryson, Adil Hakimjan, Khalid al-Odah, Maha
Habib, and Alberto Mora photos: © Witness to Guantánamo, LLC

Library of Congress Cataloging in Publication Control Number: 2019019266

For my wife, Mary Louise,
and Christopher, Liam, Colleen,
and their families

History, despite its wrenching pain,
cannot be unlived, but, if faced with courage,
need not be lived again.

—MAYA ANGELOU

There's a literary form I haven't mentioned yet: the literature of witness. Offred [in *The Handmaid's Tale*] records her story as best she can; then she hides it, trusting that it may be discovered later, by someone who is free to understand it and share it. This is an act of hope: Every recorded story implies a future reader.

—MARGARET ATWOOD

CONTENTS

AUTHOR'S NOTE

Nearly all of the quotes in this book are from interviews filmed by Witness to Guantánamo, an organization I founded in 2008 to collect and preserve the personal stories unfolding at Guantánamo Bay Naval Base. I conducted all the interviews between 2009 and 2019. Consequently, where I write that someone said or told "us," I am referring to myself and the Witness to Guantánamo crew present at the interview. The people in this book gave us consent to use their interviews in this work. The interviewing process is explained in Appendix II. The full-length interviews are held in perpetuity at the Duke University Human Rights Archive in Durham, North Carolina. Duke intends to publish online nearly all of the 158 interviews we filmed across twenty countries. Duke also intends to publish transcripts of the interviews. The stories we heard need to be told, and preserved for history.

WHEN THE PLANES HIT

On the morning of September 11, 2001, between the hours of 7:30 and 8 a.m., nineteen men carrying metal box cutters boarded four airliners. Two of the flights were leaving from Boston; a third was from Newark; and the fourth from Dulles International in Washington, DC. Earlier that morning, most of the men cleared the walk-through metal detectors and the X-ray machines that scanned carry-on items to identify weapons. In the instances where some of the men set off the alarms on the metal detectors, those men were scanned with handheld wands. They passed through. A few men had their bags checked for explosives and also passed through.

Three of the four planes were headed for Los Angeles (LAX): American Flight 11 and United Flight 175 from Boston, and American Flight 77 from Washington, DC. United Flight 93 from Newark was bound for San Francisco (SFO). Five men boarded each plane to LAX. Only four men boarded the flight to SFO. Most of the men had purchased tickets in the front rows of the planes, either in first class or business class. A few sat in coach. One man on each plane had been trained as a pilot. The others were the "muscle" men.

The man intended to be the fifth on United 93 from Newark to San Francisco, Mohammed al-Qahtani, had flown into Orlando, Florida, from Dubai in early August. He was refused entry into the US and put on a plane back to Dubai. The nineteen men who boarded the planes, and al-Qahtani, who would have been the twentieth hijacker, were part of the al Qaeda terrorist organization from the Middle East. Sixteen of the men, including al-Qahtani, were from Saudi Arabia.

As each plane reached cruising altitude, the terrorists charged into the cockpits, killing the pilots and copilots. The pilot hijackers then took over the controls.

The terrorist pilot on American 11 turned the aircraft away from its designated flight path and aimed for the northern façade of the North Tower of the World Trade Center in lower Manhattan. The Twin Towers of the World Trade Center were once the tallest buildings in the world, standing over 1,300 feet. The plane hit floors ninety-three to ninety-seven of the North Tower at 8:46 a.m. Initially, the media reported that a small plane had accidentally flown into the tower.

While television news broadcast the aftermath of the incident, the terrorist piloting United 175 from the south flew the plane into floors seventy-five to eighty-five of the South Tower at 9:03 a.m. People watching the newscasts witnessed the second strike as it occurred. The video of that second strike played over and over again throughout the day, and it is available on the internet to this day.

After the second strike, it was apparent that the US was under attack. At 9:37 a.m. the third plane, American 77, flew into the western side of the Pentagon, the headquarters for the Department of Defense. This massive five-sided structure is the largest office building in the world, employing more than twenty thousand people. It is located in Arlington County, Virginia, across the Potomac River from Washington, DC.

After the suicide hijackers took control of the cockpit of United 93 bound for San Francisco, passengers learned through cell-phone conversations with friends and family members on the ground about the attacks. Several passengers decided to organize to retake control of the plane. They coordinated a plan. At 9:57 a.m., a telephone operator heard a passenger say, "Let's roll."[1]

The passenger assault began. The passengers rushed forward to try to break into the cockpit. The terrorists screamed at each other to hold back the door against the passenger siege. A passenger yelled, "Let's get them!" There is more screaming.

With the intent of keeping the passengers off balance, the hijacker pilot rolled the plane to the left and right and also pitched the nose up and down. However, his actions did not deter the passengers from continuing to try to storm the cockpit.

The passengers must have been close to succeeding, according to cell-phone conversations between passengers and crew in the air and family and friends on the ground, and to the cockpit recorder. Realizing that the passengers were seconds away from overpowering the terrorists, the pilot turned the control wheel hard and aimed the plane downward. As the plane fell to earth, one of the hijackers was heard shouting, "Allah is the greatest! Allah is the greatest!" United 93 crashed into an empty field in Shanksville, Pennsylvania, at 10:03 a.m. It was likely headed for the US Capitol or the White House.

It was a perfect fall morning in New York City before the planes hit. The sky was a vibrant blue, with no clouds overhead. After the planes hit, the blue sky parted. Clouds of toxic smoke alternating in shades of black, white, and gray, merging with orange-gray ash, swallowed up the air. The heat of the implosion was intense—too intense for those who had survived the strikes at the towers' impact floors or above. People leaped out the tower windows to certain death to escape the unbearable heat. Those living in nearby buildings saw the bodies fall. Television viewers were not certain what they saw at first. But then they knew.

People below the impact floors rushed down the stairs to escape the burning buildings, and the toxic ash. First responders arrived to assist them. At 9:59, the South Tower buckled and collapsed. Twenty-nine minutes later, at 10:28, the North Tower buckled and collapsed.

Countless stories of rescues emerged that day and in the days that followed. Nevertheless, the heroic first responders suffered numerous casualties, as they repeatedly ran into the buildings to rescue people and dug through the burning rubble looking for anyone who was still alive. Fortunately, all but approximately one hundred people who worked below the impact zones in both buildings escaped before the towers collapsed. Twenty-five thousand people made it to safety from the towers and surrounding buildings that day.

People ran from the blasts and the dust, soot, and smoke. As the massive towers collapsed, large pieces of debris hurtled into nearby buildings.

People nearby ran out of their apartments and down the stairs, knowing not to take elevators in emergencies.

The sky turned dark again as each tower collapsed, and the thick orange-gray haze grew thicker. People could barely breathe. They covered their mouths against the fine white dust from the incinerated building materials and from the other debris and substances swirling about. The dust and ash settled in their throats. Some people knew where to run. Others walked in a daze. Millions of bits of paper were flying in the air and settling at their feet. People rushed to retrieve their children from daycare centers. They hugged their children. They called home. They shared cell phones or found pay phones that were free that day. They heard the screaming sirens behind them. As they ran, they turned their eyes from fallen body parts. A man from a restaurant covered fallen bodies with white cloths.

Doormen invited people into lobbies for shelter from the strange dust and soot. Apartment dwellers opened their doors, offering food, drink, and bathrooms. A school bus stopped for people to board. The bus headed to the harbor. A tugboat carried people to Brooklyn. A ferry carried children to New Jersey. People walked across the Brooklyn Bridge. They fled uptown. Those with vehicles hurried out of town, hoping to leave before the bridges and tunnels were closed down. People mourned, and grieved. They ran to help where they were needed. They dug in search of survivors. They bonded.

As the days passed, a burning smell remained in the air. Faces of missing persons appeared on subway walls and buildings and in parks, particularly around Union Square. People developed "fireman's cough." On May 30, 2002, the cleanup of Ground Zero officially concluded. Years later, the city offered free medical checkups. As time passed, many first responders and others who were present that fateful day died of cancer. Three firefighters died of cancer on the same day in 2014.[2] There is a famous photo of a well-dressed woman, who had worked at the World Trade Center, enveloped in orange-gray ash. The photo of the "Dust Lady" circulated around the world. She died of cancer in 2015.[3]

A total of more than 3,300 people died on September 11: 2,600 people died at the World Trade Center. Another 125 died at the Pentagon. 256 people died on the four airplanes. 412 first responders lost their lives that day. The continental US had never been attacked with such ferocity before. America was caught completely unprepared. Until then, most US officials and military personnel had been trained for a "cold war" with Russia.

President George W. Bush was visiting an elementary school in Florida that morning. He was informed of the second plane crash at 9:06. Soon after, he boarded Air Force One. The aircraft crisscrossed much of the United States for the next eight hours, stopping at air force bases in Louisiana and Nebraska. After he had boarded, he spoke to Vice President Dick Cheney about shooting down terrorist-piloted planes that might still be in the air. But it was too late. The damage had been done. The president's plane was escorted by three F-16 fighter jets, and did not return to Washington until 6:42 that evening, when it was believed to be safe.

Vice President Cheney was in the White House when the attacks occurred. He was taken to an underground bunker conference room. Secretary of Defense Donald Rumsfeld was in his office in the Pentagon but was not injured.

Many people in the US watched the news all day as the aftermath unfolded, terrified of another attack. Perhaps a biological or chemical attack would be next. No one knew what to expect. Emotions were raw. Many people, especially in major metropolitan areas, were frightened that another attack was imminent in their communities.

People living in California imagined and awaited an assault on the West Coast. The iconic Golden Gate Bridge seemed particularly vulnerable. Employees evacuated the US Bank Tower in Los Angeles, at the time the tallest building west of the Mississippi. Disneyland closed that day.

In Chicago, employees rushed out of the 110-story Sears Tower—now known as the Willis Tower—which was in competition with the World Trade Center as the tallest building. Banks, office buildings, and exchanges around the nation emptied out and closed so that employees could be with their families.

American flags were soon seen flying from windows and porches throughout the nation. American flag stickers appeared on cars. Communities held candlelight vigils and moments of silence. Radio stations played patriotic music. Sports teams canceled events. The Broadway theater district in New York City went dark. People in other cities, who had loved ones and friends working in the towers or living nearby, tried to call.

Air travel was shut down throughout the US for two days. Those who were left stranded by the shutdown tried to rent cars to drive to their destinations. Rental car companies ran out of vehicles. People who could afford the costs went to dealerships and purchased cars.

Around the nation, schools differed on policies. Some closed, others remained open. Teachers turned on the school televisions and held assemblies. Other teachers held classes as if nothing had occurred. Officials instructed their students to stay indoors. At one school, a teacher asked her students to pray. Another teacher asked students to sing patriotic songs. Parents picked up their children early, or kept them home.

Colleges shut down classes that day. In Austin, University of Texas students worried that the university was vulnerable to an attack because Jenna Bush, the president's daughter, was living on campus.

Parents of young students reacted differently. Some explained the events to their children. Others waited until their children became older or asked questions. Still other parents never discussed the attacks with their children. Today there are young people in America who do not know about September 11, 2001. Their parents did not talk about it, and 9/11 was never introduced into their classroom courses.

Nations around the world, including those hostile to the US, such as Cuba, Russia, and Iran, condemned the attacks. Foreign leaders expressed sympathy and solidarity with the US, pledging cooperation. In Germany, two hundred thousand people marched in solidarity with the US. *Le Monde* in France ran a front-page headline: "We Are All Americans." Cuba offered medical assistance.

People who were living in the United States when the planes struck remember exactly where they were at those moments. Our lives would never be the same. It was a defining moment. A friend suggested: Don't bother saving the newspaper recording the events of September 11. Save the paper that recorded the events of September 10—to remember the day before the world changed forever.

Two weeks after 9/11, an FBI special agent named Ali Soufan determined that the terrorist organization al Qaeda was behind the attack.[4] Osama bin Laden was a founder and leader of al Qaeda. He was living in the Tora Bora cave complex in the White Mountains in Afghanistan and was given refuge and support by the Taliban, the Sunni Muslim-controlling government in Afghanistan. The leader of the Taliban, Mullah Mohammad Omar, refused to assist the US in capturing bin Laden. The Taliban controlled most of the country, where it was engaged in a war with the Northern Alliance, a loose band of Afghan, Uzbek, and Tajik fighters that controlled the northeastern corner.

After US airspace reopened on September 13, planes carrying members of the bin Laden family and other Saudi nationals hurriedly departed the US. The American media reported that many Saudi family members feared for their lives after hearing reports of violence against Muslims and Arab Americans.[5] The 9/11 Commission Report said that Saudi nationals were screened and checked against various databases before they were allowed to depart, and that "no one with known links to terrorism departed on these flights."[6] In addition, the report noted that when members of the bin Laden family were interviewed, "none of the passengers stated that they had any recent contact with Usama bin Laden or knew anything about terrorist activity."

In the aftermath of September 11, the US government feared that other attacks were likely. In response, and as a demonstration to the world that the US would defend itself from further attacks, the Bush administration adopted a firm and determined stand. Five days after 9/11, on a Sunday morning talk show, Vice President Cheney told the world that to find the people responsible for the attack, we would "have to work sort of the dark side."[7] The message: we mean business; do not mess with us.

The FBI initiated a program known as PENTTBOM (Pentagon/Twin Towers bombings) immediately after the attacks. Bureau agents seized and investigated people in the US illegally who had "been identified as persons who participate in, or lend support to, terrorist activities."[8] Nearly all the men were of either Muslim or Middle Eastern descent. An estimated 1,500 to 2,000 people were detained, mostly on minor immigration violations. They were held without charges—until cleared or deported—in detention centers around the country.[9] The men spent an average of eighty days in lockup, while denied their due process rights to a hearing.[10]

On September 17, President Bush issued a secret directive authorizing the CIA to detain suspected terrorists, as identified by CIA personnel, in facilities outside the US. The practice became known as "extraordinary rendition." In executing the directive, CIA operatives would kidnap terrorist suspects, cut their clothes off with knives, fit them in diapers and orange jumpsuits, and tranquilize them. The suspected terrorists were transported to foreign prisons and CIA "black sites," prisons that were directly controlled by the CIA. Once the suspects were disappeared into those locations, they were brutally tortured.

The same day, President Bush visited the Islamic Center of Washington, DC. In embracing Muslims as an essential part of the American fabric, he said that the face of terror is not the true face of Islam and that Islam is peace. He talked about the "incredibly valuable contributions" Muslims have made to the country. He wanted Americans to know that the people who intimidated Muslims did not represent the best of America. Rather, they represented the "worst of humankind, and they should be ashamed of that kind of behavior."[11]

Anecdotally, there were countless stories of brown people, Muslims, people of South Asian descent, and people of Middle Eastern descent who were harassed in public venues and on streets throughout the country.

On September 18, President Bush signed the Authorization for Use of Military Force (AUMF), which gave the military the authority to attack the Taliban and al Qaeda network in Afghanistan. The Northern Alliance became a US ally. Beginning in October, American bombs rained on Afghanistan.

The AUMF also gave the administration authorization to detain captives. The US dropped millions of leaflets over Afghanistan, including its border with Pakistan, offering cash bounties for alleged al Qaeda and Taliban fighters.

On November 13, 2001, President Bush issued an executive order creating military commissions (also known as military tribunals) to charge and try captured alleged al Qaeda and Taliban fighters. Military commissions are creatures of exigency, used in times of war when civil courts or military courts-martial are not available or not easily accessible because of military operations. America was positioning itself for war, a "war on terror."

General Tommy Franks was commander of the US Central Command overseeing US military operations, including ground troops, in Afghanistan and Pakistan. He did not think he could manage the more than one thousand captives in his area of operations. Consequently, the Bush administration created a team of officials from various agencies to identify another location to house them. After reviewing options, the interagency working group settled on the Guantánamo Bay Naval Base on the island of Cuba, five hundred miles from Miami.

The administration liked the idea. The naval base was outside American territory, yet under American control. American officials believed that American law would not apply there, and thus the captives could not challenge their detentions in federal court. Guantánamo was a place outside the law.

On January 11, 2002, the first twenty captives arrived at Guantánamo, after a grueling eighteen-hour flight from Afghanistan. There is a military photo of the men in orange jumpsuits, shackled and kneeling outside their open-air wire cages in Camp X-Ray, the first camp in which they were held. People described the cages as similar to those of a dog kennel. The photo was our graphic message to the world: this is where you will be if you dare to attack the United States.

The administration described those captured and taken to Guantánamo as "the worst of the worst."[12] The captives were depicted as extremists, fanatics, and suicide bombers. We were told that the men were determined to chew their way through the thick hydraulic cables of the C-30 that carried them to Guantánamo, and bring down the plane.

The suspected mastermind of the 9/11 attacks, Khalid Sheikh Mohammed, was captured in March 2003 in Rawalpindi, Pakistan, and transferred among several CIA black sites around the globe.[13] He suffered 183 simulated drownings, known as waterboarding, as well as head bashings and intense isolation, and other dark cruelties. KSM, as he is also known, was transferred to Guantánamo with thirteen other "high-value" detainees in 2006. Mohammed al-Qahtani, the would-be twentieth hijacker, is also held there. A total of 780 men were held in the detention center at its peak. There were no women prisoners. All the men in Guantánamo were Muslim.

Bin Laden and his entourage initially escaped through the mountainous Tora Bora region into Pakistan. In May 2011, with the authorization of President Barack Obama, US Navy SEAL Team 6 found and killed bin Laden in Abbottabad, Pakistan.

— — —

According to J. Wells Dixon, attorney for the Center for Constitutional Rights, by the time President Bush left office in January 2009, there were 539 fewer men at Guantánamo (of those, five people had committed suicide or had otherwise died in the prison). In the next administration, President Barack Obama announced on his second day in office that he would close Guantánamo. Many people actually think that he had closed the prison, because he said he would. But President Obama did not close Guantánamo. However, he reduced the number by two hundred men (four men died, some by suicide) before he left office in January 2017. Forty-one men were still being held when Donald Trump became president, in January 2017.

As of August 2019, forty men remain in Guantánamo. One detainee has been transferred to Saudi Arabia under a plea agreement made by the Obama administration. Twenty-six of the forty men are considered "forever prisoners."[14] They cannot be tried because the evidence against them is either insufficient or unreliable—having been obtained through torture. However, these men are also considered too dangerous to be released. They are likely to die in Guantánamo, never charged, never tried, and never convicted.

Of the fourteen who are not designated forever prisoners, seven men are being tried in military commissions. Preliminary proceedings have been ongoing for these men for more than a dozen years. There is no assurance these seven suspects will ever have a trial.

Five other men were cleared for release during Obama's tenure, but were not released before he left office. President Trump shows no interest in releasing them.

Two men have been convicted. One is serving his sentence, the other is waiting to be sentenced.

Of the 740 men once held at Guantánamo but now free, nearly all were never charged with a crime. Nevertheless, many spent a decade or longer suffering physical and psychological torture in the prison. Although it is sometimes difficult to distinguish psychological torture from physical torture, psychological torture includes such sufferings as prolonged sleep deprivation, hot and cold temperature manipulation, and long-term isolation. The detainees told us that psychological torture was more common at the prison than physical torture.

Guantánamo, situated on a forty-five-mile spit of land on the southeastern coast of Cuba, has become more than a detention center for alleged terrorists, in reaction to the attacks on September 11, 2001. It is more than a naval base housing nearly ten thousand soldiers and personnel, complete with McDonald's, Pizza Hut, KFC, Subway, Starbucks, Jamaican jerk chicken, a movie theater, and Navy Exchange, or NEX, shops. Guantánamo is a metaphor for much that has gone wrong after 9/11.

A Place Outside the Law highlights the human side of Guantánamo. People who were held captive in the prison or who worked at the base saw their lives deeply transformed by the experience. I learned this firsthand in my role as founder of Witness to Guantánamo. Starting in the fall of 2008, I set out to film and document the stories and the voices of Guantánamo. The people we interviewed took important time out of their lives to sit down with us and tell their stories.

For a decade, my team and I filmed their stories. We were a small operation with a filmmaker, creative director/editor, fundraiser/media outreach person, producer, and me as director/interviewer. Everyone was part-time. We interviewed 158 people across twenty countries, recording more than three hundred hours of film. Fifty-two of the interviewees were former detainees. We also interviewed prison guards, interrogators, interpreters, chaplains, medical personnel, military and civilian lawyers representing the detainees, prosecutors, journalists, high-ranking military officials, high-ranking government officials, and family members of the detainees. No one else in the world has done this extensive work. Witness to Guantánamo gives the most comprehensive picture to date of life at Guantánamo.

Some of the people we interviewed were more forthcoming than others, revealing personal stories. Others focused on their experiences and lives in the prison, and kept their personal lives separate. All the voices and stories combined create a mosaic, a larger and more defined picture, and a better understanding of the place we know as Guantánamo. (Appendix II describes the origins of Witness to Guantánamo and discusses how we found people to interview and why they agreed to participate.)

Our films are the only records for many of the people we interviewed. That is, some interviewees only recorded their stories with us, and with no one else. Since we began this project, some of the people featured have died. There will come a time when these filmed stories will be the only ones we have of many of the people who were in Guantánamo. Their voices will speak to future generations. And their witness will remind future generations not to repeat what has happened there.

Hopefully, these stories will be shared with our friends, relatives, children and grandchildren. Perhaps they will share the stories with others.

These are the stories of people affected by America's response to that fateful day. They are the stories of the human toll when America strayed from honor.

A PLACE OUTSIDE THE LAW

In fall 2003, Tom Wilner was a high-powered Washington, DC, attorney working for a large firm. A spokesperson for twelve Kuwaitis who were held in Guantánamo asked Wilner to represent the men. Wilner agreed. He joined forces with a handful of other courageous attorneys who represented detainees when the public was still reeling from the events of 9/11. In those early days following the attacks, few attorneys were willing to stand up on behalf of the men in Guantánamo. The lawyers who did were branded "unpatriotic" and received hate mail and death threats. It was not until summer 2004—when Wilner and the handful of other attorneys won their case in the US Supreme Court—that many more lawyers agreed to represent the detainees. The case was *Rasul v. Bush*.[1]

The petitioners in *Rasul* argued that the detainees had the right to challenge their detentions in federal court, in what is known as a habeas corpus hearing. A habeas hearing is not about the innocence or guilt of the person being held. It is not a criminal proceeding. It is a civil proceeding and has a lower standard. A habeas petition asks that the court consider whether there is sufficient evidence to continue to hold the prisoner. This habeas right to challenge the government's continued detention of an individual goes back more than eight hundred years. It was established in England by the Magna Carta, or Great Charter, in 1215. The framers adopted the right to habeas corpus and incorporated it into the US Constitution in 1789.

Wilner and the other lawyers raised several arguments. One concerned Cuban iguanas. Wilner explained that iguanas are considered a gourmet delicacy in Cuba. But when Cuban iguanas crossed the border into the Guantánamo Bay Naval Base, American law protected them under the Endangered Species Act. In fact, someone who injured or killed a Cuban iguana in US territory could be fined thousands of dollars.

In contrast, Wilner pointed out, human beings held in the detention camp in Guantánamo were not protected under American or international law. He reasoned that if the Supreme Court did not grant review of his clients' cases, human beings at Guantánamo would have fewer safeguards than the Cuban iguana.

The Supreme Court agreed to review. A year later, in June 2004, much to the surprise of Bush administration officials, the Supreme Court ruled in favor of the detainees.

Although Wilner and the other attorneys thought that they had won and that the administration would now abide by the law, it was not to be. The administration pushed back by substituting administrative proceedings for federal court hearings and by adopting new legislation to block all habeas hearings.[2] The government intended to keep Guantánamo beyond the reach of the law.

Part I of this book provides stories and perspectives on how the law was brushed aside in Guantánamo. Military and civilian lawyers, detainees, an interpreter, a prison guard, and a reporter share their experiences in a place outside the law.

We begin with a brief overview of the men who were brought to Guantánamo.

CHAPTER 1

COMING TO AMERICA

After the attacks on September 11, 2001, America dropped leaflets over Afghanistan and its border with Pakistan offering bounties for "Taliban and al Qaeda fighters [to] rid Afghanistan of murderers and terrorists." One leaflet read "Get wealth and power beyond your dreams." Another said "This is enough money to take care of your family, your village, your tribe for the rest of your life—pay for livestock and doctors and school books and housing for all your people."[1]

Those kinds of rewards encouraged Afghan and Pakistani soldiers to pick up Arabs who were not from the local community, as well as tribal enemies, and sell them for bounty to the US. They were generally paid $3,000 to $5,000.[2] Feroz Ali Abbasi, a former detainee from the UK, told us that he believed the US paid $30,000 for him.

Indeed, Pakistanis and Afghans became rich selling people to the Americans. Emile Nakhleh, a CIA expert on political Islam, told us, "Frankly, had the United States not paid the Pakistanis for every guy they got, most of them would not have been [in Guantánamo]."

The kinds of men who were purchased and brought to Guantánamo varied. Before 9/11, the Taliban functioned as the government of Afghanistan. Many of the Taliban soldiers brought to Guantánamo had joined the Taliban army prior to 9/11, before the US and the Taliban had become enemies. Other Afghans in Guantánamo were farmers, shopkeepers, or tribal enemies—tribes living in Afghanistan and Pakistan had seized and sold members of enemy tribes to the US.[3]

Afghan and Pakistani soldiers also sold Arabs from other countries who were living in Afghanistan and Pakistan. The Arabs were in these two countries for any number of reasons. Some believed that they could find a job or other economic opportunity, begin a new life, and perhaps marry a local woman.[4]

Men arrived in Afghanistan and Pakistan to teach in Islamic schools, work for Islamic nongovernmental organizations (NGOs), or contribute other good deeds engaging in charity work. To many Muslims, the mission of a young man is to help others. Khalid al-Odah, the father of one of the Kuwaitis who was held in Guantánamo, explained his son's commitment to charitable work: "Fawzi, my son, is a good person. He wants to help the others. And since he was in high school he has, together with his friends, contribute some charity, money, and make a project for poor people outside Kuwait."

Al-Odah explained that the young men would give money to charities and identify the kinds of projects they would like to support. "It's a small project," al-Odah explained. "What they contribute every year does not exceed $2,000. But it gives them the opportunity to share with others and to help others." He explained that his son became a teacher after graduating from a university.

"And he has a long period in summertime which is a very long holiday. So, he wanted to continue doing charitable work and travel outside Kuwait. He did that in 2000. He went to Pakistan. He knows that there is a lot of Afghani refugees on the borders between Pakistan and Afghanistan."

A few of the men fled to Afghanistan because they were facing criminal charges, or they had been convicted and were awaiting sentencing in their home countries, or had been sentenced and wanted to leave after their sentences were completed. One man we interviewed had been tried and convicted in his home country for being a member of a gang that physically attacked women who did not fully cover themselves in public. He left for Afghanistan sometime after he had completed his sentence.

There were men who believed in the ideology of al Qaeda and wanted training in an al Qaeda camp. Al Qaeda was a militant Islamic organization headed by Osama bin Laden, initially based in Sudan. The militant group focused on eliminating what it considered corrupt Islamic governments. It declared a holy war against the US because of its large presence in the Islamic world. In 1996 bin Laden established al Qaeda's base in Afghanistan under the protection of the Taliban.

Some men may also have joined al Qaeda for economic reasons. The jobs al Qaeda provided, such as chauffeur or cook, were well paid for the region.

After they had been released from Guantánamo, four of the men we interviewed left their homelands to fight in Syria for the al Qaeda affiliate Jabhat al-Nusra. Three of these men were killed in Syria. If the US government had not obtained evidence against these four men in violation of the Constitution, the men could have been lawfully prosecuted and convicted. The men would then not have been able to return "to the battlefield" to do further damage.

Other men traveled to Afghanistan specifically *to* join the Taliban. The Taliban was not the same as al Qaeda. The Taliban was a religious faction that practiced a fundamentalist form of Islam. It emerged in Afghanistan after the Soviets pulled out in the mid-1990s. As the Taliban gained power and control over the nation, it imposed harsh rules that ruthlessly subjugated and oppressed women, excluding women from all forms of public life. In late 2001 the Taliban—which controlled nearly all of Afghanistan—refused to extradite bin Laden to the US after the 9/11 attacks.

Ayub Mohammed, a Sunni Muslim Uighur from China, came to Afghanistan when he was sixteen, on the first leg of a hoped-for journey to America.[5] He told us that he planned to make his way to Turkey and then emigrate into the US. Other Uighurs came to Afghanistan to learn the basics of armed combat that they could use against the Han Chinese when they returned home. (China has dominated East Turkistan, the home of the Uighurs, since the mid-twentieth century.)

Most, but not all, of the men in Guantánamo were captured in Afghanistan and Pakistan. They were first detained at airfields, either at Kandahar or Bagram, Afghanistan. They were then transported to Guantánamo. Some were brought to the prison from other countries.

Six Algerian men who had been living in Bosnia and had been charged with planning an attack on the US embassy in Sarajevo were seized by the American military after the charges were dropped. They were flown directly to Guantánamo. Two other men were captured in Gambia and taken to a CIA black site in Afghanistan known as the Dark

Prison. As the name implies, everything was pitch-black. They lived in total blackness for weeks, crawling, bumping into walls, trying to locate their food, and knocking over their "honey buckets," a euphemistic term for pails used to collect human waste, or slop buckets. From the Dark Prison, the men were delivered to Bagram and then to Guantánamo.

Fourteen men who were labeled "high-value" detainees and tortured at prisons in countries such as Syria, Jordan, Egypt, Morocco, and Thailand—under the CIA's extraordinary rendition program—or at CIA black sites in such places as Afghanistan and Lithuania—also under the CIA's extraordinary rendition program—were transferred to Guantánamo in 2006.

Secretary of Defense Donald Rumsfeld called the men in Guantánamo "the worst of the worst."[6] A 2006 study by Mark Denbeaux of Seton Hall University Law School concluded—based on America's own data—that US forces captured no more than 5 percent of Guantánamo detainees. In addition, only 8 percent of men captured were considered al Qaeda fighters. Fifty-five percent of the captives never committed any hostile act against the US.[7] They were not "on the battlefield."

The United States military had neither the skills nor the expertise to sort out the dangerous men from the harmless in those early days following 9/11. Consequently, the US was willing to purchase people, hold as many as it could, and sort them out later. America did not know many of the people it held in Guantánamo. Sometimes, military officers confused and misspelled the names of the men. And sometimes the men gave false identities.

The pressure on the military to deter another possible 9/11 attack was intense. Purchasing the men with bounties gave some comfort to members of the military, to the Bush administration, and to many people. The message was that America had captured the terrorists. The government and military were keeping us safe. The Bush administration capitalized on our fears and violated American principles and values by holding the captives in Guantánamo without charges for years.

When the administration chose Guantánamo, it believed it had found a place outside the law—a place under American control but where federal courts could not interfere.[8] However, Guantánamo was not an obvious choice from the start. Members of an interagency working group in fall 2001 considered and rejected a number of other locations.

The Pacific island of Guam, although isolated, was rejected because it was a US territory and had a federal courthouse. American bases in Europe were rejected because European Union countries were subject to the jurisdiction of the European Court of Human Rights. Non-European countries that were willing to house the detainees had substantial infrastructure issues and costs. Diego Garcia, an atoll south of the equator, was too far away from Washington, DC. Housing captives on ships at sea would not work. There were too many captives.

It was not until November when someone in the working group suggested the detention center at Guantánamo Bay, Cuba. It was offshore, but close to the mainland. The naval base had housed Cuban and Haitian refugees in the 1990s. An infrastructure was present, and the captives could be moved to the island immediately. By being close to the US mainland, Guantánamo was easily accessible to government and military officials. In addition, the prison was on an island thousands of miles away from the homes of the detainees. The group believed this would deter the detainees from any hope or thought of escape. Secretary of Defense Rumsfeld later publicly described Guantánamo as "the least-worst place we could have selected."[9]

Brad Berenson, associate counsel to President Bush, told us how senior-level appointees in the White House, Justice Department, State Department, and Defense Department were all convinced that the detainees would not have the right to challenge their detentions. He could not recall "a single lawyer involved in these debates at the time who believed either (a) that habeas corpus jurisdiction did extend to Guantánamo Bay or (b) that the courts would say that it did, whatever our personal beliefs about whether it did or did not work." Essentially, the administration was surprised by and unprepared for the Supreme Court's *Rasul* decision, which held that the detainees did have access to federal courts to challenge their detentions.

There is a long history to America's control of Guantánamo that goes back more than a century. The United States Navy entered Guantánamo Bay, Cuba, in 1898, during the Spanish-American War. We never left. In 1903, the US and Cuba entered into a lease guaranteeing that "the United States shall exercise jurisdiction and control over and within" forty-five square miles of land and water along the southeast coast of the island, housing the Guantánamo Bay Naval Base.[10] A treaty in 1934 affirmed Cuba's ultimate sovereignty over the territory, while confirming US control. The treaty required that both parties agree to the termination of the lease. Over the years, Cuba has sought to terminate the lease, and has refused to accept the annual lease payment of "two thousand dollars in gold coin." The US has rejected every effort by Cuba to terminate the contract.[11]

The detainees spent somewhere between a few weeks to several months in the makeshift detention centers at the Bagram and Kandahar airfields in Afghanistan before they were transported to Guantánamo. The first twenty men were flown to Guantánamo on January 11, 2002.

Nearly all arrived between 2002 and 2004. The fourteen "high-value" detainees, who had been held under the CIA's extraordinary rendition program, were transferred in 2006. The last man was sent to Guantánamo in March 2008, while President Bush was in office.

It took eighteen hours for planes to fly from Afghanistan to Guantánamo. Most stopped at the Incirlik Air Base in Turkey to refuel. When the planes arrived on the leeward side of Guantánamo, the men were taken to a bus that transported them to a utility boat. The boat ferried them across Guantánamo Bay to the windward side, where the detention center is. The windward side is also the heart of the base, where most of the activities occur.

The detainees gave variations of the same story. All were stripped of their clothes and dressed in orange jumpsuits. Their legs were shackled to the floors of planes, and their hands were shackled to their waists by belly chains. They wore mittens, woolen caps, earmuffs, or noise-blocking headphones, and blackened goggles. Sometimes they wore hoods.

Although some men were required to lie on the floors of planes, most were forced to sit upright on hard benches. They were not permitted to move or talk to others. The pain of sitting up straight for more than eighteen hours on the hard benches was unbearable. The lucky ones were given sedatives.

If a man needed to go to the bathroom, a guard unshackled him from the floor and walked him to the toilet. The male or female guard observed the man doing his business, while the detainee's arms remained shackled to his waist. On other flights, men were not allowed to leave their benches. They wore diapers.

When UK lawyer Gareth Peirce saw American government photos of the men shackled and chained on the cargo flights and dressed in orange jumpsuits, she thought "that the foolishness of the Americans to give pictorial depiction of what they were doing" would have an enduring impact. "And curiously, I think the rest of the world got it more than Americans," she added.

The men had little to eat on the flights. Those we interviewed seem to have been fed the same things: peanut butter sandwiches, an apple, and juice or water. Their hands were shackled to their waists and they could not raise their arms to their mouths. Sometimes an officer would bring a sandwich up to the mouth of the detainee. Some guards merely placed the sandwiches in the hands of the detainees, expecting the detainees to raise their hands to their mouths. That did not work, as former detainee Ruhal Ahmed of the UK explained.

Ahmed told us how a soldier lifted his earmuffs and told him that she was going to place a peanut butter sandwich in his hand so he could eat it. The smell of the peanut butter sandwich was "mouth-watering" to Ahmed. He was starving and savored the idea of eating the sandwich. But, he continued, "I'm looking down and I'm thinking, how am I supposed to eat that? And I'm there for maybe half an hour trying to eat it. I'm trying everything, going forward, trying to lift my arms up, and I'm thinking, damn, what things you have to do to eat food. So, I'm there and basically she came to my ear again and she lifted my muffs and then she goes, 'Don't you want to eat it?' I said, 'Well, how am I supposed to eat it?' She goes, 'What do you mean? Put your hands in your mouth.' And I thought, there's no point explaining.

"She took the sandwich, threw it in the bin, because everybody had the sandwiches and I think they threw everybody's in the bin, because nobody could eat it. Then they came again. They put an apple [in my hands] and I thought, how ridiculous, and how, like—you guys were just thick or stupid or something like that. And I just thought, damn, I'm missing out on my apple. I missed out on my peanut butter and now I'm missing out again. So then, they took the apple, threw that away and they gave me a glass of water, and I thought, are you having a laugh? Is it supposed to be funny? I could hear—sometimes [because if you move your shoulder, the earmuffs would move], so I could hear things. And they were saying, like, 'Oh, they hate it, no one's eating.' And I thought, you stupid idiots!"

Ruhal Ahmed was one of the Tipton Three—three men from the town of Tipton in the West Midlands of the UK who were captured and sent to Guantánamo. Shafiq Rasul, who became known as the lead petitioner in the Supreme Court case *Rasul v. Bush*, which granted detainees the right to challenge their decision, was another.[12]

Feroz Ali Abbasi was another UK citizen held in the prison. He was in the first group of twenty people who arrived in Guantánamo on January 11, 2002. Ali Abbasi and the other early arrivals were housed in Camp X-Ray—a patchwork of outdoor eight-by-eight wire-mesh cells. Each cell had a toilet hole and a bucket for water. Metal pipes for urinating were added later.[13] Although the cells were covered with corrugated metal, the men were exposed to the tropical sun and all outdoor elements. Three months later, the military constructed permanent indoor prison facilities known as Camp Delta, and relocated the prisoners there.

On the plane to Guantánamo from Afghanistan, Ali Abbasi thought he was coming to America. People had told him so. But upon landing, his first views of Guantánamo did not look like America. So he decided that he must have been taken to a place where he would be quarantined.

"I thought to myself, well, you know, like animals when they're being brought from abroad into a country, you have to put them in quarantine. My basic understanding, you have to keep them in a situation, where they get diseases or something like that. I thought to myself this must be quarantine. They're going to hold us here for a short period of time to work out whether we've got any diseases or something. And then we're going to be sent to America."

Abbasi was one of the most thoughtful, smart, and self-aware people we interviewed. He was always trying to make sense of each moment, as well as of the full event.

Uighur Ayub Mohammed was also housed in Camp X-Ray. He described to us his first impression when he was taken to one of the cages. There were two buckets in the cage, one with water and one empty.

"I thought [the cage] was a bathroom. We felt they brought us here first so we could use the toilet and then they'd transfer us somewhere else later. And then later, they didn't come, and then about an hour or two later the food came, and we ate the food."

But he wondered why he and the others were not moved to another cell. He whispered to the men around him, "Are they going to move us somewhere else or not? This is a toilet; how do we lie here?" When it became apparent that they were not going to be moved, he and the others noticed an iron bed, with two sheets and a towel. Ayub Mohammed recalled, "And we started our life there like this."

Brandon Neely was a twenty-one-year-old prison guard when the first planeload of twenty detainees arrived on January 11, 2002. The military had prepared him and the other guards to be afraid. The guards were told that these men were the "worst of the worst." Neely is a big person in physical stature. But in his mind the captives were giants, monsters perhaps. He could not imagine what he would see.

Members of the United States Marines had earlier escorted the first group of men off the plane and onto a bus that would take them to the prison. Prison guards were assigned to Camp X-Ray to escort the detainees off the bus. Neely and another soldier escorted the second detainee off the bus. Neely described the initial moments: "Plane landed and they came on the radio, five minutes out, and they came back on the radio, thirty seconds up. You can see bus coming and there is a Humvee in front of us with marines and a 50 Cal Mount and a Humvee in the back with the 50 Cal Mount. And the bus pulls into Camp X-Ray and you can hear the marines just yelling and screaming at detainees on the bus. Then the door opens and they started throwing detainees off. And I happen to be the second guy in line doing escort. They had the K-9 there too and the dogs barking. So, it was loud. It was chaotic. Before the bus ever pulled up, everybody was quiet. You could clearly hear a pin drop in the whole camp. Then when the bus pulled up, it was just loud. It was all chaos."

The first detainee who came off the bus was hobbling. He was missing a leg. The team of two guards grabbed him, one man holding each arm, and dragged him to the holding cage. Meanwhile, the marines on the bus threw the detainee's prosthetic leg after him, onto the ground.

Then the second detainee came off. He had two legs. As with all the detainees on the bus, he was still wearing his blindfold and earmuffs. Leg shackles and handcuffs were attached to his limbs. Neely and his partner took control of him. They yelled and screamed at him and forced him down on his knees.

Neely and his colleague lifted the detainee and escorted him to the holding area. They told him to sit, cross his legs, and put his head down. Then the two guards returned to the line and waited for the next detainee to come off the bus. The process continued until all the men departed the bus.

"I can remember one detainee just like sobbing, just crying. They put him in the holding cell and then we're telling him to shut up. But most of them—they're probably so tired from the plane they're just going with the flow," Neely added.

Later, the guards nicknamed the detainee with the prosthetic leg "Stumpy." It was not the only time that the guards ascribed names to the detainees. There was "Wild Bill" and "Half-Dead Bob." Another detainee, who had attempted suicide and was close to brain dead, was called "Timmy," after the disabled character in the animated television show *South Park*. A few detainees were assigned seemingly more respectable names, such as "Professor" and "General."

In our interviews, we heard many stories of how military personnel reacted to what they saw and experienced in the detention camp. One person, who will remain anonymous, told us of a guard who expressed his empathy with the detainees. The guard wished he could do something for the detainees. However, as the guard saw it, there was nothing he could do other than tell the detainees that there were people in the military who sympathized with their plight, hardship, and misery. The guard added that he was only a soldier and had to follow orders—or he would be in the cell next to the detainee.

CHAPTER 2

RIGHT SIDE OF THINGS

After the attacks on 9/11, Mohamedou Ould Slahi was seized by the Mauritanian secret police at his family's home. The police told the family that Slahi was in a safe place. The family presumed this meant that he was in a police station in Mauritania. But he was not. Slahi was in Guantánamo.

His family was fortunate. They learned of Slahi's fate through an article on Guantánamo in the German magazine *Der Spiegel*. Slahi's brother, who was living in Germany, had seen the article.

Other families were not as fortunate. Many families had heard nothing from their loved ones after the US bombing of Afghanistan following the 9/11 attacks. The families thought that their husbands, sons, and fathers had been killed in the bombings. But many of the men had not died. They had been captured by Afghan and Pakistani soldiers and sold for bounty to the Americans. Then they were disappeared into Guantánamo.

Because the US refused to release the names of its prisoners, many families did not know the fate of their loved ones. It was not until May 2006—more than four years after the first twenty detainees were transferred to Guantánamo in January 2002—that the US officially released the names of the detainees. And it is possible that the government would not have released the names even then were it not for US Navy staff attorney Lieutenant Commander Matt Diaz.

As a young man, Diaz was a high school dropout working as a full-time dishwasher, going nowhere. He and his girlfriend were living in a motel off a freeway in San Bernardino County, in Southern California. Three people—his father, the motel manager, and one of the cooks in the restaurant—were very concerned about him. Each of them individually encouraged Diaz to enlist in the military and find direction. He followed their advice.

Diaz took college courses while in the military. Later he pursued a law degree to become a judge advocate general officer in the navy. ("Judge advocate general," or JAG, is the term used for military attorneys.) He enrolled in JAG school and obtained an LLM, or master of laws, degree. While working toward the degree, Diaz took a semester of international law classes. When the opportunity arose to choose a foreign station, he decided on Guantánamo, rather than Afghanistan or Iraq. He began his work in Guantánamo in July 2004.

Diaz was working at his desk as deputy legal advisor at Guantánamo in early 2005 when he was copied on an email from a human rights attorney in New York. The attorney had requested that the government release the names of the men held in Guantánamo.

The Bush administration denied the request. Diaz was torn. He believed that all families should know whether their sons, husbands, and fathers were being held in Guantánamo. But he knew that the list was classified and could not be officially released.

There were other families besides Slahi's who had heard the news about their loved ones from various sources. Australian Maha Habib heard the news that her husband was alive through the media, specifically radio and television.

In the case of Kuwaiti detainee Fawzi al-Odah, his father, Khalid al-Odah, knew his son had been traveling with a friend in Afghanistan and Pakistan. The friend told Khalid al-Odah by phone that Pakistani military officials were holding Fawzi. Fortunately, the father knew the Kuwaiti minister of foreign affairs, who had connections with the US government. He revealed to the father that Fawzi had been transferred to the American military and was in Guantánamo. The friend was later seized and also transported to Guantánamo.

Families also heard about their loved ones from the men who were released from Guantánamo. The men provided human rights organizations with the names of people they had met in the prison. Sometimes the released men contacted detainees' families directly. In several countries, as in Kuwait, local government officials formally informed the families. However, other countries were not as quick or willing to reveal the whereabouts of the missing men. These countries, like Mauritania, told the families that they could not disclose or confirm anything about their loved ones.

There were some instances where the Red Cross delivered a postcard from the detainee to the family—provided the family had a permanent address and was not living in a country torn by war. Some families first heard the news through such postcards. However, it took anywhere from months to more than a year for the cards to reach recipients. And cards were heavily censored; on some postcards, nothing appeared but the word "Dear." In addition, the United States had a policy of keeping certain detainees hidden from the Red Cross.[1] Those detainees never sent cards.

It was with this background that Matt Diaz's story begins. He was working as a staff lawyer in Guantánamo when habeas attorney Barbara Olshansky sent the request for the names of all the detainees still in the prison. Olshansky was a lawyer for the Center for Constitutional Rights (CCR) in New York City.

The CCR was the first nonprofit organization to courageously take a stand for America and the rule of law after 9/11 by agreeing to represent the detainees. It was a huge step for the group, which knew that it could be labeled "unpatriotic" and possibly lose funding from supporters. But CCR's president, Michael Ratner, and its board believed that America's values and principles mattered most, especially in wartime. They decided to stand up for what is right, for the Constitution and due process. CCR and the handful of lawyers around the country who challenged Guantánamo policy in those early days after 9/11 received hate mail and death threats. Nevertheless, they persisted. CCR was the driving force behind *Rasul v. Bush* in early 2002.

In December 2004, Olshansky wrote an email to the Joint Task Force in Guantánamo and the Southern Command in Miami. SOUTHCOM is in charge of the southern region, which includes Central America, South America, and the Caribbean. She requested the names of all the detainees still held in Guantánamo. The recipients of her email were under the supervision of the Department of Defense (DOD). Diaz received a copy.

In the email, Olshansky asserted that in not revealing the names, the government was in violation of the Geneva Conventions. The United States and every nation in the world had signed the conventions. She also believed that the military was denying the men access to counsel, as required by *Rasul*.

The DOD denied her request. At the time, it did not provide a reason. A year later, when Diaz was tried in a military court-martial for releasing the classified names, a lawyer for the DOD testified that detainee policy was to not release names of people who were confined during wartime. (That detainee policy was in violation of the Geneva Conventions. However, in February 2002 President Bush had declared that the Geneva Conventions did not apply in Guantánamo.[2])

Diaz did not have the authority to make the decision to release the names. Moreover, arriving in July 2004 and being in Guantánamo for less than six months, he was still on a steep learning curve in understanding how everything worked. His tour of duty was to end in January 2005. (The government cycled most of its military personnel through every six months, and few people had a complete grasp of operations before they left the base.)

Consequently, after seeing that the DOD had denied Olshansky's request, Diaz believed that the government might never release the names. Diaz thought to himself, "I'm on the wrong side of things here."

"Knowing that we were not going to release the names, knowing who my relief was going to be, and just knowing the general atmosphere that we're operating in, there's no way these guys were ever going to be identified," he said. He asked himself whether there was something he could do. "I know you can't do it through proper channels because it's just top-down. There's no way this is going to be done properly," he said to us.

Diaz struggled with his conscience. He knew that there were many families still wondering what happened to their loved ones and whether they were still alive. Diaz believed that but for him, the families might never know.

"And, could I sleep or live with myself for the rest of my life knowing who knows how this would turn out? Would these guys have been un-identified forever, indefinitely as their detention is? So, I mean the only way that would really do it was to actually release the names."

Once he decided that the names had to be released, Diaz resolved to do it quickly, before he changed his mind. "I did it in a hurried manner. I guess that's how I left the prints on it."

He could not leave the island with the list. He and all his belongings would be searched. "So how could I do it without it being traced back to me?" he recalled asking himself. "I mean, because there's still a concern about, you know—I could be prosecuted. It could ruin my career."

In January 2005, on the night before he was to leave the base at the end of his six-month tour, he downloaded the list, minimized it, printed it, placed it in a greeting card, inserted the card inside an envelope, ad-dressed the envelope to Olshansky, sealed the envelope, carried it to the post office, and mailed it.

"It's hard sometimes to think of what I was thinking at the time, as I was going through it," he said. "But, once I threw it in there, then it's like there's no turning back. I mean it's in the mailbox now. And so then I returned to my quarters and got ready, because there was a farewell the last night there."

When Olshansky received the card, another lawyer in the office ad-vised her that it "was a trap." The colleague was afraid that if the envelope held classified information, the government would hold Olshansky, and possibly CCR itself, accountable.

Olshansky recalled that CCR president Ratner wanted to go "straight to the *New York Times*, like the Pentagon Papers," and offer the document to them. (The Pentagon Papers were highly classified DOD documents on the Vietnam War that were leaked to the press.) But because others in CCR were afraid that the letter Olshansky received could compromise CCR if the organization held the information, the lawyers decided to seek advice from outside counsel. Outside counsel told them that the document could be top-secret material and retaining it could "constitute treason."

In response, Olshansky suggested that CCR ask federal district court judge Colleen Kollar-Kotelly to hold the document—with the stipula-tion that if CCR won the right to the names, the judge would unseal the contents. The judge refused. However, she agreed to have the document held in the court security office in Crystal City while the case was being litigated. But the court security office would not consent. Instead, it informed Olshansky that federal agents would show up at her office the next morning at 6 a.m. to collect the document and all copies.

Olshansky told us how she was "really a klutz" after the phone call with the security office. "Coffee spilled all over the envelope. You couldn't really read the handwriting anymore," she said. The next morning, a "guy in a black trench coat" arrived to collect the document.

The investigation continued for a year, while the authorities sought to identify the person who sent the names. During that time, Olshansky went to southern Africa to work on human rights issues. When she arrived back home, naval police welcomed her. They took her into custody and brought her to the Norfolk naval base. They held her for nearly one month as a material witness. (A material witness is alleged to hold information material to a criminal proceeding and may be arrested.) Olshansky explained to the military authorities that she did not know who Matt Diaz was. They did not believe her.

Diaz was arrested and initially charged with improperly mailing classified information; conduct unbecoming an officer (for giving classified information to a person unauthorized to receive it); several counts under the Espionage Act, including the willful disclosure of national defense information with the intent to harm his country or advantage another nation; and several other counts, for releasing the information reasonably believing that it could harm his nation or advantage another country.

He could have received a sentence of thirty-six and a half years for the initial charges. The most serious charge, of intent to harm his country, was dropped. By the time he went to trial, the maximum sentence he could have received was twenty-four years.

At Diaz's court-martial, Barbara Olshansky testified that the Center for Constitutional Rights had filed a class action hearing challenging the detentions, and thereby already had the information in the list. She also asked and was permitted to present a "victim impact statement." She described Diaz as "being a hero of the most traditional American kind, like a true patriot who believed in the rule of law." It may have made a difference. The prosecutor asked for seven years imprisonment. The jury of military officials decided on six months of prison time.

I asked Diaz whether he had any regrets.

"Well, there are a lot of regrets that I have. Primarily, to my family, for putting them through that, and taking away a lot of stuff that they could have had that they can't have now because of what I had done. But also, on the professional side: the person that followed me, or others that follow in my position—I mean, they may not have that trust that the commanders are supposed to have in their lawyers. So yeah, it's a regret there, that I set them up for having that on them."

On the other hand, it was not a simple case of black and white to him.

"But then, I don't know. I had to weigh that on not knowing [when] these names were [ever] going to be released. What if that never happened?" He worried that because President Bush had been reelected to a second term, and the administration was fiercely pursuing its litigation and congressional strategy to block any rights for the detainees, the names would never be released.

"So, could I have lived with myself if I didn't do that? It's like the impact on me and my wife and daughter at that time versus these 551 individuals, versus these JAGs that may be not [seen as] trustworthy in the future. So, as I think through it, those are the things that I [considered in thinking], how can I continue to live with myself?"

When he was released, Diaz was hired as a teacher in Florida. He was laid off before his classes began. He then applied for a teaching job in New York City, but that too was unsuccessful. Fortunately, a stranger who took an interest in him helped him find a job with the Bronx Defenders in New York as a paralegal and legal aide. In 2008 Matt Diaz was awarded the Ridenhour Prize for Truth-Telling.

In linking our conversation to the truth-telling prize, Diaz reflected further on his actions. "So, maybe [I would] reconsider, which is sad, because if we don't have the people that are going to stand up for the truth, then who knows what the government's going to be doing or continue to do if people aren't willing to take these actions, knowing that there's not going to be some support on the other end of it and make it a softer landing."

After he was hired by the Bronx Defenders, Diaz applied for readmission to the Kansas state bar, where he had been licensed to practice law before all this happened. A hearing panel of Kansas state lawyers unanimously recommended that his license be reinstated.[3] The Kansas

Supreme Court, pointing to Diaz's disclosure of classified information, rejected the hearing panel's recommendation and disbarred Diaz from the practice of law.[4]

Did Matt Diaz's actions make a difference? The United States did not officially acknowledge the identities of the men in Guantánamo until it released the first batch of 558 names in April 2006, fifteen months after Diaz sent the greeting card. The US released a second batch of 201 names one month later in May 2006. The names were made public in response to a Freedom of Information Act (FOIA) request filed by the Associated Press in January 2006 and a subsequent lawsuit filed in March 2006.[5] It is possible that Diaz's actions in mailing the names spurred the United States' response to the AP's FOIA request. We will never know for sure.

Matt Diaz did not give up on his future. On May 2, 2018, he was sworn in to the New York state bar. He now works at a public defender office in the Bronx.

CHAPTER 3

CHINA'S SHADOW

The first time I met Rushan Abbas, I could not keep my eyes off the stunning brooch that was secured on a necklace she wore. When I commented on it, she reached for it, pushed out a flash drive, and smiled.

"Purchased from Swarovski," she said. Ten years later, Abbas told me she still wears it, and it serves her well.

It was summer 2009, and Witness to Guantánamo was about to begin our first round of interviews in Tirana, Albania. We had flown Abbas from her home in the Washington, DC, area to meet us. We were in Albania to interview four Uighurs and one Uzbek. She met us in our hotel for breakfast.

The Uighurs are Turkic-speaking Sunni Muslims whose native home is a country formerly known as East Turkistan. After the Chinese officially assumed control of East Turkistan in the mid-1900s, the Uighur nation was renamed the Xinjiang Autonomous Region in Central Asia. The Uighurs still refer to the region as East Turkistan.

When the Chinese gained control of the region, they sought to destabilize and destroy the unique Uighur indigenous culture. The Beijing government encouraged and incentivized Han Chinese to settle in East Turkistan, start their own businesses and promote and expand the Chinese culture into the Uighur community.[1] The schools taught Mandarin, while the Uighur language was rejected as an official language. Today, the eight million Uighurs are a minority population in Xinjiang.

In the past two decades, firefights and other violent protests against Chinese domination have erupted in the region. The Chinese have increased their surveillance and repression of the Uighurs and have responded with brutal force to any Uighur uprising. China labels the Uighur separatists as terrorists. Some number of the twenty-two Uighurs who were captured after 9/11 had traveled to a village in Afghanistan for military training, particularly training on small arms and rifles. The men had planned to return home and use their newly learned skills against the Chinese. However, several of the Uighurs had other plans. They were living in Afghanistan, with the goal of migrating to and settling in Turkey.

Abbas was born into a Uighur family in Urumqi, the capital of Xinjiang. She had been a student at the local university and had formed a student organization promoting Uighur rights. When she graduated college, she was labeled a political liability by the Chinese government. Her father was afraid that she would be arrested. A scientist and professor with influence, he arranged for her to attend Washington State University in the US. In 1989, at age twenty-one, she enrolled as a visiting scholar and worked in a plant pathology lab. Abbas knew only a few words of English when she arrived. Five months later, she took the GRE exam and was accepted as a graduate student at the university. While there, she married her professor. They had three children.

In 1997 Radio Free Asia (RFA) added the Uighur language to its broadcasting service. The following year, Abbas was hired to be the voice of RFA to western China and the Uighur region. She worked for the RFA until 2000. The work changed her life.

After Guantánamo opened, in January 2002, an American contractor contacted Abbas and asked her to become an interpreter at the prison. The military needed someone to interpret for the twenty-two Uighurs who had been captured. Abbas was the only American citizen who spoke English, Mandarin, and Uighur, the military believed.

Eighteen Uighurs had been living in the mountains of Tora Bora in Afghanistan when the US shelled the area after the attacks on 9/11. The men fled into Pakistan, where they were turned over to Pakistani officials. Two other Uighurs were arrested in Pakistan, but in a separate incident. The remaining two Uighurs were captured near Mazar-i-Sharif, Afghanistan, and first held in a nineteenth-century fortress in Qala-i-Jangi.

Initially, Abbas declined the request to serve as a military interpreter. She was afraid of "these jihadists," she told us. Her husband then reminded her that when she became a citizen, she had pledged to serve her country. She changed her mind and has never looked back.

She arrived in Guantánamo in late April 2002 and lived on the base until December of that year. In one of the interrogations, one of the Uighurs recognized her voice as the voice of Radio Free Asia.

"You're Rushan Abbas," he said.

The interrogator became unnerved and asked Abbas how the Uighur detainee knew her. Would that compromise the interrogation? he wondered. Could the detainee's knowledge cause harm to her in the future? The detainees were not told the names of the interpreters.

After the detainee explained how he knew her, Abbas assured the military that the men were comforted to hear a familiar voice. The Uighur then explained that their complaints were with China, not with the US. In fact, the military officials themselves were beginning to realize that the Uighurs were not a threat to the US. Several of the Uighurs had gone to Afghanistan to arm themselves against the Chinese, not to wage war against the Americans. Indeed, the Uighurs believed that the US was their inspiration against the repressive Chinese government.

The men explained to Abbas that when they were transferred from Pakistani to US soldiers, they were elated. They understood that the US would hold them for a short time to question them. But once assured that the Uighurs were the enemies of China and not the US, the US military would release the men, they thought. That did not happen. The American military held the Uighurs in Guantánamo for years, some of them for more than a decade.

China wanted the men back. To the Chinese, the Uighurs were terrorists, and there were clear indications that if the men were repatriated, they would be tortured and executed as traitors. Alan Liotta, the director of the office of detainee policy of the Department of Defense, told us of a situation where another country returned a Uighur to China: as soon as the man exited the plane, he was tried at the bottom of the steps, convicted, and executed on the tarmac.

There were two reasons the US did not immediately release the men to other countries after determining that they were not a threat to America. Both reasons concerned China.

The first was that China had pressured nations throughout the world not to accept the Uighurs into their countries. Because of China's power, its trade opportunities, and its not-so-subtle threats, most nations turned down US requests.

The second was that the US was planning to invade Iraq and did not want China to interfere. China agreed, but asked in return that the US officially brand the Uighurs as terrorists.[2] China claimed that the Uighurs belonged to a Uighur independence group known as the East Turkestan Islamic Movement, or ETIM. China further maintained that ETIM was aligned with al Qaeda and the Taliban. To mollify China, the US added ETIM to its Terrorist Exclusion List.[3]

The US also agreed to allow the Chinese to interrogate and, in the process, intimidate the Uighurs in Guantánamo. When the Americans first interrogated the Uighurs, the Uighurs trusted the US and revealed names of their family members and other personal information. The US had assured the Uighurs that it would not disclose the information to the Chinese government. Ayub Mohammed told us that in relying on these American assurances, "we said everything."

When Chinese officials later interviewed him, the Chinese knew his name, address, family members, and other personal information. In fact, the Chinese knew the personal information about each of the Uighurs, one of the Uighurs told us. The Uighurs believed that the Chinese had been given access to documents and transcripts of the American interviews.

The Uighur families in China were harassed and made to suffer while the men were in Guantánamo. Later on, when the men were released to other countries, their families were not permitted to leave China to join them. The Uighurs believe that the US lied to them, and discarded them as so much collateral damage, in exchange for political support from China.

It was not until 2006, four years after the men arrived in Guantánamo, that the first five Uighurs were transferred to Albania. The last three Uighurs were transferred out of Guantánamo in 2014—more than a dozen years after they had arrived. The Uighurs described themselves as pawns in the global chess game between the US and China.

In 2009, during his first year in office, President Obama was intent on transferring as many as four to eight of the Uighurs into the United States, specifically to a Uighur community in northern Virginia. After the

FBI interviewed the Uighurs still in Guantánamo, two men were selected to start the process. But when certain Republican members of Congress got wind of this plan, they created a media frenzy.[4] It was the NIMBY, or "not in my backyard," argument. "We don't want these terrorists in Virginia," said a congressperson.[5]

According to Liotta, the director of detainee policy, the Uighurs could have been more of a threat than most people understood. Although the Uighurs were not a danger to Americans, many of the Uighurs had been trained in a terrorist camp in Tora Bora. If the Uighurs were permitted into the US, they could apply their training and skills in attacking Chinese officials or Chinese assets in America, Liotta explained. For example, if Uighurs attacked the Chinese Embassy in Washington, the incident would severely interfere with US–China relations, he said.

Obama backed down with his plan to release the men into the US. Greg Craig, President Obama's White House counsel, found a home for four Uighurs in Bermuda. Two of the men had been selected for transfer to Virginia. Lawyers for the Uighurs chose the other two men. Craig and Abbas flew with the men to Bermuda.

That same year, 2009, the lawyers for the Uighurs sued in federal court to require the government to transfer the remaining Uighurs into the US. They argued that because the men were not a threat to America, they could no longer be held in Guantánamo. If no country would take the Uighurs, the US was obligated to accept them.

Judge Ricardo Urbina of the US District Court for the District of Columbia agreed with the Uighurs' position. He explained to us that he had wanted to bring the Uighurs into his courtroom and ask the various interested agencies—the CIA, Homeland Security, the Department of Justice, and the Office of the US Attorney—to "help structure the conditions on which they would be released into the community." But the government would not allow the Uighurs to be brought from Guantánamo into the courtroom for the hearing.

Judge Urbina ruled that because the Uighurs were not "enemy combatants," they had the right to be transferred out of the prison. As the judge saw it, if there was a right, there had to be a remedy. And if no country would take the Uighurs, they should be released into the US.[6] In making his decision, Judge Urbina was not worried that he could be accused of releasing alleged terrorists into the US. "I needed to do the right thing," he told us. That was his job.

The US Court of Appeals for the District of Columbia Circuit, which oversees the district courts in Washington, overturned his ruling.[7] The appeals court held that only the president and Congress had the power to release people into the US, not the federal courts.

The Uighurs appealed the court of appeals ruling to the Supreme Court. The Obama administration feared that the Supreme Court might overturn the court of appeals and agree with Judge Urbina's decision to settle the Uighurs into the US—if the administration did not find a home for every Uighur outside the US.

At the time of the lawsuit, all but one of the Uighurs had been offered resettlement in Palau, an English-speaking tropical island of twenty thousand people in the Pacific Ocean near Guam. However, Palau would not accept Arkin Mahmud. If Mahmud had no place to go, the lawsuit would proceed.

Mahmud and his brother Bahtiyar Mahnut were both held in Guantánamo. (The brothers' last names were spelled differently by the American military. Before they were captured, their last name was Mahmoud.) Their story is compelling.

Mahnut had left home for Afghanistan and had become part of the community of Uighurs who were in the mountains in Tora Bora and then fled to Pakistan. When his mother did not hear from him, she sent another son, Mahmud, to Afghanistan to look for him. Mahmud was captured by the Northern Alliance.

The Northern Alliance was commanded by General Abdul Rashid Dostum, an Uzbek warlord.[8] The Northern Alliance aligned with the US after the 9/11 attacks. Mahmud was held with approximately four hundred mostly Taliban prisoners in a nineteenth-century fortress at Mazar-i-Sharif, Afghanistan. While he was held, a massive riot broke out, and the Taliban took refuge in the basement of a pink classroom building, known as the Pink House, in the fortress.

To force the Taliban to surrender, Dostum's men dropped grenades into the air ducts, followed by fiery diesel fuel. When neither worked, they pumped cold water into the basement, forcing the men to stand in the frigid water thick with vomit, blood, and feces. Seven days after the incident began, only eighty-six of the original four hundred men—suffering from dehydration, hunger, and hypothermia—emerged. Mahmud survived along with "American Taliban" John Walker Lindh.[9] Mahmud was later flown to Guantánamo.

Unfortunately, Mahmud's mental state deteriorated when he was captured, and he continued to decline while in Guantánamo. No country, including Palau, would agree to take him. Countries that were considering accepting the Uighurs claimed that they did not have the resources to provide the necessary ongoing and critical care needed. Mahnut would not agree to a transfer without his brother. (The administration had allowed the men the option of refusing a transfer out of Guantánamo.)[10]

Dan Fried, President Obama's special envoy for the closure of Guantánamo, talked to the Swiss government, which consented to take the two brothers. As the home of the International Committee of the Red Cross/Red Crescent and the Geneva Conventions, Switzerland believed it could take Mahmud on humanitarian grounds, and that China would not be as offended as it would with most other countries.

Now that Palau would take every Uighur except Mahmud, and Switzerland would accept the two brothers, the Supreme Court turned down the Uighur petition.[11] The two brothers were transferred to Switzerland. However, only six Uighurs agreed to go to Palau. The other Uighurs decided to remain in Guantánamo. They were holding out for a country that would provide them with better employment opportunities and a larger Muslim community. They also yearned for a nontropical climate—that is, a country with four seasons similar to those of their home country of East Turkistan. They did not want to move from one tropical island like Guantánamo to another one like Palau.

Rushan Abbas continued with her story. After working for one year as a government interpreter in Guantánamo and realizing that the Uighurs were not enemies of the United States, she resigned and returned to California. At the urging of the military, she agreed to work in Guantánamo for two additional months in early 2003. But she was determined not to continue working for the government after that, because "all the interrogators already made the decision that the Uighurs were innocent and they were at the wrong place at the wrong time."

In 2006, when Boston attorney Sabin Willett went to Guantánamo to represent the Uighurs, the men asked that he bring Abbas with him as his interpreter. From then on, she became a critical part of Willett's legal team. Abbas was involved in negotiations between the lawyers and the government whenever Uighurs were transferred to other countries.

Over time, Abbas became a surrogate mother to the Uighurs in Guantánamo. When she traveled to the naval base, she brought home-cooked meals with her because "they will never see their mothers again."

In her 2010 interview with Witness to Guantánamo, Abbas expressed disappointment in how the US had failed the Uighurs. She had been the perfect immigrant coming from a repressive regime to America, the land she understood to be the shining light to the world. She became an American citizen, raised three American children, and worked for the American military. Yet, she watched as the America she loved abandoned the Uighurs in Guantánamo. America's legal system did not protect her people. Abbas reminded us about the framers of the Constitution and the principles for which they stood. "What happened in Guantánamo was not what I understood of the Constitution," she said. "I often think that, what if our forefathers—they see, they know what's happening today in Guantánamo—how they feel about this?"

When President Obama announced on his second day in office in January 2009 that he would close the prison within one year, Abbas recalled, she was "so excited, I had tears in my eyes." She believed that President Obama would "correct the mistake [made by President Bush] and do the right thing." But during our interview she was disheartened. It was nearly one year after Obama announced that he would close Guantánamo. His deadline was fast approaching, and Abbas knew "it's not going to happen." Guantánamo would not close. (In fact, Obama never closed the prison in his eight years in office.)

Abbas continued: "And in my twenty years in United States, I always want to see the great side of the United States. But the last eight years, what I have endured, what I have experienced in Guantánamo, was not the side that I want to see of my country."

Shortly after Rushan began working with Willett, China confiscated Abbas's father's passport. Although her father had a green card, he could no longer visit the United States. She never saw her father again. When he died in 2010, she did not feel it was safe to attend his funeral. Because she was closely connected to the Uighurs in Guantánamo, she believed that the Chinese government considered her a threat also, and possibly even a terrorist. She worried that if she returned, she could be arrested, persecuted, and perhaps even executed. Her friends thought that China might arrest her to show the world that not even an American citizen was safe.

Nearly two decades after the opening of Guantánamo, Abbas does not see an opportunity to return to China. If anything, the Chinese persecution and suppression of the Uighurs has increased a hundredfold. Approximately one million Uighurs are now held in internment camps. The people in the camps have been subjected to reeducation and indoctrination programs by the Chinese authorities. The Uighur language is forbidden in the camps. Their Muslim religion is branded as divisive. Orphanages have been built to house children of people detained. A German expert characterized the actions in Xinjiang as a systematic campaign of cultural genocide.[12] Observers have said Xinjiang is becoming a massive internment camp.[13] In addition, China has created a state-of-the-art surveillance and policing system to monitor every movement of the Uighurs.[14]

Opposing the camps, Abbas led a protest in front of the United Nations in the spring of 2018. In September 2018, she spoke before the Hudson Institute, a conservative think tank in Washington. Six days after the talk, her sister and aunt disappeared from their homes in China. Abbas believes that they were taken to the internment camps in retaliation for her advocacy on behalf of the Uighurs.[15]

Although Abbas has become disenchanted with the US' and the world's unwillingness to stand up to China on behalf of the Uighurs, she believes that there is a silver lining. Before 9/11, the world knew little or nothing about the Uighurs. The capture of the twenty-two men brought Uighur life and culture into the global spotlight and drew attention to the harsh suffering and persecution that the Uighurs have endured under Chinese rule.

The men were depressed and demoralized in prison. As Uighur Abdul GhapparAbdul Rahman expressed to us, their "golden years" were passing by. Still, as Abbas saw it, their lives in Guantánamo had also made a huge difference for their people. Because of their sufferings in the prison, the world now knows the story of the Uighurs.

Guantánamo changed Abbas's life. She not only became an interpreter and substitute mother to the Uighurs, she became a powerful and outspoken advocate for all the Uighurs under Chinese oppression. She has become the voice for the twenty-two Guantánamo Uighurs, and serves as one of the most powerful voices of the Uighurs today. She told us: "Yes, of course, I'm glad I said yes [to becoming an interpreter]. I had lifetime experience, got to know so many different things that I had no idea. And I helped twenty-two people with their times in incarceration in Guantánamo."

Abbas was booked on the same flight as my wife, Mary Louise, and me when we left Palau at 2 a.m. for Guam. From Guam, we would fly to Hawaii, and then home to the Bay Area. Abbas was to travel with us to Hawaii and then fly home to the Washington, DC, area. When Mary Louise and I transferred in Guam, we did not see her on the plane. We wondered where she was sitting. In fact, we did not see her again until seven hours later, at the Honolulu airport.

And when we saw her, she was steaming. Her anger had not subsided in the seven-hour flight. She told us that she had been pulled aside in Guam and interrogated by American customs officials. They wanted to know why she would travel fifteen thousand-plus miles for a two-day trip. She asked why they were interested. They answered that she knew why.

Customs officials then asked her why she came to the US from China when she was twenty-one. And they asked about the many trips she had taken to Cuba. She explained that she had been working as an interpreter in Guantánamo for the US State Department in Cuba. She emphasized that she had government clearance. Apparently, that made no difference. The interrogation continued. They also asked her about a plant she had brought into the country many years earlier.

In telling the officials about her work with Witness to Guantánamo, she added that I, as founder and director, was on the plane. They could talk to me if they wanted confirmation on our work. Customs did not seem interested in contacting me. Finally, after delaying the plane, they allowed her to board.

Our filmmaker, Johnny Symons, was still in Palau. I emailed him about the incident. As he boarded the flight from Guam to Honolulu several days later, customs officials pulled him out of line. They apparently had Abbas's answers in front of them. When his answers mirrored those of hers regarding our work, they let him board without issue.

That was the only time that Symons was ever stopped on our trips to twenty different countries. Neither Mary Louise nor I was ever stopped and pulled aside in our near-decade of travel with Witness to Guantánamo.

Not all the Uighurs have remained in the countries to which they were transferred. Some, to their fortune, have been able to leave their adopted country and resettle in a more suitable environment. Others have done the best they could, and made a home for themselves in their new lands.

Four of the five Uighurs transferred to Albania in May 2006 still live there today. They married women they met on the internet or knew through connections back home. Jobs have been hard to find in the Albanian economy. One of the men, Abubakir Qasem, volunteered to work in a restaurant making pizzas when he arrived. After a few years, Qasem started his own pizza establishment. His work is supporting him and his family today. The fifth Uighur, Adil Hakimjan, was granted asylum in Sweden a year after he had arrived in Albania. His sister, who was a refugee from China, lived in Sweden. Hakimjan lives in Stockholm, raising a family and holding two jobs.

Ayub Mohammed, one of the Uighurs living in Albania, is married to a Canadian woman. Their children are Canadian citizens. Mohammed applied for permanent resident status in Canada, but Canadian immigration officials denied his request. In late spring 2019 the Federal Court of Canada ordered a new hearing. The outcome of the hearing could also affect two Uighurs who are living in Bermuda and who are also married to Canadian women.

The six men who were transferred to the Pacific island of Palau in October 2009 now live in Turkey, a Muslim country with a similar language and a more agreeable culture. Palau is a relatively poor country, and work was difficult to find. The nation relies on tourism, particularly deep-sea diving. Because they had limited economic opportunities, the men felt that they were transported from one island prison to another. All six lived in an apartment building owned by the president's brother. There was one mosque, a tiny Muslim community, and one halal restaurant.

In 2013, four years after they had arrived, one of the six men managed to find his way out of Palau without a passport. It is believed that he had the assistance of a rich hotel owner, as well as local officials.[16] One year later, the five others made arrangements to leave. It is assumed that they also had the assistance of local officials. Four traveled through Japan to Turkey. The fifth tried to leave through South Korea but was stopped in transit. The Chinese government demanded that South Korea extradite him to China. The US intervened, and he was permitted to return to Palau. In March of the following year, he left Palau, also for Turkey.[17]

When four other Uighurs were resettled in Bermuda in June 2009, they were provided jobs at a golf course. However, they were subsequently laid off and had difficulty finding new jobs.[18] Since then, times have improved, and today they are employed in construction and landscaping. Each man is married with children. They met their wives through social media. The US and Bermuda helped bring their wives into the country.[19]

Bermuda is a British overseas territory, and the UK is responsible for its foreign relations and defense. When Bermuda agreed to resettle the men without first informing the UK, the UK government was irate.[20] The UK refused to provide travel documents and European Union (EU) passports for the men. However, by 2019 three of the men had obtained passports and could lawfully travel off the island.[21]

The two brothers, Bahtiyar Mahnut and Arkin Mahmud, were resettled in a small town in Switzerland in March 2010. There is a tiny mosque, but no Uighur community. The closest Uighur community is in Geneva, two and a half hours away. Mahnut is working in a factory and has documents that allow him to travel throughout the EU.[22] Mahmud has not been working, but is doing much better.[23]

Two Uighurs transferred from Guantánamo to El Salvador in April 2012. Two years later, they were able to leave and resettle in Turkey. It is not clear whether they were assisted by Salvadoran and/or US officials.

The last three Uighurs in Guantánamo were transferred to Slovakia in December 2013. They live in a small town in the central part of the country. There is no mosque in all of Slovakia, and no significant Muslim community.

There was one other ethnic Uighur in Guantánamo, Sadik Ahmad Turkistani. He was born and raised in Saudi Arabia. Military officials in Guantánamo believed that he had tried and failed in an attempt to kill Osama bin Laden before the attacks on 9/11.[24] The Taliban captured him and held him prisoner. Following the attacks on 9/11, the Northern Alliance freed most of the Taliban's prisoners. However, Northern Alliance soldiers sold Turkistani to the Americans. He was transported to Guantánamo in early 2002. Rushan Abbas, who was working at the military base in 2002, told me how military officials found it ironic that the man who had tried to kill bin Laden was being held as a prisoner in Guantánamo. Turkistani was repatriated to Saudi Arabia June 24, 2006.[25]

The president of Palau described the story of the Guantánamo Uighurs as "biblical."[26]

— CHAPTER 4 —

LAWLESSNESS

In the fall of 2014, I presented my work with Witness to Guantánamo to fellow faculty at my law school. At the end of the presentation, as people were left with their thoughts, one professor broke the stillness.

"What about the law?" he asked.

Based on all that I had heard from interviewees over the course of the project, the question did not require a complex answer.

"There was no law," I responded. That is, government officials purposely selected Guantánamo because they believed it was outside the law. As the government saw it, the detainees could be held indefinitely without charges, and under any conditions chosen by their American captors. There was no law to protect the detainees.

The only rules that applied were the rules the government invented in support of its actions. In effect, the rules in Guantánamo were made up on the fly and changed with the day. There was no predictability. To the extent that legal considerations posed an obstacle, they were overridden, circumvented, or ignored.

Erwin Chemerinsky, dean and law professor at the University of California, Berkeley, was the first lawyer to file a case on behalf of the detainees in Guantánamo.[1] His thoughts on Guantánamo when he spoke to us in 2010 reflected those of many lawyers and legal scholars: "To me, one of the aspects of the Bush administration position, the most repugnant, was that there was a group of people in a place where no law could apply. Their position was the Geneva Conventions didn't apply to these individuals. United States constitutional and statute law didn't apply to these people. So, the government could do whatever it wanted. That kind of lawlessness is the antithesis of the rule of law. And the idea that now, for eight years, individuals have been held without due process in the Constitution is disappointing beyond words."

The notion of indefinite detention is "something I never would have expected, something I think a lot of people never would have expected, and it's something that is hopefully intolerable to people. I think it's something that we will come to regret for a very long time if we don't regret it already," J. Wells Dixon, senior staff attorney for the Center for Constitutional Rights in New York and a Guantánamo expert, said.

He likened Guantánamo to infamous prison islands like Devil's Island, which housed French political prisoners in French Guiana, and Robben Island, off the coast of Cape Town, where South African president Nelson Mandela was imprisoned during apartheid. Dixon feared that the policy of indefinite detention could become part of our national heritage.

The concept of holding men indefinitely, without charges of any crimes, created a lawlessness that allowed the government to do anything it wanted. But it also motivated lawyers who believed in the Constitution to challenge the Bush administration's detention policies.

Australian attorney Stephen Kenny represented two Australian detainees in the very early days after 9/11. He was horrified when he realized that the military was transporting his clients to Guantánamo "deliberately to be beyond the law." To him, the idea of "taking people and treating them in that manner by a country such as America was quite a shocking thing."

"You don't have a right to say, 'Wait a second, I'm the wrong guy.' You don't have a right to challenge anything about the conditions under which you're being held. You don't have a right to say, 'I didn't do anything wrong, no, no, no, no, no.' And they can just hold you forever," habeas attorney Joe Margulies, who was also one of the first attorneys to represent detainees after 9/11, told us.

When JAG defense attorney Major Yvonne Bradley first went to meet UK detainee Binyam Mohamed, she was frightened.[2] Although she had represented a sizeable number of people on death row, including serial killers, in her civilian life, she was told by the military that the detainees were far worse than any defendants she had ever seen before. The military had portrayed the detainees as monsters. In the back of her mind, Bradley was thinking, "I'm going to see a real terrorist." These are "vicious individuals."

"And I remember the first time going in to see Mr. Mohamed, at that particular time, I'm kind of embarrassed to say this now, I was really scared to go in to meet him. And I had no reason to be scared, given my background, given my criminal background. But I remember walking in there and thinking, wow, I'm scared to, what I—you can't even say to this individual."

Bradley felt very differently after she left that meeting. She said, "I think it was at that point when I started putting together—after meeting Mr. Mohamed and seeing him, seeing his demeanor, and looking into his eyes and seeing his body language—that he was probably more scared of me than I was of him. I realized for the first time that whatever I knew about Guantánamo, whatever I read about Guantánamo, whatever information they had about Binyam [Mohamed] was likely not true. And that was the first time when it just hit me how fear and propaganda can make such a difference on how people understand things. And I was probably more mad coming out of that cell with Binyam than I was scared when I first went in to meet [him]."

That first meeting with Mohamed caused Bradley to do some soul-searching. It rocked her faith in government, she told us. Though she sometimes second-guessed herself, questioning whether she was over-reading the situation, she was committed to doing the right thing.

As Bradley saw it, there was no sense of justice in the prison. However, if the military continued to promote the term "full and fair justice," people would accept it. She further observed that military officials were making up charges as they went along, as well as making up policies as they went along. "The rule of law had been broken," she said.

Bradley compared Guantánamo to both *Alice in Wonderland* and *The Twilight Zone*. Each episode of *The Twilight Zone*, the science fiction and fantasy television series in the late 1950s and early 1960s, ended with a surprising and sometimes chilling ending. Guantánamo had that sense of a fantasy world to Bradley: "You don't know what's real. It's absolutely madness. I didn't understand that at the time."

After three men allegedly committed suicide at Guantánamo on the same evening in June 2006, the military canceled Mohamed's hearing scheduled for the following week. Mohamed was not told why, and Bradley was unable to meet with him to explain. When she visited him a month later, she wanted to bring news articles of the suicides so he would understand why she did not show up that day. Trust was important in building her relationship with him, and the articles would assist her in documenting why she missed the meeting. However, when she arrived at the detention center, the military confiscated the articles, tagging them as contraband. She was also instructed not to mention the suicides to Mohamed, presumably because the suicides were a "national security concern." In their meeting, she tiptoed around the issue as she tried to explain why she had not been there a month earlier. But Mohamed asked directly about the suicides.

"So now it makes me look foolish because he's thinking I'm not being honest with him."

He knew about the suicides, yet even then she could not discuss the suicides with him. How could her relationship with him be based on trust if he was wondering why she was not telling him something he knew?

"And that was the continued type of madness, when we talk about this so-called prison system of Guantánamo and how it's so different from the real world," she said. "I can't even ever imagine [that I] can't talk about something that's important to the client or explain to him why [I wasn't] here. How do you explain to someone that their hearing was canceled without telling them it was based on the suicides, and I can't talk about the suicides? It was that type of madness."

The more fantastic Guantánamo became to her, the more passionate Bradley became in her representation. "It gave me the determination that I was going to represent this individual fully, zealously, because I thought what was about to take place then in Guantánamo was a travesty of justice."

Bradley also described to us her reaction when she first read Binyam Mohamed's charge sheet. She thought it was missing something.

"I'm reading through these charges," she said. "I'm waiting for, you know, whom did he murder, what mass destruction did he cause? I'm waiting for a war crime, and all I see is this one long conspiracy, and everyone's name that you could connect at that time to the alleged al

Qaeda organization was on the charge sheet—Khalid Sheikh Mohammed [self-proclaimed mastermind of 9/11], Osama bin Laden, Richard
Reid [known as the 'shoe bomber,' who tried to blow up a plane with a
bomb in his shoe]. It made no sense to me. And then at the very end, it
said that he was apprehended at Karachi Airport going back to London.

"And after reading this complex conspiracy, I remember either email-
ing or calling Clive [Clive Stafford Smith, the civilian habeas attorney
representing Mohamed]. I said, 'Clive, I don't think you sent me everything, because this [charge sheet] doesn't make sense. Where is the
crime? What you've given me doesn't state a criminal activity that's a war
crime.'

"And then Clive said, 'That's it.'"

When we interviewed Chicago attorney Candace Gorman, she explained how Guantánamo was outside the reach of the law through
another lens—the failure of the federal courts. That was so, even after
the Supreme Court ruled in *Rasul* that the men had the right to habeas
hearings to challenge their detentions in federal courts.

Consistent with the theory of habeas, the federal courts had an obligation to stand up to the president and release the men when there was
insufficient evidence to hold them. Instead, the judges bowed to the government's argument that national security concerns trumped the rights
of the detainees, Gorman noted. Federal judges were afraid to make decisions that could result in releasing an alleged terrorist. In essence, to
Gorman and many other habeas lawyers, the federal courts abdicated
their role.

Federal judges deferred to the government no matter how weak or
meager the evidence was against the detainees. As long as there was
"some evidence," courts would agree with the administration and not
order release.[3] It was sufficient that the government characterized the
evidence as classified information that could not be revealed because of
national security concerns.

Gorman explained that she was very disappointed in our court system. When she became involved she "had confidence in the courts at
that time. I really thought that our courts would do the right thing. And
it has been eye-opening to me to see how the courts have just crumbled

before the executive branch, and that they are just unwilling and unable to stand for the rule of law." The failure of our courts to stand up when necessary "goes to the very fabric of our country," she added.

Gorman volunteered to represent detainees after the *Rasul* decision was issued in 2004. Earlier, she had won a significant settlement in a case that she had taken to the Supreme Court. She used her fees from the settlement to pay for her work and expenses, including flights, in representing two detainees in Guantánamo.

Military attorney David Frakt was one of several people who described the military hearings in Guantánamo as "kangaroo courts." A kangaroo court is seen as a rigged trial, where the legal proceedings are a sham—although the government attempts to give the impression that the process is fair. Kangaroo courts offer no impartial justice. The verdict is decided in advance and, invariably, to the detriment of the accused.

Frakt told us that when he first arrived in Guantánamo to act as defense counsel for a juvenile detainee, a colonel in the office gave him this advice: "Don't get your hopes up. Don't think for a minute that you can win one of these cases. You just save yourself a lot of heartache because you can't win. It doesn't matter if the facts are on your side, if the law is on your side. The system is rigged. It's a kangaroo court. So, it's just not going to happen."

A military commission—or tribunal—is a military court created in exigent circumstances when military courts are not available, such as on a battlefield. Military commissions may provide fewer rights. Many military lawyers and human rights advocates have argued that the military commissions in Guantánamo are not proceedings during exigent circumstances. Guantánamo is not a battlefield. Hence, tribunals in Guantánamo are obligated to provide rights equal to those rights provided to service members in court-martial proceedings, or in constitutionally created federal courts.

During the Bush administration years, six prosecutors working in military commission cases quit or requested reassignment.[4] Yvonne Bradley believed they quit because "the system was broken."

Colonel Morris Davis was one of those six prosecutors who resigned or requested reassignment. A chief prosecutor, he resigned because he believed that the justice system in Guantánamo did not dispense justice. Davis described a conversation he had with William J. Haynes, general counsel to Secretary of Defense Donald Rumsfeld. Davis explained that he was pressured by Haynes to bring in convictions.

In the meeting, as described by Davis, Haynes told Davis that the military commission trials in Guantánamo were on the same plane as the Nuremberg trials. (The trials prosecuted Nazi war criminals in Germany after World War II.) Davis reminded Haynes that not everyone who was tried was convicted at Nuremberg. It appeared that Haynes had not considered the possibility that there could be an acquittal in the military commissions in Guantánamo. Davis explained: "And I remember he was sitting across from me and he kind of rocked back and said, 'Acquittals? Wait a minute, we can't have acquittals. We've been holding these guys for years. How are we going to explain that? We can't have acquittals. We've got to have convictions.'"

JAG attorney Lieutenant Colonel Colby Vokey similarly experienced the absence of law while representing a detainee in Guantánamo. Vokey represented Canadian citizen Omar Khadr in military commission proceedings. Khadr was fifteen when captured in a firefight in Afghanistan.[5] He was accused of killing an American soldier in the fight, although there was no direct evidence. Khadr spent much of his adolescent and young adult years in the prison. Although he was a juvenile, he was not separated from the adult population. In fall 2012, after a decade in Guantánamo, he was transferred to a Canadian prison. In March 2019, a judge in Alberta, Canada, ruled that Khadr had completed his sentence and lifted all remaining restrictions on him.[6]

Vokey explained that when he filed a brief on behalf of Khadr, one of two things happened: either the government never replied to his brief, or the government's responsive brief cited no law. He explained: "You can be citing Ukrainian law for all the good it would do to you. . . . If we did get any answers back from the [judge at the military] commissions, they would be remarkably free of any kind of legal ruling."

Vokey believed that Secretary of Defense Rumsfeld and his legal staff invented new laws for the military commissions. He agreed with Morris Davis that the system was "designed to convict."

"It was like walking into a third-grade class and saying, 'Okay, class, for fun today, I want you to write the laws for some country.'"

— CHAPTER 5 —

UNDERMINING HEROES

Beginning with the opening of Guantánamo in January 2002, the government sought to obtain intelligence it believed detainees might have regarding another attack. In addition to using harsh and cruel methods, including torture, when questioning detainees, government interrogators pretended that they were lawyers sent to represent detainees.

"There was a very concerted effort on the part of the interrogators to undermine the trust and confidence in the lawyers. And some of it began with the interrogators going in and posing as lawyers," habeas lawyer Clive Stafford Smith told us.

Until the *Rasul* decision in June 2004, the detainees had no access to lawyers who could legitimately represent them. Even though legitimate lawyers were available after *Rasul*, detainees continued to be mistrustful of people who appeared at the prison and said that they were lawyers who had come to represent them,

To assure clients that they were not government agents, lawyers sometimes visited the men's families before meeting clients in Guantánamo. With the help of the families, the lawyers collected photos and personal information to bring to their first meetings. Attorney Joe Margulies told us how he asked Maha Habib, the wife of Australian detainee Mamdouh Habib, to tell him three things that only Mamdouh would know about their lives and children.

Maha told Margulies where she and Mamdouh went on their first date, the first gift that Mamdouh had given her when they were dating, and where their other children stayed when she and Mamdouh spent the night in the hospital caring for their oldest son. Margulies repeated this to her husband, Mamdouh.

"And he looked at me for a long time and then he dropped his head and started to cry, and the tears are just falling down. He looked back up, tears in his eyes, and said to me, 'Joe, we have so much work to do.' That's when I knew, okay, now I have a client," Margulies recalled.

The military erected bureaucratic hurdles to make life for the detainee who met his lawyer more onerous than it was for the detainee who did not meet his lawyer. A detainee who wanted to meet his lawyer would be taken to the waiting cell hours—sometimes days—before the meeting. He was required to wait alone in his solitary cell until the time of the meeting. After the meeting, the detainee would again be moved to a solitary cell. In addition, guards subjected the detainee to intrusive body searches both before and after the meeting, arguably for security purposes.

There were times when the military brought the wrong detainee to the meetings, habeas lawyer David Remes told us. It was never clear whether this was a deliberate military tactic or a result of confusion over names. The government had classified the names until March 2006, making it difficult for attorneys to verify identities. Because Arabic names can be spelled differently when translated into English, the military sometimes confused the names.

If officials brought the wrong client to a meeting, lawyers did not always have the flexibility to set up another meeting with their actual client before it was time for the lawyer to leave the base.

Someone who wishes to remain anonymous explained: "So now you have an unhappy detainee who was brought in to see a lawyer that he doesn't know. And you have an unhappy attorney who came all the way from the mainland, and it's the wrong client." Both lawyer and misidentified detainee are upset and annoyed. Moreover, the wrong detainee had been held in a solitary cell for hours or days and had been subjected to intrusive body searches, all for nothing.

Habeas attorney Stafford Smith explained another approach that interrogators used to damage the lawyer-client relationship. "Interrogators would say, 'If you have a lawyer, you're never going to get out of here. If you just talk to us, we're your ticket out of here.'"

The interrogators "would point to people who had already gone home, who hadn't had lawyers—which there were quite a lot. By the [first] time we got [to visit the prison in November 2004], there had been two hundred people released already," he added.

Detainees were transferred home for reasons that had nothing to do with their lawyers' filing papers and obtaining hearings in federal court. When leaders of countries that supported President Bush's policies asked Bush to release their detainees, Bush would oblige. In other situations, detainees would be released if their home countries agreed to imprison the men when they were returned.

Over time, many detainees realized that it did not seem to matter whether they had a lawyer or not. They would be released only when the US government decided to transfer them from the prison. Even winning a habeas case in court did not guarantee that a detainee would be released. The US government had the final say. Consequently, some detainees abandoned their lawyers, seeing no value in maintaining the relationship.

"A lot of attorneys were fired by the detainees because the message from the detainees was that you're not really coming to help me. You're coming to really abuse me as much as the United States government is abusing me," an anonymous interviewee explained to us. This interviewee wanted us to understand that the detainee did not benefit from meeting with his attorney, but actually suffered. By being placed in solitary confinement and body-searched before and after the meetings, detainees were being "punished" for meeting with their lawyers. No matter how often a detainee met with his lawyer, nothing seemed to change. The detainee remained in prison until the government said otherwise.

There were other military and interrogation tactics that undermined lawyer-client relationships. One was telling a detainee that his lawyer was Jewish. The interrogators believed that this information would motivate the Muslim detainee to abandon his attorney.

A detainee asked habeas attorney Tom Wilner, "Tom, do you mind me asking what religion you are?"

"I'm Jewish," Wilner replied.

"Interrogators told me don't trust your lawyer, because he is a Jew," the detainee said. "You know that Jews are not good to Muslims."

Wilner asked the detainee whether the fact that he was a Jew bothered him.

"Oh no, not at all. It doesn't matter to me. It depends on what kind of person you are," the detainee replied.

"What did you say to the interrogator?" Wilner asked him.

"I looked at him and said, 'There are good people and bad people in every religion.'"

Habeas lawyer Stafford Smith described a variation on this story. The military told Stafford Smith's clients that their lawyer was Jewish. (His father was Jewish.) But the military also told the clients something else.

"Oh, Clive, do you know what they're saying about you?" a detainee said to the lawyer.

Stafford Smith assumed that the detainee would say he was Jewish.

"What is it? Please tell me." Stafford Smith asked.

The detainee responded, "Oh no, it's too embarrassing," and turned red.

Stafford Smith asked him again.

"Please. Please tell me what it is."

The client answered, "They are saying that you, Clive, like to have sex with men."

Stafford Smith wanted to discuss how people should not care about people's sexuality, and how the military was playing off people's prejudices. However, he did not want to spend his client's limited meeting time. So he pointed to his wedding ring and said it was not true.

"But it was that sort of stuff that they did all the time," Stafford Smith said.

Lawyers also questioned whether the military was listening in on privileged lawyer-client conversations. There were closed-circuit cameras in each meeting room, but the military claimed that the cameras did not record sound. Lawyers were told that the cameras were there to monitor activities, such as a detainee becoming violent.

"Neither lawyers nor detainees believe for a second that the government does not listen in on conversations," Center for Constitutional Rights lawyer J. Wells Dixon said. Other attorneys had similar views.

"The idea that they weren't listening in was silly and, of course, they were listening in and in fact we caught them at it," Stafford Smith told us. He explained that, after a first visit, the military interrogated Joe

Margulies's client "about exactly the things he had just been talking to Joe about, and they weren't very good at it. And so it was clear that they were listening in."

In later years, lawyers representing the high-value detainees found that smoke detectors in the lawyer-client meeting rooms contained hidden listening devices.[1]

The military also made attempts at antagonizing the lawyers. For example, Stafford Smith was accused of providing "contraband" underwear to his clients. Stafford Smith wrote a blistering and humorously sarcastic letter to the Department of Defense explaining how that was not possible. He explained that anything the lawyers take into the meeting is searched. Furthermore, there is a camera in the meeting room observing all activities. He suggested that a soldier who had been issued that particular brand of underwear was likely the culprit.[2]

Habeas attorney Candace Gorman flew down to Guantánamo in 2006. For five days, she tried to visit her client. Each day the military challenged the information she provided about her client and refused to bring him to a meeting—although his name was on the government's list of detainees. No matter how hard she tried, the military denied her a visit. Gorman returned home without seeing her client. When she filed papers complaining of her treatment, the military responded that "counsel did not really want to see her client and instead preferred to go bird watching."[3]

Attorneys also had to abide by strict government procedures that interfered with the attorney-client privilege. Lawyers had to obtain security clearances before they could fly to the base. Sometimes, it took six months to obtain the clearances. These added requirements were justified on national security grounds.

Attorneys were subject to an agreement known as a protective order. Among other things, the protective order restricted the materials that lawyers were permitted to bring into meetings. They could not bring laptops. They could bring only pen and paper. At the end of the meeting, a guard collected the attorneys' notes and sent the notes to a secure facility in the Washington, DC, area. Once the notes were reviewed for classified information, the unclassified notes were returned to the attorney. Attorneys were permitted access to the classified information at the facility, but could not use any of it in a document.

There were a few bright spots for detainees who met with their lawyers. One was when lawyers brought food to the meetings. Uighur Rushan Abbas, who interpreted for the lawyers representing the Uighurs, brought Uighur home-cooked meals to the meetings. Many lawyers purchased pizza, sandwiches, or other food from McDonald's and other franchises on the base and brought it to the meetings.

A change from daily prison fare appealed to the detainees. The chance for conversation and the opportunity to hear about their families were both very appealing reasons for the detainees to meet with their attorneys. The meetings were a reminder of their humanity and the world outside.

— CHAPTER 6 —

FAUX LAW

For years, we have been searching for the derivation of the term "enemy combatant." We knew the term had no legal meaning, but we wondered how it became part of the legal lexicon after 9/11. Now we know.

Six months after 9/11, "enemy combatant" appeared as the Bush administration's designation for al Qaeda and Taliban captives. The term permeated the media. People who studied international law and human rights law knew that the term had no legal meaning under domestic or international law. Under the Geneva Conventions, the universe of combatants is two: "lawful combatant" and "unlawful combatant." "Enemy combatant" was nothing more than a generic term. In fact, many scholars of international law believed that the US deliberately created the term in order to circumvent the protections of the Geneva Conventions.[1]

No matter how hard we tried, we could not find the derivation of the term. That is, until we sat down with William Lietzau, an expert in international law and the law of war. Lietzau is highly respected in his field. He was instrumental in creating the "elements of crimes" for the Rome Statute—the underlying document for the International Criminal Court. A marine in uniform, he was legal advisor to the Department of Defense during the Bush administration, where he was called upon to develop the rules for military commissions to prosecute al Qaeda and Taliban captives. He was also a legal advisor in the Obama administration and later became deputy assistant secretary of defense. He told us the answer.

First, some background. The United States is a signatory to the Geneva Conventions, as is every country in the world, including Afghanistan.

Under the conventions, lawful combatants are entitled to prisoner of war (POW) status. Soldiers in the armed forces or related militias are lawful combatants.

The International Committee of the Red Cross/Red Crescent (ICRC)—whose humanitarian mission is to protect people in armed conflicts from cruel, inhuman, or degrading treatment, including torture—is the guardian of the Geneva Conventions. The ICRC recognizes only lawful and unlawful combatants. It does not recognize the term "enemy combatant" as legitimate.

Lawful combatants, or POWs, have powerful protections when captured. They have the right to not be interrogated, disclosing only name, rank, and serial number. They must be repatriated at the end of hostilities. Lawful combatants can kill and be killed on the battlefield.

Although unlawful combatants are not entitled to POW status, they still have rights. They can be interrogated, but they cannot be mistreated or tortured. An example of an unlawful combatant would be a civilian, not a member of the armed forces or related militias, taking up arms. Spies are also unlawful combatants. Unlawful combatants who kill an enemy soldier can be tried for murder.

The US military's goal at Guantánamo was to obtain actionable intelligence to thwart another attack, including chemical and biological attacks. Consequently, the US did not want to provide POW status to any of the men captured. The US intended not to let the Geneva Conventions interfere with brutal and harsh interrogation of the captured men. In February 2002, President Bush declared that the Geneva Conventions did not apply to the men in Guantánamo.[2]

By applying the term "enemy combatant" to the captives, the US was avoiding all Geneva Convention humanitarian protections for the detainees—whether they would have qualified as lawful or unlawful combatants. Without these protections, the men could not assert the lawful rights guaranteed them by international and domestic law. If the detainees were not protected by the law, the US believed it could mistreat and torture them with impunity.

When asked for the origination of the term, the Bush administration pointed to a 1942 Supreme Court case, *Ex parte Quirin*.[3] In the case, the court uses the term "enemy combatant" generically and interchangeably with several other terms, such as "unlawful combatant" and "unlawful belligerent." It is a sloppy decision in which terms are tossed about without deliberation. The case does not give authority to the administration to ignore or bypass the Geneva Conventions.

Fortunately, after years of searching, we identified in an interview with Lietzau the true source of the creation of the term "enemy combatant." Lietzau confirmed that the *Quirin* case was not the source of the term.

When I asked whether he might know who first thought of using it, he uneasily admitted, "I hesitate to say I was responsible for it, because it's been so resoundingly criticized since."

The term "enemy combatant" first surfaced when Paul Wolfowitz, deputy secretary of defense, was asked to appear on a national news show.[4] Lietzau was asked to be present during a practice session, to assist Wolfowitz in preparing. During the session, someone asked Wolfowitz how the detainees could have fair trials if the president had, in various memos and statements, already designated the detainees as "unlawful combatants."

Wolfowitz needed an answer. Lietzau first suggested that Wolfowitz use the term "unlawful combatant" less frequently. Lietzau explained that "unlawful combatant" caused confusion because it implied a prejudgment of the detainee's guilt, even though the term did not mean that. Lietzau added that America was holding people not because they were criminals, but because they were the enemy.

Wolfowitz asked Lietzau whether there was another term that he could substitute for the confusing term "unlawful combatant." Lietzau suggested that he use the generic term "'enemy combatant,' [because] it then designates them with the appropriate adjective to describe why we're holding them. We're holding them because they're the enemy, not because they've done something unlawful. A lawful combatant or an unlawful combatant can be held just as well."

After the session, Lietzau went to William J. Haynes, general counsel to Secretary of Defense Donald Rumsfeld, and Chuck Allen, deputy general counsel for international affairs DOD, and asked them to approve the use of the term "enemy combatant" as a descriptor for the detainees. Lietzau told us that "everyone was fine with it, [and] they found it in *Quirin*. And that became the term that was then used."

Quirin was a post hoc rationalization. "I'd like to say I was so well versed in *Quirin* that I pulled it directly from the case, but no. It was logic. It was the English language." Lietzau was "thinking in terms of what the American people would understand."

Lietzau is a smart and thoughtful man. He had no intention of instilling the term with the power to circumvent the Geneva Conventions. Indeed, Lietzau stated that "no one involved in the terminology change ever intended that it be so imbued." To Lietzau, "enemy combatant" was a descriptive term.

Nevertheless, that practice session changed the terminology for the men we captured in Afghanistan. From then on, they were enemy combatants. When I wrote to Colonel Lawrence Wilkerson, Secretary of State Colin Powell's chief of staff, about how the term "enemy combatant" originated, he replied that the unintended consequences of the term—as Martin Luther King Jr. said in another context—"roll down the mountain like mighty waters."

CHAPTER 7

WARRIOR JOURNALIST

"**F**undamentally, I'm the Guantánamo correspondent," Carol Rosenberg said during her interview in November 2011. If you were looking for understatements, this quote would rise to the top. If it were not for Rosenberg's tireless energy and relentless search for the story, those of us who have been studying the detention center in Guantánamo Bay would be vastly uninformed. She has been our lifeline to the lives, policies, contradictions, and cruelty of Guantánamo.

For most of her career, Rosenberg was a reporter for the *Miami Herald*. She was born in 1959 in North Dakota and grew up in New England, and she now lives in Miami Beach. She was initially based in the Middle East. In 1999, the *Herald* assigned her to cover the Southern Command, the Pentagon's office in Miami that oversees the Southern Hemisphere, known as SOUTHCOM. She held the title of military affairs correspondent. Her first assignment that year was to report on the removal of a minefield by the US Marines in Guantánamo.

In December 2001 Rosenberg heard that SOUTHCOM was setting up a prison in Cuba, to be used as a "relief valve." The military said that there were too many prisoners held in Bagram and Kandahar air bases in Afghanistan, and detainees would have to be transported to Guantánamo.

Rosenberg saw a document requisitioning construction of two thousand cells. She picked up the phone and questioned someone in the military about the need for that many cells for the prisoners. He replied that they would actually not need that many. Rather, he said, they were going to bring in about a hundred "really important" prisoners. Looking back, Rosenberg realizes that although the military was not using the term then, it was thinking of housing "the worst of the worst" in Guantánamo.

She and her editor thought it was "strange" that the Pentagon was going to build a prison system in Guantánamo. They decided that she should cover the story, and not return to the Middle East. As she explained it, "This was our piece of the war on terror, journalistically." Events of 9/11 happened in New York, DC, and Pennsylvania. With Cuba in the *Herald*'s backyard, and with many Cuban Americans living in Miami, the editor believed that the Guantánamo story was the *Herald*'s to cover. The newspaper would "own" the story even before she went to the naval base. (The paper has continued to invest in the story throughout the years.) Rosenberg flew to Guantánamo a few days before the first prisoners arrived.

On January 11, 2002, the day of the first detainees' arrival, Rosenberg and other reporters, along with their military escort, sat on a hillside overlooking the airstrip. It was hot, and they had brought water and hats. They were there an hour before the C-141 Starlifter cargo plane arrived carrying the first twenty men from Afghanistan. Boats patrolled the Caribbean coast while a helicopter with gunmen flew overhead. As Rosenberg told us, the military had never done this before and wanted to be certain that they had the necessary security.

Rosenberg described how she watched as the men in orange jumpsuits, blackened goggles, sound-canceling headsets, surgical masks, and mittens that were taped together shuffled off the plane one by one. They were chained at the ankles. When they walked down the ramp, their legs buckled, and they fell down on their knees.

The men then boarded a white school bus that had the seats removed. Their legs were chained to shackle points on the bus floor. The bus was driven to a ferry that carried them across Guantánamo Bay. The bus was then driven down Sherman Avenue—the main street of Guantánamo— past the movie theater, a McDonald's, and the church on the hill. They finally arrived at Camp X-Ray.

Rosenberg knew that "it was important to get it right for history. There were no cameras. There was no CNN, and we [the pool of reporters present that day] needed to write and describe the day Guantánamo opened." Because news photographers were banned, this was a writer's story.

While still in Miami, the military offered to embed Rosenberg at the base. Then, they retracted their offer but permitted her to stay one hundred of the first hundred and fifty days. Other reporters came and went, taking the tightly organized and restricted three-day-plus-tour and then writing the same bland officially sanctioned stories. Rosenberg stayed and has spent much of her time in Guantánamo ever since. She describes her work as writing "the first draft of history."

Rosenberg has immersed herself in the Guantánamo system—which changed as military officials issued improvised rules that changed daily. By being present day after day, she has unearthed important and even incredible stories.

In one instance, she met a soldier who told her that during prayer among the detainees, a one-legged detainee was leading the service. He was shouting out to the prisoners in a language that did not seem to follow the liturgy. The military interpreters believed that the detainee was telling the detainees, "Be strong, man. We're going to prevail, man."

Rosenberg wrote a story that said a loose structural command organization was evolving around prayer time. When the next group of reporters came into Guantánamo, they asked the general in charge about her story. Rosenberg told us what happened.

The general "sort of shrugged the question off and was a little bit cynical or skeptical of this article. . . . [Yet] a couple of days later, when he had the next briefing, he announced that, in fact, there had been some sort of a loose organization evolving in the camps around prayer time," she said.

"I believe one of the reasons I was allowed to stay down there as long as I was and report, as detailed and extensively as I was, is because the people who were running, who were supervising the camps, were Southern Command in Miami," Rosenberg said. "And every morning they picked up the *Miami Herald* and the paper was one of the pieces of intelligence as to what was going on at Gitmo. They would read things in the paper about what it was like, and that was important to them. I mean, they were getting their dispatches from their people." But they were also getting their information from Rosenberg.

The military revised one of its policies after Rosenberg wrote another story, about how she had seen detainees in jumpsuits, flat on stretchers, carried to interrogation huts from Camp X-Ray. "I remember saying to the colonel, 'What is this?' And he said, 'They were chained at the ankle. They were moving, you know, in baby steps. And it was taking forever to get them to and from the interrogation booth. And there was no mistreatment there; it's just efficient. It's more comfortable for them. It's hard for them to walk the distances from their cells to the interrogation booth, so we're getting them there.' And I said to him, 'This looks terrible.' And he said, 'No, no, no, it's okay. This is what we're doing and they're going in this way, they're not just coming out this way. Nothing's going on in the interrogation booths.' And I said, 'There may be the best explanation in the world, but I'm going to include this in the story I'm writing.'"

She wrote an article that appeared on page 3 of the *Miami Herald*. She believes that somebody at SOUTHCOM must have picked up the paper the next morning and said, "Get rid of the stretchers," because the stretchers disappeared. Pretty soon, they were using golf carts. And the men taken to and from the interrogation huts were sitting up.

Pentagon officials who worked in Washington and not at SOUTHCOM were not always charmed by Rosenberg's continuous presence at the base. They even suggested to her editor that she be replaced. According to Rosenberg, she had too much knowledge, or she was too aggressive, or she was too interested. There were others in the military who said that her work was important and that she should continue reporting.

And she has. Rosenberg flew down to the base as often as she could, and she petitioned to stay as long as she could once there. She never imagined that it would last for more than a few months. She noted that there were years when she was nearly the only reporter in Guantánamo, because people had lost interest. Most reporters went down once and never returned.

Rosenberg believes that if she were not reporting from Guantánamo, someone else would. "It was too important. It's too uncharted, it's too different. This isn't like anything that we've ever done in this hemisphere. This is 9/11! I mean, all of America was inventing from the morning of September 12th. So, if we hadn't done it, somebody else would have for sure. Very important stories have been written by other reporters who have gone through Guantánamo."

Certainly, other people have written important stories. But the fact is no one else has stepped up to do the heavy lifting, day after day. Even when the days were uneventful, Carol Rosenberg was there in the event something did happen.

At the end of the interview, she pulled out charts that she had brought with her. They begin before Guantánamo opened on January 11, 2002. The first date is January 6, when the command arrived to set up the detention center. The media arrived on January 9.

She explained that because the military switched out units every six months to a year, there was no institutional memory. Rosenberg and the charts provided that memory. She told us of an incident when she had to correct a military official who stated at a military briefing that there had been no amputations at Guantánamo. She took him aside and said, "Sir, I was here when they briefed the first amputation," a month after the detention center opened.

It's likely that, since 9/11, Rosenberg has lived in Guantánamo for more days than she has lived at her home in Miami Beach. She is still covering the naval base and detention center today. In summer 2018, she moved from the *Miami Herald* to the Washington bureau of McClatchy, a company with nearly thirty newspapers, including the *Herald*. In February 2019, when McClatchy was trimming its staff and offering retirement packages, she moved to the *New York Times*.

Carol Rosenberg has devoted the best years of her life to Guantánamo. Her uncompromising stories are the first drafts of history. The whole world is forever grateful.

EXPECTED AND UNEXPECTED CONSEQUENCES

CHANGES AND TRANSFORMATIONS

A prison guard converted to Islam. A prosecutor quit the naval base and entered a monastery. A human rights lawyer left the country with her family. The "King of Torture" apologized. He was one of three interrogators who crossed the line in their treatment of detainees. A detainee told us how Guantánamo saved his life. Men in the prison explained how they found silver linings among their grim experiences. Family members of detainees revealed their indomitable spirits.

After Guantánamo, people saw and experienced the world differently. The chapters in part II tell the stories of how people's lives changed forever.

CHAPTER 8

FACEBOOK FRIENDS

When Brandon Neely sat down to interview with us in Houston, Texas, he brought his wife. She knew much of his story, but it seemed that he wanted her to hear him share his story with us. Maybe he would recall something new, something he had not told her before.

Neely had signed up with the military before the events of 9/11. "When I joined, it was quiet. There was nothing going on around the world. I wasn't doing much. I was stocking groceries forty hours a week and I knew I needed change. I wanted really to go to college. I've been out of school almost two years. Because, you know, I grew up in a military household, so I figured I'd go get some training, something I want to do."

Neely received his military training. But everything changed after 9/11. As a private, he was assigned to be a prison guard in Guantánamo. (Later, he was elevated to private first class.) Neely was part of the first wave of soldiers to arrive at the detention center before it opened on January 11, 2002. His job was to escort the second detainee off the bus, a story described earlier in this book.

One of Neely's duties during the six months he was in Guantánamo was to walk through the cellblock each day and check on the prisoners. Military officials instructed the guards not to speak to the men. But when Neely heard several detainees speaking English, he could not resist. Perhaps conversing with the men would reduce his boredom. In his conversations, he discovered that the young men in the cells were similar in age and "were doing the same thing I was doing just two weeks ago."

"I spoke to Ruhal [Ahmed, a detainee from Tipton, a town outside London]. We were talking about girls, nightclubs, music and that we had listened to a lot of the same music. I mean, this could be a guy that I would probably hang out with back in the States, but here he is in Guantánamo. At the time I thought everybody was guilty, so I was just like, he just had to do something to get here. Here we were at Guantánamo, but on opposite sides of the cage."

Neely also conversed with several other English-speaking detainees, including Shafiq Rasul, who was also from Tipton.

Two years after he had completed his military service, Neely returned home and joined the Houston police force. Because he continued to be interested in Guantánamo, he noticed a story in the media about the Tipton Three. Neely turned to his Facebook account.

"I was like, yeah, I remember those guys. Just for kicks, I put in Shafiq [Rasul's] name, and there it was. It just popped up with his picture and I said, man, no way this guy is on Facebook. So, I sent one message and we just started talking through [Facebook]. It was just weird." Neely said, "You find everybody on Facebook now."

I asked him whether he still communicated with them.

"I talk to Ruhal [Ahmed] and Shafiq [Rasul] through Facebook and text message, you know, maybe a couple of times a week, and we exchange photos of the kids, just normal conversation. Since we're past the whole awkward stage, I would say that we're friends."

Neely flew to London in January 2010 for what he described as a reunion with the men he used to guard. That meeting is memorialized on YouTube.

When I asked Brandon Neely whether he was surprised in how he had once been a prison guard and had now become a good friend of the former detainees, he replied, "I used to be very close-minded. I've always said if I could change—anybody could change. I now look at stuff differently. I try to look at the whole picture instead of just one side of it. I really realized like not everything that the media says is what it is, and I've kind of opened myself up to different ways of life, 'cause not everything was the way they do it in Texas or any other place. I don't know anything about their religion or kind of people. But now I'm just open to it all. I guess I'm more open to change and different cultures and different people and that part of it was positive. . . . I just look at it all different."

CHAPTER 9

CONVERT

Before arriving in Guantánamo, Terry Holdbrooks's military police unit went to visit Ground Zero in New York City, where the towers fell.

"I can only imagine that the purpose behind that was for propaganda, you know. Take us to the place where 9/11 happened, then tell us that Islam and Muslims are to blame. Take us to Guantánamo, obviously everyone is going to be riled up and it's going to be an effective means of getting the job done," he told us.

When Private Holdbrooks became a Guantánamo prison guard in summer 2003, the military described the prisoners as "the worst of the worst and a bunch of towel heads and dirt farmers and such." He explained why the military used such phrases.

"They didn't want us to trust them or develop any kind of friendship or relationship with them whatsoever. . . . Don't have conversations with them. Don't befriend them."

However, many of the detainees were friendly to Holdbrooks, and he was encouraged by their openness to strike up conversations.

"I spent most of my time talking with detainees. If I was ever going to have an intelligent conversation, it was with a detainee. So, you know, talking about their lives, about where they came from, what society, education, and religion is like in the rest of the world. How often are you going to be in a place where you can meet people from forty some-odd different countries? It just wasn't something I was going to pass up. I had to, you know, I had to take use of the opportunity," he said.

Similar to the realizations of prison guard Brandon Neely, Holdbrooks recognized that "these individuals maybe listen to some of the same music that I do or they've watched the same movies, you know, we speak the same language, we're really not all that different. So, I don't understand why everything the military has told me is not equally up here."

Becoming friendly with some of the detainees, observing their practices and learning about their lives and their Muslim faith had a powerful effect on Holdbrooks. He began to limit his drinking, changed his diet by eliminating pork and greasy foods, and cut down on the number of cigarettes he had each day. His health improved. He also tried to change his speech, using more descriptive words and eliminating profanity. And he worked on being more positive about others. "These are important in Islam," he added.

At the time he was becoming more interested in the lives of the detainees and in their faith, it was also "right about that time my wife and I had truly hit our lowest point in our marriage." It caused him to wonder what he was missing in life, and how other people dealt with life-affecting and life-transforming issues. He was feeling miserable during this period in his life, he told us.

But while feeling miserable, he would look at the detainees and observe that they were "always smiling and happy despite the interrogation, the abuse, and the being away from their families. They are still happy."

Holdbrooks would wonder, "What are you guys so happy about? What do you have to be happy about? You have the same food, seven days a week. It's awful. It's hot out here, you don't have any air-conditioning. What are you happy about?"

And he would answer his questions: "They got faith. It's just a test. It's all it was for them—a test. And seeing them have that cohesion, that brotherhood, that unity, that I didn't even have with the military."

Islam began to "make sense" to him. It felt right. "So, I should really just go with this wholeheartedly," he thought.

He talked with a man known as the "General," one of the leaders of the detainees in the prison, about converting to Islam. "He blew me off the first time," Holdbrooks said. Holdbrooks persisted, and ultimately the General consented.

It happened on a midnight shift in December 2003, six months after Holdbrooks had arrived in Guantánamo. The prison was quiet and no other guards were around. Holdbrooks stood in the hallway outside the General's darkened cell and said his Muslim statement of faith, his Shahada.

Holdbrooks was in Guantánamo for another six months. During that time, many of the detainees knew of his conversion. He kept it secret from the military, but he did reveal it to two of his closest friends. Holdbrooks left the military with the rank of specialist.

Holdbrooks wrote to me in spring 2019 that he is still practicing his Muslim faith.

CHAPTER 10

FLIGHT (I)

Before he became a prosecutor on the Guantánamo military commissions, Lieutenant Colonel Darrel Vandeveld served in Iraq. His assignment was to pay reparations to the families of people American soldiers had killed. He drove up and down the war-torn roads tendering the money to each family. As he explained, "The price of human life, it turns out, in lower Iraq in 2005 to 2006 was around $2,000 per person." He looked up and added, "It's awful, awful to sit here and have to say that."

When he completed his duties in Iraq, he flew home to Pennsylvania. Once home, Vandeveld had what he called "readjustment difficulties."

"I was very irritable—quick to anger. I'll never forget. I came home. I took my youngest son to a Toys R Us. Got out of my car. I opened up my car door and it barely touched the door of the car next to me, but there happened to be some fellow sitting there and he kind of scowled, and I just went nuts—'Come on, get out of that car!' And here's my nine-year-old watching."

Vandeveld could not sleep, his mind constantly returning to Iraq. He felt he was not finished, and that he needed to "go forward" to survive. "You know, I would succumb to a war I had survived if I didn't continue in some other capacity to press on."

He had a lot of guilt that he did not die. "You made it home, and it could have been you. Couple of times, it could have been me. Well, every time we went into Iraq it could have been me, or it could have been somebody next door."

Not managing well in his civilian life, he pressed military officials to send him back into active duty. When the military sought JAG attorneys to prosecute alleged terrorists in Guantánamo, he leaped at the chance.

"I didn't go down to Guantánamo with the purest of motives. The *clearest* of motives—yes. But in retrospect, in hindsight, having had time to contemplate this and reflect on my conduct and my point of view, yeah, I was something of a monster."

When Vandeveld arrived in Guantánamo, he was still a fervent believer in the global war on terror. He never questioned what he had heard—even when he learned that the CIA tortured suspected terrorists.[1] To Vandeveld, the military's policy of "need to know" governed. He did not need to know. He trusted America's leaders. He believed that they had the intelligence to make the right decisions.

But in 2007, when Vandeveld was assigned to prosecute juvenile Mohamed Jawad, everything changed. (Jawad's age was never conclusively determined.) Jawad had been accused of throwing a hand grenade that injured two US service members and an Afghan interpreter who had been riding in a jeep in Kabul.

Major David Frakt, a Harvard Law School honors graduate and JAG defense attorney, was opposing counsel. (Frakt was subsequently promoted to lieutenant colonel.) Jawad was not "the worst of the worst," Frakt told Vandeveld. He urged Vandeveld to thoroughly review the evidence against Jawad.

At first, Vandeveld was dismissive of Frakt's claims. Jawad was guilty, Vandeveld was certain. The Afghans had turned him over to the Americans, and Vandeveld had Jawad's handwritten confession. Frakt explained that Jawad spoke Pashto, not Farsi, the language in which the confession was written. Furthermore, Jawad was illiterate, and could not sign his name. Rather, Jawad had been told that the document was his release paper. He was instructed to put his thumbprint on it. He did. But, as Frakt pointed out, Jawad was not thumbprinting a release paper but a confession written in another language.

Jawad's case proved life-changing for Vandeveld.

"I became like someone who had been wearing a mask and suddenly I took it off," he said. "And there staring me in the mirror was not Darrel Vandeveld—this hard-charging soldier who was going to single-handedly win the war on terrorism—but somebody possessed of humanity, who could extend that humanity to even someone who is an enemy, a dirty little terrorist, from a dirty little crappy foreign land. A land that's a pile of rocks."

Vandeveld began to reexamine his beliefs. He told us how Frakt encouraged him to appeal to his greater sense of reason, and not to the hatred, intolerance, bias, and predispositions that he had. It did not take long for Vandeveld to realize that he would have to leave his post as prosecutor at Guantánamo.

He boarded a plane for Washington. Upon landing, he made his way to a Benedictine monastery, where he contemplated the course of life for a few days. He sent a note to John Dear, a Jesuit priest.

"I just said simply, 'I'm a prosecutor at the commissions in Guantánamo and I have grave reservations about what I'm doing and what our country is doing. Tell me what to do.'" Dear responded immediately.

"'What you're doing is participating in evil,' Dear said. 'This is something that God does not want you to do. Stop, resign, and start your life over.'

"Talk about being thunderstruck!" Vandeveld told us.

After leaving the monastery, but still in DC, Vandeveld took action. He wrote an email to the army judge advocate general and identified the flaws in Jawad's prosecution. He cc'd the chief prosecutor and asked to be reassigned.

Soon after, Vandeveld went public, resigning from his position as prosecutor and denouncing the military commission process. In response, the military required him to remain in his "furnished quarters," an apartment in Rosslyn, Virginia, until further notice. He was confined for three months in what the military described as a "house arrest." His government-issued Blackberry phone was shut off.

Vandeveld believed that the order to stay in the apartment was clearly unlawful. He said that he would have lost it had he not gone out.[2] He went running along the Potomac, visited the Smithsonian, and went to bookstores and readings. During this time, a military official issued media "talking points" on Vandeveld. Frakt described the talking points as very personal and nasty, designed to discredit Vandeveld because of his resignation and his public denunciation of the military commission process.

While he was under house arrest, Vandeveld provided a declaration and testified remotely via video teleconference at Jawad's pretrial hearing in Guantánamo. He testified that he believed Jawad's confession was fraudulent and had been the product of coercion, if not torture. He also explained that not all the evidence in the case had been turned over to the defense. The charges against Jawad were dropped. Jawad was repatriated to Afghanistan, after nearly seven years in detention.

The military released Vandeveld from active duty. He had accepted a job as director of a public defender office in Pennsylvania.

The military also began an investigation that could have resulted in a denial of his pension and other benefits. Ironically, during the time of the investigation, the military was looking for a judge advocate certified as capital case qualified. Vandeveld was identified as one of the few people with that designation. "In a turnaround from attempting to toss me," Vandeveld said, he was called up to defend Sergeant John Russell, who was accused of killing five fellow service members in Iraq.[3]

After the murder case ended, Vandeveld retired with a full pension. He did not return to the director position in Pennsylvania, instead becoming a part-time public defender. He also accepted a position teaching part-time at a local university. Vandeveld and Frakt became close friends. They worked on a number of military criminal trials together on behalf of defendants.

Since he left the military, Darrel Vandeveld has hiked the pilgrimage route of Camino Santiago several times. Known as the Way of Saint James, it is a network of routes over a distance of five hundred miles from the French border to the Cathedral of Santiago de Compostela in Spain. The cathedral is the home of the shrine of Saint James the Great. Today, people from all over the world walk the paths on their spiritual journeys.

CHAPTER 11

FLIGHT (2)

When Gitanjali (Gita) Gutierrez returned home from her first trip to Guantánamo, she could hardly sleep. She had dreams of people chasing her and her clients. She and her clients were all trying to escape. In the days, weeks, and months that followed, Gutierrez recalled, "I would dream that I was being interrogated or that I was watching someone being interrogated, and I would sit straight up in bed and start yelling and wake myself up."

A year later, when she was representing another client who had been severely tortured, "he was the first thing I thought of every morning and the last thing I thought of when I went to bed—that he was still there. And I had a very full life, and family and children that were involved in my life, and a lot going on—and that still was the dominant thought for my day."

Not knowing what else to do, she immersed herself in her work. She worked nonstop. For nearly two years, Gutierrez did not take a vacation. She thought that if she worked harder every day she could make a difference for the men she was representing. At the end, it made no difference, she concluded.

When she sat down to interview with us in 2011, Gutierrez described herself as a human rights activist with a law degree. Her "primary goal was to affirm the humanity of the person." Adopted and raised in rural Kentucky, she is of South Asian heritage. She graduated from Cornell Law School in June 2001, three months before the 9/11 attacks. In 2003, while on a two-year fellowship, Gutierrez began working with the Center for Constitutional Rights in New York on the *Rasul v. Bush* case. When her fellowship ended, she joined CCR as staff attorney.

Gutierrez was the first habeas attorney to fly to Guantánamo. It was September 2004, three months after the Supreme Court ruled in *Rasul* that the detainees had the right to challenge their detentions in federal court.

While working with the detainees, she asked CCR to provide psychological training and counseling for her and the other lawyers. She understood that people who work with torture survivors might experience secondary trauma. CCR provided the training. However, counseling could not resolve all her problems. The work was too intense. And she could not share her concerns and work with lawyers in her office who did not have security clearances. In addition, government restrictions, such as the protective order delineating what lawyers could and could not do, interfered with her doing the best she could for her clients.

The protective order, between the government and the lawyers who represented detainees, restricted lawyers from revealing their clients' memories and experiences of torture. That is, the lawyers could not reveal the words they heard from their clients, unless the government consented. The administration characterized evidence of torture as classified sources and methods.

Barred from publicizing what happened to her clients, Gutierrez felt that she was complicit in the system and that her ability as a lawyer was being destroyed. "I was being used in a system to conceal torture," she told us.

She became further distraught after she realized that President Obama was not going to close Guantánamo. She watched as some men were released while others were not. The process seemed haphazard and arbitrary. She was concerned that several of her clients might never leave the prison. They would become "forever" prisoners and die there.

She became more convinced than ever that her work was ineffective. She got to the point where she was feeling as hopeless as her Guantánamo clients. To her, Guantánamo was "like seeing a very ugly side of this country. . . . How could this happen? It was the antithesis of everything I've ever learned about being a lawyer—everything I've ever learned about being the citizen of a democracy, as much of a democratic experiment as this country is."

Gutierrez's disillusionment in her country's policies increased. "I never had a rosy picture of the United States, but I believed in this country's diversity, and I believed in our ability. I believe in social justice movements in this country, and that's changed for me in these ten years."

Moreover, seeing some judges express the same racist biases as those voiced by members of the public alarmed her. The courts were there to check racism, not reflect it. As she explained, the courts were supposed to check the executive from doing "something to someone just because they're not a citizen."

She also worried for herself, and never went anywhere without her passport.

"I have not parted company with it since that first visit because, more than anything else, that visit made me understand that if the United States thinks—doesn't think you have citizenship, they will do whatever they want to do to you. And because I'm not a white American, I always have it with me."

In 2011, ten years after graduating from law school, Gutierrez resigned from CCR. She moved with her husband and family to Bermuda. She explained that because she did not want to be complicit in the government's actions, she thought it best to leave the country.

We interviewed her soon after the move. She intended to continue to use her law degree. She felt privileged to have the degree and described it as a very important tool.

She also expressed her concerns about her children's experiences and perceptions in America. She did not want her children "growing up with the exaggerated threat of terrorism hanging over them all the time. I don't want them to see friends who are Muslim and South Asian and Arab and immediately associate them with the stereotyping that happens in the United States. I want them to know what's going on in this country, but I don't want this to be the point of reference for them."

Gitanjali Gutierrez retained her citizenship and worked for several years as a US lawyer after her move. In 2015, she was appointed Bermuda's first information commissioner, an independent, nongovernmental office that promotes and reviews public access to actions and decisions by public agencies.

— CHAPTER 12 —

FROM PRIDE TO SHAME

On October 6, 2005, Specialist Damien Corsetti returned home from Iraq. He wore so many ribbons that he "looked like a general." Within twenty-four hours of his return, he was placed in handcuffs and arrested for mistreatment of detainees at Bagram, Afghanistan, where he served as an interrogator before he went to Iraq. Corsetti was known as the "King of Torture."

When he was arrested, Corsetti was confused and angry. He had joined the military because he believed in America. He had always trusted that the military would approve only what was right. He did what the military and America had asked of him. He believed that he had done nothing wrong. In fact, military lawyers had approved his harsh interrogation techniques, after he specifically questioned the legitimacy of the methods. Yet now the military and the full powers of the United States government had turned on him. Corsetti said he had gone "from pride to shame."

Years after he was arrested, he spoke into our camera and apologized for his actions. "I've apologized, and I'll continue to apologize. . . . You need to continue to apologize until nobody needs to hear it anymore."

Corsetti, Marshal Skaggs, and Glendale Walls worked at the Bagram air base as interrogators. The young men formed a close friendship there. Corsetti and Skaggs had known each other professionally for a year before they were at Bagram together.

Colonel Brittain Mallow, Army commander, Criminal Investigation Task Force, described the military interrogation program in the early days after 9/11 as "chaotic."[1] There was no protocol, and even senior officers did not have a great deal of experience. Yet there was tremendous pressure on them to produce results. The message from the top to the interrogators was "find me something that works."[2] In essence, the message was, find a way to stop another feared attack.

Because the military left the men to their own devices, they experimented. Their superiors countenanced, if not actively encouraged, their experimental methods. Their superiors often looked the other way when the interrogators crossed the line. The boundaries were never clarified. These three individuals were not trained for the job.

The military used experimental interrogation approaches at both Bagram and Kandahar bases, where detainees were held before they were transferred to Guantánamo. The military used untried interrogation methods in the early days of Guantánamo, too, after the camp first opened, in January 2002. However, according to the detainees, the interrogation methods in Guantánamo were focused more on psychological abuse than on physical abuse.

For more than two years after September 11, 2001, the military and law enforcement agencies such as the FBI did not see eye-to-eye on intelligence gathering. Law enforcement agencies used a rapport-based approach in gathering evidence. They wanted to get to know a detainee and show empathy, believing that a detainee would be more likely to tell the truth if a relationship was built between the interrogator and detainee. Law enforcement agencies also believed that cruel interrogation techniques and torture were illegal and did not result in credible evidence.

However, law enforcement agencies and the military had different goals after 9/11. The agencies looked for evidence of past crimes and terrorist activity; the military was focused on obtaining actionable intelligence to stop another attack. The military felt it could not wait to build a relationship with a detainee. It needed intel immediately.

With this background in mind, we consider the three young men in Afghanistan who were ill prepared to become military interrogators after 9/11.

Reprieve, a highly respected London-based human rights organization that advocates on behalf of prisoners worldwide, collected data on the treatment of prisoners at Bagram air base in Afghanistan from 2002 to 2003. Reprieve described Bagram as a cavernous converted aircraft hangar. There were metal cages surrounded by coils of razor wire. Some cages were no larger than one by two meters (approximately three by six feet). Approximately twenty people were in each cage, sleeping on foam mats spread on the ground. The detainees rarely saw daylight. Plastic buckets served as toilets. There were also a half-dozen plywood isolation cells. Along one wall was a catwalk for guards and interrogators to observe the detainees.[3]

Reprieve uncovered mistreatment that included the shackling of detainees; stripping detainees naked; forbidding them to look at each other; stepping on the neck of a prostrate detainee; kicking a detainee in the genitals; forcing a detainee to kiss the boots of an interrogator; forcing a detainee to pick bottle caps from a drum filled with a mix of excrement and water; depriving detainees of sleep for weeks; forcing them to stand while a bright light shined into their eyes; chaining detainees to ceilings and doors; forcing them to stand or kneel for hours while wearing hoods or spray-painted goggles; subjecting them to electrocution; beatings with whips or baseball bats until unconscious (a practice referred to as "beat down"); feeding detainees very little; adjusting detainees' room temperatures from 100 degrees to 10 degrees; dousing detainees with freezing water in the winter, resulting in frostbite and amputation; subjecting them to light deprivation, snarling dogs, mock executions, and threats of rape; placing detainees in prolonged isolation for up to a year; interrogating them while they could hear the terrifying screams of others; and desecrating the Quran.[4]

Since Corsetti left the military, he has tried to redeem himself and become a better person. Each time we interviewed him, he became progressively more reflective and self-aware, which is why he continued to speak to us and why we spoke to him three times, more than anyone else. But when I first met him, he was scary.

Because we had never met, we decided to get together before the interview at a café near my hotel, located in Georgia. It was 8 a.m. on March 4, 2013. As soon as we sat down, Corsetti ordered a Bloody Mary. He began by revealing that he went to see his psychologist the day before. He had sought counseling to assist him in preparing for the interview. He said that the military had assessed him at 100 percent post-traumatic stress disorder. But obtaining the 100 percent PTSD rating was a huge struggle. At first, the military would not even acknowledge that he had a serious case of PTSD. But Corsetti pursued the matter and eventually won.

"Sometimes, I lose it," Corsetti said, explaining that on certain days he would wake up in the morning and stay home all day. He knew that if he left the house, he would not function well in public places. To say that I was nervous about sitting across from this large and intimidating person—the King of Torture—would be a ridiculous understatement.

In our early, stilted conversation, I noticed his leg twitching feverishly under the table. It never stopped. Within a few minutes, he went out for a smoke. Fifteen minutes later, he took another cigarette break. It was now 8:45, and he asked to order a second Bloody Mary. I soon thought— if he had another drink, who knew what he would be like during the interview?

I panicked that the interview would implode before it even started. Holding my breath, I suggested that instead of another drink, we head over to the hotel for the interview. He agreed. He smoked another cigarette as we walked.

At the hotel, we began with a voice check. Johnny Symons, my filmmaker, could sense Corsetti's tension and uneasiness. When the interview began, Corsetti continued to be agitated and anxious. His legs did not stop shaking, sometimes violently. We took lots of breaks so he could go out for a smoke. At the first break, I was certain that Corsetti would not return. But he did.

As the interview proceeded, Corsetti's demeanor changed. His stress level moderated. He was relaxing, and became more at ease. At the end of the interview he apologized, expressing regret on camera for his harsh mistreatment of detainees at Bagram. "I recognize the [detainees] as human beings and as my equals on this earth, with the right to exist and be happy just as much as I do," he said.

Earlier, I had wondered whether the trembling legs, incessant smoking, and Bloody Mary were signals of his own worries and tension in knowing he would be telling his very personal story on film to a stranger. But because Corsetti was trying to atone for his deeds and become a more thoughtful, generous, and caring person, the interview had been therapeutic for him.

He spoke to me because he believed that telling his story on film would help him get better and help him express regret for what he had done. He apologized again at the end of his second interview, six weeks later. In a third interview, more than two years later, in July 2015, he told us he was doing much better in managing his life. In my limited observations over the years, I thought he had appreciably improved. The tensions that existed in the previous interviews had dissipated. He seemed relaxed and comfortable chitchatting with us, both before and after the interview.

When he was young, Corsetti said, he had "wanted to do my own thing. I was bored with society's norms." He grew up outside Washington, DC, in a middle-class family, but school was not for him. "I would rather smoke pot and play Nintendo than go to class, and so I was really lacking a lot of discipline."

In September 2000, at the age of twenty and realizing that he would not obtain college and graduate degrees, he decided that to obtain decent work without the education, he needed a security clearance. His choices were to work either for a defense contractor or a government agency. He chose the army because of its counterintelligence program. It was very important to him to have a top-secret clearance for jobs after leaving the military. His long-term goals did not include the military. He had higher ambitions.

"I wanted to be James Bond."

When Corsetti enlisted, in 2000, he asked to be assigned to intelligence services. He intended to circumvent combat. An intelligence officer collects evidence from a suspect or target. The officer may also recruit assets or engage in espionage. The duties do not normally include interrogations.[5]

But after 9/11, everything changed. The military needed hundreds of new interrogators. Corsetti's supervisors redirected him into interrogating "high-value detainees." A high-value detainee is presumably someone who knows or has access to actionable intelligence. However, after 9/11 the term was arbitrarily used in its designation of individuals, because the military did not have sufficient information on many of the people captured. The military made mistakes in its initial assessments.

Corsetti's training as an interrogator was limited to two weeks. He arrived in Bagram on July 29, 2002, when he was twenty-two years old. His mission was to obtain actionable intelligence from the detainees.

The way Corsetti saw it, the US sent him as an agent of America's anger—he was there to carry out America's demand for revenge, he said.

He was also personally "super angry," after seeing the damage to the Pentagon on 9/11 while living in Washington.

He believed in his country and was convinced by his superiors that he was doing the right thing. He was even under the impression that if he did not take an aggressive stance toward the prisoners, he was not performing his duties. America's emotions were raw after 9/11.

But Corsetti was conflicted. "I'm going to go over there and I'm going to have to go kill some poor motherfucker, and he's going to be trying to kill me, and what good can come of this?"

When he first arrived, he was terrified—"I was scared of the whole horror of war." But he had a job to do.

"It was my job at that prison to be the big scary guy for everybody."

Corsetti used "fear up harsh"—a technique in which the interrogator may appear threatening and overpowering in order to impress on the detainee that he has something to fear. And he employed "other not-so-nice techniques."

Interrogation tactics and procedures similar to "fear up harsh"—such as "fear up,"[6] "pride up and ego down," and "ego down harsh"[7]—were all designed to not only instill a sense of fear, but to quash the detainee's sense of self. JAG Colonel Manuel Supervielle has described these tactics as "ad hoc [and] very helter-skelter."[8]

Although the military used these imprecise terms for interrogations, the interrogation approaches in Bagram were limited only by the imaginations of the interrogators.[9]

"Some of the [techniques] were in the [army field manual], some of them we created while we were [in Bagram]. They were encouraged there. . . . We were given extreme liberty to try to pioneer different things to do," Corsetti told us. He and another interrogator came up with a procedure they called "casual cruelty."

"Casual cruelty was a way of dehumanizing the prisoners. You would use them as furniture. You would—my favorite thing to do would be to have them kneeling next to me and I'd pull out their pocket on their shirt and use it as an ashtray. Not even acknowledge their existence and just play cards in front of them for two hours or read a book or just take away the humanity of the prisoner and it broke their will pretty quickly as it would, you know, if you can imagine," Corsetti explained. Other teams of interrogators later adopted the procedure.

Everything a detainee received was a privilege bestowed by the interrogator, including clothing. Detainees went to the restroom, ate and drank, and slept with the interrogators' consent.

If he did not like what he was hearing from a detainee, or if the detainee chose to say nothing, Corsetti had no problem turning up the heat. He would pluck hairs out of a detainee's chest or put his crotch up against someone's face. He would make them sit in a stress position for five hours without moving. Stress positions, which were in themselves dehumanizing, included requiring the man to kneel with his hands behind his head, sit on an invisible chair or against a wall, or stand with his feet more than shoulder width apart.

Corsetti added to the stress positions. He sat by the detainee smoking and dumping his ashes into the man's pockets. He kept one detainee kneeling for two hours, while he read a book and spat on him. When a sergeant testified at Corsetti's trial that Corsetti sat on a detainee's chest, Corsetti admitted it "sounds like something I would do," even though he could not remember doing it.

Corsetti believes that his methods led to intelligence that saved American lives.

"I mean, I definitely got good intelligence while I was there. I saved—at the time, immediately, through direct action of intelligence I gathered—I know I've saved lives. I know I've saved US lives. I know I've saved lives outside of the United States as well."

On the other hand, he wondered whether his actions in obtaining the intelligence led to the recruitment of terrorists and "in the end cost more lives" than he saved.

At the start of his job, Corsetti believed what the military had told him—that all the men captured were connected to the attacks on 9/11 and were high-value detainees. After all, he thought, why would the government lie to him and bring him people who were not involved? After working for a few months, gathering insights into a possible next attack, he began to wonder whether all the men he interrogated were actually connected to the attacks. It seemed to him that a number of the captives were swept up in a wide net and did not belong in Bagram. They had little to nothing to offer.[10]

Around the same time, Corsetti and a few of his colleagues began to question the tactics they used to obtain the information. He wondered out loud whether they were violating the Geneva Conventions (GC), which forbid torture and other cruel treatment and require humane treatment of all captives. Corsetti's supervisor arranged a meeting with the military's JAG lawyers. The military lawyers assured Corsetti and the other interrogators that they were not violating American law or the GC, and that they could continue with their interrogation techniques. This advice may have been based on the fact that on February 7, 2002, President Bush determined that the GC did not apply to the prisoners captured in Afghanistan.

Because Corsetti had received training in the GC before he arrived in Afghanistan, he questioned the legal advice. But he believed that if he did not comply—after being advised that his interrogation practices were legal—he would be disciplined and perhaps prosecuted for not following orders. Consequently, he continued the abusive intelligence-gathering techniques.

Later, those same techniques became the basis of Corsetti's arrest and trial for abusing prisoners. "I was given awards for those techniques, and then I was turned around and charged for them a few years later," he said.

After Corsetti had served seven months in Afghanistan, he was sent to Iraq. He worked as an intelligence officer and conducted interrogations. He was one of the first interrogators to arrive at the notorious prison at Abu Ghraib. He told us that he was not aware of the abusive actions by the military police (MPs) that were occurring in the prison before photos of the torture at Abu Ghraib were released in spring 2004. The photos provided visual evidence that Americans clearly engaged in torture and included images of naked men lying on top of each other, of a hooded man standing on a box with electrical wires fixed to his hands, and of a female MP holding a leash attached to a naked man's neck, dragging the man along the floor.

On Corsetti's thigh is a tattoo of the Statue of Liberty. She is holding a gun to her head. A tear is running down her expressively sad face. Corsetti asked an artist to tattoo this image after President George Bush won reelection in 2004 because he could not believe that our country would reelect a president who had led us down the path of torture.

"I got a tattoo the day after he got re-elected—the Statue of Liberty shooting herself in the head, kind of like death to liberty, look what you fuckers have done." It was the beginning of his transformation from the person he had been to the one he became.

— — —

On October 6, 2005, Corsetti returned home from Iraq and was arrested for mistreatment of detainees in Afghanistan. He was charged with maltreatment, assault, and dereliction of duty, and performing an indecent act with another person, all during the period from August 2002 to February 2003.[11]

Factually, he was accused of sitting on top of a detainee, throwing garbage on him, and putting cigarette ash on him; walking across a detainee's handcuffed hands and pulling hairs out of his chest; pulling the head and beard of a detainee; removing a detainee's pants to expose his genitalia to a female interrogator, and bending him over a table and waving a bottle in close proximity of his buttocks; striking the detainee in the leg, groin, and chest with his hands and knees; and showing a detainee a condom and his penis and saying, "This is special for you. This is your god" and "I'm going to fuck you," and placing his penis near the detainee's face and placing his groin against the detainee's buttocks.[12]

The charges were based partly on statements by Guantánamo detainee Ahmed al-Darbi.[13] Sergeant Jennifer Higginbotham, who had worked with Corsetti in Bagram, testified at his trial that she had witnessed Corsetti pulling a detainee's beard and sitting on a detainee.[14] She also testified that there was no standard operating procedure for interrogations when they first arrived.[15]

Corsetti has disputed that he ever pressed his penis against someone's face. It was either an exaggeration or a mix-up in interpretation, he said. He admitted that he used the detainee's shirt as an ashtray, poured water over him, and made him pick up feces with latex gloves and cardboard. Corsetti also confirmed that detainees were hung by their wrists.

When he was arrested, Corsetti was confused and angry.

"I felt like, you bastards made me go do things that completely violated my conscience and changed forever who I am as a human being, but I went along with it. [Now you will] charge me for the very same things you gave me awards for."

He was home, but he felt like a stranger, as though he did not belong and would never be accepted again. And to see *People of the United States v. Corsetti* on paper—"I got a lot of animosity towards the American people, like, you sons of bitches, like, really? And now you're going to call for my head. You're going to call me a monster."

What did Americans expect? he asked. They had sent him to Afghanistan to "get even." He followed the military's marching orders. And now they wanted to punish him for it.

The other interrogators who were charged for their actions in Bagram agreed to plead to certain charges, and/or agreed to testify against him, Corsetti told us. He was also offered a plea bargain, but he turned it down. He explained that he could not plead guilty to crimes he did not believe he had committed. He added that he would have pleaded to some of the charges, including an assault—pulling a man's head by his beard. But he would not agree to plead guilty to something he did not do or to a tactic that the military's JAG lawyers told him was not torture or cruel treatment. Even if the tactic had been wrong, he had obtained JAG approval.

I asked Corsetti to describe the moral and ethical violations that he admitted committing.

"I started not looking at these people as human and looking at them as numbers, and looking at them as evil. But these people, even the terrorists, are not evil. They're good and evil. They have good and bad in them, as all of us do. We all have our demons and, hey, they chose a different way, but you can't really say that you wouldn't have turned out like that if you were raised and sent to a madrassa and raised in the environment that they were raised in. You can't say that you would be any different. . . . I didn't treat human beings like human beings. . . . I worsened humanity during a time of my life."

Corsetti added, "I do want to clarify that I'm not innocent of everything they accused me of. [Yet], on a legal basis, I was innocent of everything they accused me of. . . . [even though I did] some horrible things. Legally, not really. Legally, on paper, I didn't. But on a moral level, ethical level, I definitely did, you know."

He believed that his behavior, as well as that of the other interrogators, was standard policy. "Basically, just everything that we did was acceptable—that this is not the work of this loose cannon, rogue wolf Corsetti. This was institutionalized, and this is how shit went down." He added that the military made decisions "facilitated through a system."

Corsetti was charged in 2005. The court-martial was in 2006, before a jury of military officials. He told us that he had thirteen charges in nine different counts against him. He was looking at a twenty-three-year federal indictment.

Corsetti called his parents and asked them to find a top civilian attorney to join his appointed military attorney in his defense. He told his parents that if they did not want him to be in prison for a major portion of his life, they needed to find and finance the civilian attorney. They found one. Even with the addition of a civilian attorney, Corsetti continued to believe that he would be convicted.

During his trial, he was self-destructive. He took multiple drugs and even attempted suicide. Before and during the trial, "everybody kept telling me, 'Oh, you're just under a lot of stress 'cause of your trial. Once your trial's over, you'll be back to yourself.'"

At the end of the trial, Corsetti was acquitted of every charge, including those to which he would have pleaded in a plea deal. He was honorably discharged from the military October 1, 2006. "I was so convinced [that I would be convicted] that when they brought me in to read my verdict, my knees buckled and I just completely collapsed and started crying. And it wasn't that it was over and it wasn't that I got away. I was crying because I had lost all faith in my fellow soldiers, all faith in them," he told us.

When I asked him why he thought he was acquitted, he credited the result to "jury nullification." Corsetti believed that the jury was composed of military personnel who had been in special operations and personally understood what he had gone through at that time in 2002. Consequently, Corsetti believed that the jury did not want to convict him, even when the facts supported some of the charges.

After he was acquitted, Corsetti felt like a stranger in his home country. "I don't know if I will ever feel accepted here again. I really felt pushed away by the people of this country. It really hurt. It really hurt."

When he was released from the military, Corsetti was unable to deal with his return to civilian life. He was undisciplined and violent. He bounced around strip clubs and biker bars, living what he described as a rough life for three years. He started taking heroin. "The trial, war, treatment all became one," he said.

"I don't know that if it was just the drugs. Though, at that point, I was in such a deep depression that I never really snapped out of that for a few years after my trial was over. I mean, it still sits with me today. It was probably two years after it was over before I started to feel any better."

I asked him what it was that pulled him out of his deep depression and drug use.

"Well, my wife left with my child, and I don't blame her. I was an animal. I used to beat the shit out of her. So, I totally understand. I'm glad she left me. I would never have started my progression in life had she not left me."

The Veterans Administration (VA) medical personnel had tried to get him to see a psychiatrist, but Corsetti did not trust psychiatrists.

"They just want to medicate you and it really does no good. . . . You're trading my cocaine for a Xanax, and that's all you're doing. I still have my problems, you're just masking them."

Things finally changed when he met a social worker at the VA who had served in Vietnam and was a perfect listener without judgment. They bonded. Meetings with the social worker were therapy. The meetings, he said, "really started me talking, which was nice because I had tried to talk about these events before my trial and it was almost as if I had a physical reaction; my throat would close up and my eyes would well up with tears, and I couldn't get any words out. I would just sit there and cry, and I wanted to talk. I wanted to tell people something other than, 'Do you know what I've done?' I wanted to actually tell people what I had done."

Therapy prompted him to go into rehabilitation and leave the hard drugs.

I asked Corsetti whether he regretted entering the military.

"No, I mean it definitely—it made me accountable. Made me [get] to the point where I was willing to be accountable for myself because you're forced to be accountable for your actions. And I needed that, and I needed the direction. I needed the discipline at the time. I really didn't have any of that. I was not, by no means, at twenty years old—I was not a man. I was still very much a child at twenty, with a child's mind, and wanted to do childish things."

But he also wanted people to know that he was not unique, and that many other young men might have reacted similarly.

"I guess I'd really want to emphasize to people that, hey, this could be you. If you were taken from your situation and put into this, don't think that your decisions would be greatly different than my own. I wasn't this person when I went there. I became this person, and it was through the environment I was in that that happened."

Becoming accountable was transformative for Damien Corsetti. It was why he was able to apologize on camera to the people he harmed, each time I interviewed him.

"I look back at my life and I'm very pleased, very pleased with who I am today. I'm pleased with how I treat people. I'm pleased at the father that I am to my children. I'm pleased with the son that I am to my parents. And I'm very happy with that. And I wouldn't be this person, who I am, had I not gone through all of this just horrible experience. And at the same time, as mad as I am that I had to go through it, I'm very grateful because it ultimately led me to a point where I am okay with myself."

Damien Corsetti's experience and ultimate transformation may not be typical of the military interrogators in Bagram. But he is not unique. In the following years, the government prosecuted and convicted three former military interrogators and three guards in Bagram for mistreating the detainees.[16] Interrogators were also accused in the deaths of two Afghan detainees, Dilawar and Habibullah.[17]

When we interviewed Damien Corsetti the third time, his two friends and fellow interrogators, Marshal Skaggs and Glendale Walls, were visiting him. He asked each of them whether they would speak with us. Walls agreed. Skaggs would not. Corsetti then suggested that Skaggs observe our interview with Corsetti. In the room, before Corsetti's interview began, Skaggs emphasized to me that he had never spoken to anyone, other than his girlfriend of more than a dozen years, about his experiences in the military, and that he would not speak to us. He was unequivocal.

At the end of Corsetti's interview, Skaggs looked up and said that he had never expected that our interview style would be so open-ended, allowing Corsetti to tell his full story in his own words, in the way he wanted to tell it. No judgment. And no agenda. Skaggs was inspired.

At first, the woman who has been with him for years—whom he credits with saving his life—was leery and did not want Skaggs to talk to us. He asked her to look at our Witness to Guantánamo website, where she could read about our mission to document the stories and watch video clips of many of our past interviews. She did, and that changed her mind. Skaggs flew to San Francisco with his brother to tell his story.

Marshal Skaggs was twenty years old when he joined the army, before 9/11. He hoped to use the money from enlisting to pay for college. It did not quite turn out that way. Similar to Corsetti's experience, Specialist Skaggs was assigned by the army to become a counterintelligence agent. However, after the attacks on 9/11, Skaggs was moved into an interrogation unit. He was sent to Bagram in 2002, with less than two weeks training and with no exposure to the Afghan culture he was about to enter.

Skaggs hated his job as an interrogator. The work became more and more oppressive, as the days, weeks, and months wore on. He hated the job and the people he interrogated. They were the reason he was there, he said, and he hated them for it. "We didn't want to be there," he said. "We were pissed at them, so it went from like kind of being malicious and cruel to being angry. And when you factor all of that stuff in, you know, we weren't gathering any intel. And we wouldn't even really talk to them, we would just put them in stress positions, we would pour water on their head, we would berate them, we would degrade them. . . . We would kick the Quran or we would make them kick the Quran around the room. You know, just complete sacrilege. And then we would just simply write in our reports 'no actionable intel' or something like that."

Soon it was not even about the intel. "[We thought] you're the reason why we're here—you and your stupid, fucked-up country. We don't really like you. We think you're an ignorant fool, so we're going to laugh at you and we're going to make you do stuff that you don't want to do for the sole reason of laughing at you," he told us.

The interrogators were convinced that it did not matter to whom they were talking. Every detainee was "bullshitting" them. To the interrogators, these people were simply "ignorant."

"You know, these people obviously have no idea how to live. This is what I thought. If you can imagine living about five hundred, six hundred, seven hundred years ago, that's what Afghanistan is like; it really is. When we got there, it was a culture shock, and it was interesting for about the first two hours and then after that it became just tiresome," Skaggs said.

About midway through his interview, Skaggs asked for a break. He had been extremely nervous. His shaking hands expressed the tension, as did his faltering voice. When he returned from the break about ten minutes later, he was much calmer and focused. His body language, his facial expressions, and his hand motions had all changed. The nervousness was gone. After the interview, Skaggs told us that he had phoned Corsetti during the break for advice. Corsetti advised, "Tell him everything."

Skaggs said that he was a drinker and abused drugs. He explained that he found comfort in one thing, "cutting myself with the sharpest thing that I could find." Cutting became habitual, "just something that I just had to do."

Skaggs did not know why he did it. He said the most accurate way he had heard the experience described was of a balloon filled with too much air; a person cut himself to release the pressure.

He knew he was not well. But "you don't ask for help. You've seen people do that kind of stuff, like talk to somebody about that—they get on Prozac and now they're not employable, so they go home."

Skaggs said "it became much worse when I was drinking, but I was always drinking, so it was always pretty bad. And like once I found out that they're planning on sending me back to Iraq six months after my ETS [expiration of term of service], though I'm supposed to be out then, I just—I became just inconsolable. I wouldn't listen to anybody."

The cutting became much worse after he learned he would be sent back to Iraq. Soon after, one of his roommates found Skaggs slumped over a chair, with blood all over the floor. Skaggs had passed out and was sent to the hospital. He was in a psychiatric ward for a week. But Skaggs was glad that he did not have to deploy. He received his ETS.

Skaggs was so thrilled to be released that when the military asked him whether he wanted his veteran's benefits, he said no. "I just need to get out. . . . That would fix everything."

For Skaggs, the process of getting the compensation, even if it required only an extra three days in the army, was not worth it.

However, his release from the army did not "fix everything." When he got home, he went into psychiatric care for a week. But because he was no longer in the military, the care did not continue. He received no further care or counseling. "Nobody contacted me from the VA or anything. I just left. And that was the last I heard from the army."

Skaggs refused to talk to family members. He was drinking every single day, all day. "They were really worried and they talked to me about it, and I just—I just shook my head and just walked away, like I just—I wouldn't talk to them. I had a pretty, pretty huge alcohol problem. And that went on for about ten years."

During that time, he suffered from alcohol poisonings, requiring hospital admissions. Unlike his colleagues, Skaggs was never charged for any alleged abusive crimes he may have committed regarding the detainees. He believed it was because he was nice to the interpreters, who had initiated the charges and were also witnesses at the trials.

Today, he drinks "very sparingly" and is back on his feet. Although unemployed, he sees himself as a "househusband" to his girlfriend.

At the end of his interview, it seemed that a huge weight had fallen off Skaggs's shoulders. He described how he had remembered things he had forgotten for ten years. Over that decade, he had nightmares. Now he wondered whether the nightmares would begin to diminish. He thanked us for the opportunity to tell his story. Our student intern drove him back to his hotel. He repeated to her how grateful he was.

I had spent the past eight months listening to more than a dozen stories that were raw, intense, and sad. Skaggs's story may not have been any worse than any of the others I had heard that year. However, the second half of his interview affected me in a way I had not expected. It reminded me of another man I know who had been a cutter when he was a few years younger than Skaggs. Somehow, that memory exhausted me. It made me realize that I could not continue at the pace I was on if I could not separate the stories I was hearing in the interviews from the experiences and stories of dear, personal friends. Skaggs's story brought it all to the surface for me. I gave up interviewing for nearly six months after hearing his story.

Specialist Glendale Walls did not know Skaggs and Corsetti before the three worked in Bagram. His training had been different from theirs. Walls had been trained as an interrogator, but, as with nearly all interrogators before 9/11, his training was in Cold War tactics, for interrogating Russian captives.

When Walls had two months left of training, 9/11 happened. Yet during those two months, the military did not revise and update its interrogation program. Walls completed his training without the knowledge and preparation necessary to understand, approach, and interrogate people who were part of "irregular forces," such as al Qaeda. He also lacked an understanding of Middle Eastern and North African cultures.

When he arrived in Bagram, Walls was told by his supervisors that the prisoners were not to be treated as "prisoners of war." Rather, they would be designated "prisoners, or persons, under US custody," or PUC. Walls explained that by using terminology other than "prisoners of war," the military could avoid being bound by the Geneva Conventions.

In Afghanistan, he understood that the interrogators could police themselves: there would be no serious review by superiors. His superiors instructed him to be "harsher" and "rougher." In response, he ended up grabbing a detainee named Dilawar by his shirt and walking him around the interrogation room. Walls told us that it was against his nature to be physical with someone. He believed that he had betrayed Dilawar's trust by committing that act.

Dilawar was a twenty-two-year-old taxi driver and farmer. He was profiled in the Academy Award–winning documentary *Taxi to the Dark Side*. Dilawar was one of two detainees known to have died in detention in Bagram. He had been arrested by Pakistani militia in his car along with three other men and was turned over to US forces. Dilawar and the others were accused of firing rockets at a US base.

Walls described how Dilawar had been put on a sleep deprivation regimen. The detainee was secured to the ceiling of his cell by his wrists, high enough for him to stand. His feet were on the floor, but he could not bend his knees. He was held in that position for four days. Dilawar was permitted only "two hours of sleep" per day, and the hours did not have to be consecutive. Walls noted that "it could have been ten minutes here, stretched throughout the day."

Walls did not understand that this abuse could lead to Dilawar's death. "In my eyes, like I had no reason to believe that he'd ever die from anything that was going on, that I was aware of."

At some point, Dilawar hallucinated that his wife had visited him. After that, Walls asked that Dilawar be cut down because he was basically speaking just gibberish at that point. Dilawar was barely present anymore, Walls told us.

One of the military police officers admitted to giving Dilawar "peroneal knee strikes" while the detainee was hanging from the ceiling. Walls described these as strikes to the back of the knee. The strikes eventually formed a blood clot that went to his heart, which may have been what killed him. According to the autopsy report, his legs ultimately became "pulpified," and the blunt trauma killed him.[18]

The military charged Walls with assault and battery for his treatment of Dilawar. He accepted a plea deal that led to two months confinement in a military jail, reduction in pay grade, and a $750 fine. He also received a bad conduct discharge.

Only the lower enlisted military personnel were charged with crimes, Walls said. "Everything rolls downhill, as they say. And it definitely didn't splash anywhere higher than us. The people that were telling us to do it stayed in the military . . . advanced their careers, and I'm sure they didn't have any second thoughts about us."

His bad conduct discharge was basically "one step higher" than a dishonorable discharge. He lost all benefits, including his pension, GI bill benefits for education, and VA healthcare. Walls could not receive military assistance and support for medical care, including counseling and therapy. He was also demoted to private.

Walls did not obtain private healthcare until ten years after the "assault and battery" incident. When he left the military, he found a job as a delivery driver for Domino's Pizza. He then trained in a Goodwill program, in computer repair. Later he found a job at a call center and subsequently moved into tech support for a cable and internet service. He became a supervisor, but was fired. He would not reveal what caused him to be fired.

Walls has had flashbacks. He said he would be "driving down the road, and all of a sudden I think I'm looking at the end of the street, it looks like, you know, the mountains of Bagram, you know, just out of nowhere. Who knows, I might have run a red light while I did it. . . . But don't be near me if I'm standing next to the street when a car backfires. I might throw you down looking for cover."

In addition to flashbacks, Walls has had very frequent nightmares, especially of Dilawar. In many of his nightmares, Walls speaks to Dilawar about what Walls did and how he did not do enough for him. "That's my fault."

Even though Walls was his interrogator when Dilawar died, Walls does not believe that he directly caused Dilawar's death. As the interview closed, Glendale Walls said, "If you could talk to Dilawar right now, I guarantee you he'd say I was the only friend he had in that place."

— CHAPTER 13 —

PAYING RESPECT

When she first arrived in Guantánamo in February 2004, Jennifer Bryson was approached by an interrogator who intended to play earsplitting, assaulting, pounding "headbanger" music and flash bright strobe lights while interrogating a detainee. Bryson, who was the first female team chief and the first civilian team chief in Guantánamo, was the interrogator's new supervisor.

"I remember the request said the music will only be up to such-and-such decibel and research has shown that this level cannot harm the hearing. I was absolutely disturbed, and baffled, and perplexed, because this had absolutely nothing to do with how I had been trained. This had absolutely nothing to do with what the army had taught us was allowed," she told us.

Knowing that she had to establish her credibility with the interrogator and make it clear that she was in charge, she consulted another team chief for confirmation of her position. She told the team chief that she did not want to approve the request, but that everyone around her assumed that this kind of behavior toward the detainees was not uncommon and would continue. The team chief was relieved that she was taking a stand against the interrogator's headbanging music technique. "Thank God, finally somebody. You're absolutely doing the right thing," he assured her.

As a graduate of Stanford University with a PhD in Arabic and Islamic studies from Yale, Bryson was not a typical member of the interrogation team at Guantánamo. In the Guantánamo environment, she believed, those sorts of degrees were not enthusiastically welcomed. In addition, as the first female team chief, she received annoying, grating, and sexist comments. One administrator in her training program said, "You're a woman; they're not going to speak to you. There's no point in you getting this training." That proved not to be the case, she told us.

I met Bryson in 2011, after a US Navy SEAL team killed al Qaeda leader Osama bin Laden in his residence in Pakistan. Former vice president Dick Cheney and other high-level Bush administration officials claimed that America had learned of bin Laden's residence from the torture interrogation of an al Qaeda courier.

Bryson, as with most Guantánamo interrogators, had intended to keep her former interrogation work hidden from the public. But when Cheney made those comments, Bryson felt compelled to go public, to speak out against torture and clarify that torture did not lead to discovery of bin Laden's home.

"I watched a resurgence in public support for cruelty and then torture in interrogation, and the implication that torture was what got us information we needed for bin Laden—and that it was just fine, and it was something we needed to have for US national security. And I was so repulsed and frightened and frustrated to see this. And especially those who were advocating this were not interrogators. They weren't people who would actually know what interrogation is. And I also found it morally repulsive as a human being and as an American." She also wanted to educate the public on the rapport-based approach to interrogation.

Interrogators who use the "rapport-based" or "rapport-building" method concentrate on the individual. They learn about an individual's background—for example, likes and dislikes, family, childhood, favorite sports, favorite foods, schooling—in order to develop a line of questioning that will better elicit cooperation, Marion (Spike) Bowman, FBI senior executive, told us.[1] Techniques could include playing chess, drinking tea, and talking about the prisoner's interests. Rapport-based interrogators believe that when an interrogator cruelly abuses or tortures a prisoner, the prisoner tells what the interrogator wants to hear, rather than the truth.

"Human beings are human beings," FBI profiler Jim Clemente told us.[2] He agreed with Bryson's approach—that the essence of interrogation is human interaction. Relationships matter, as does building trust. As an FBI behavioral analyst, Clemente had visited the detention center in October 2002 to evaluate the military's harsh interrogation plans.

Jennifer Bryson emphasized the position of women relatives in the Muslim culture, realizing that her gender could play an important role in interrogation practices.

"I knew that women in their culture were really very important, but often important within a family context. I would describe the role that I played, generally that of perhaps being an aunt to a detainee, a cousin, a daughter, a little sister, depending on the age of the detainee and what felt appropriate with that detainee."

Bryson dressed modestly and acted professionally. Because the detainees knew that she was not a Muslim, she chose not to wear a head scarf. She wore long sleeves and long skirts or loose-fitting pants. Her manner of dress was a personal choice that she believed was very important in her relationship with the detainees. She worked with Saudi detainees, one of whom had been involved in planning the attacks on 9/11. But no matter the detainee, she was always courteous and gracious. She succeeded in having conversations with all her assigned detainees, including men who had indicated at the start of the interrogation sessions that they would not talk to a woman.

Food is exceptionally important in the culture, she explained, and food was very important in her interrogations. Sometimes she would bake for the men. She always had tea available and poured the tea for the men into china cups.

She began each session by greeting the detainee in Arabic—"as-salamu alaykum," "peace be upon you"—and conducted her interrogations in Arabic—her choice. After the greeting, she would check in on the detainee, asking whether he had any concerns. She wanted him to know that she was interested in him. She saw her approach as basic common sense.

If the detainee did not want to talk, Bryson would change topics and tell stories. Stories provided a window to the humanity of each person, and stories assisted her in building individual relationships and personal connections. Trust between her and the detainee mattered most.

Since she left the Department of Defense in 2008, Bryson's life has been spiritually based. She is currently director of the Islam and Religious Freedom Action Team in Washington, DC, and serves on the advisory council of the Center for Women, Faith and Leadership, which supports women of faith in leadership roles. Bryson was the founding director of the Zephyr Institute, a community dedicated to "understanding the human person and the common good," where she served from 2014 to 2016.

On her website, she writes that she is a convert to Roman Catholicism. When she sat down to interview with us, she mentioned that she periodically visits a monastery.

CHAPTER 14

FOR HIS SON

The second time detainee Mourad Benchellali sat down with us, in Lyon, France, in July 2015, he showed us a photo of his young son. He wanted his son to be proud of him. Benchellali is working hard to make sure that wish comes true.

It was different when we first met Benchellali in 2009. He was still reeling from his experiences in Guantánamo and his arrival back home. More than anyone else we met that summer, Mourad Benchellali helped us understand the long-term psychological damage that Guantánamo prisoners suffered.

"The feeling of being always depressed, always under stress, having nightmares, thinking about it all the time, as though it could never leave our mind. So to resume a normal life, as if that hadn't happened, that has become impossible. So there is that already, the psychological trauma," he explained.

Of course physical torture existed in Guantánamo. However, Benchellali believed that the prison had been designed specifically to psychologically crush and destroy the detainees through such experiences as stark isolation, sleep deprivation, temperature manipulation, and denial of simple comfort items, such as blankets, pillows, toothbrushes, and toilet paper.

Benchellali was the only former detainee we interviewed twice. When we returned for the second visit, he was in considerably better spirits. He had found purpose in his life.

— — —

Benchellali left his home in Lyon for Afghanistan in July 2001, two months before 9/11. At the age of nineteen, he was young and naïve. He had never been away from home, and did not know what awaited him. He had left home at the urging of his older brother, who, along with the family, had been drawn to radical Islam. After American forces bombed Afghanistan in response to the attacks on 9/11, Benchellali fled to Pakistan. He was picked up by local militia and sold for bounty to the Americans. He spent two and a half years in the Guantánamo detention center.

The Americans released him in 2004, knowing that the French authorities would hold him on terrorism charges upon his arrival home. In France, he was convicted of criminal association with a terrorist enterprise and served seventeen months in prison.

While Benchellali was in Guantánamo, his Algerian immigrant parents and his two brothers were arrested on terrorism charges in France. When he returned, he was held in the same prison as his mother, but was not permitted to see her. His parents were deported back to Algeria upon their release from prison. Benchellali's French conviction was overturned in 2009 on the grounds that the "information gathered by French intelligence officials in interrogations at Guantánamo Bay, Cuba, violated French rules for permissible evidence." There was no other proof of wrongdoing.[1]

Benchellali wrote a memoir of his experiences, *A Journey to Hell*, in 2006.[2] He described how he had made a major mistake in listening to his brother and following him to Afghanistan.[3]

As was the case with many former detainees, Benchellali had difficulty finding and keeping a job. Guantánamo detainees were often stigmatized when they returned home. When an employer agreed to hire him, his coworkers rebelled, refusing to work with an alleged terrorist. He was let go. Over the years, he has learned to lay tile, and he has been supporting himself and his son with his work.

Benchellali told us that he regained his faith in mankind after Guantánamo because of one man who believed in him: Dr. Pierre Dutertre of Amnesty International. Benchellali credits Dutertre's nonjudgmental support and sincere concern for him as the reason Benchellali did not become a terrorist. "I had every reason in the world to become radicalized," Benchellali said. But Dutertre taught him to believe that there were good people everywhere, and that there were people who cared for him.

When we sat with Benchellali in 2015, he explained how his life changed. He has found a way to thank Dutertre and others by paying forward. He holds speaking tours for young people who might be thinking of joining terrorist organizations. His hope is to discourage vulnerable French youth from making the same mistakes he made.

Rather than lecturing at these programs, Benchellali modestly tells his story and shares his experiences. Joining a terrorist group is not a simple action, he explains. There will be risk and danger in what the young audience may be thinking will be an adventure.

"I simply tell them my story—this is what I saw in Afghanistan. I tell them about being tortured. I tell them about bombings. I tell them how groups enlist you, [how] people used to tell me that suicide attacks were a part of our religion. So, I tell them all of this, and I say, 'Be careful, here are the dangers you may run into over there, as I did. I don't want what happened to me to happen to you. But you have to decide for yourself.'"

Unfortunately, his life in Guantánamo continued to shadow him. In June 2015, Benchellali prepared to fly to Quebec to speak to a gathering of young people. As he was about to board the airliner in France, a border control officer blocked his path. He was informed that the US denied him boarding privileges because the flight path was over US territory. All former detainees are barred from traveling to the US. Flying over US airspace would be a violation of the ban.

Later that fall, he found a flight to Toronto that did not enter US airspace. However, upon landing he was detained at the airport and returned to France. He was "scared when they put me in jail and forced me to wear this orange suit," he emailed me. "But I will never give up what I'm doing for the youth. It is more important than ever."

When ISIS—also known as the Islamic State in Syria and Iraq—was attracting young followers, Benchellali initially received speaking invitations not only from youth groups but also from government officials in France. That changed after November 13, 2015, the day that terrorists attacked a concert hall and restaurants in Paris, killing more than a hundred people. After the attacks, many schools and government agencies withdrew their invitations. The government also questioned Benchellali's actions and took a DNA sample from him.[4] Nevertheless, he persisted with his work.

In 2017 Benchellali joined a think tank and consulting company designed to counter radicalism and extremism. The company's five partners offer their services and expertise to governments, private companies, and individuals.[5] The company was formed by Nicolas Hénin, a French former journalist who had been captured and held for ten months by ISIS while he covered the war in Syria. American James Foley and other American and European hostages shared a cell with him. They were all made to wear orange jumpsuits.[6]

In partnering with Hénin and the others to counter fanaticism and extremist movements, Benchellali is working hard to transform his life away from the image of the Guantánamo terrorist and its accompanying legacy. In seeking a new and productive life after Guantánamo, Mourad Benchellali is dedicating himself to saving young lives. He wants his son to be proud of him.

CHAPTER 15

GUANTÁNAMO SAVED MY LIFE

"**G**uantánamo saved my life," Uighur Adil Hakimjan said to us when he sat down in Stockholm for an interview in 2014. We had never heard those words from anyone before, nor had I expected to ever hear them.

When Hakimjan was captured in Pakistan after 9/11, he feared that the authorities would deport him back to China. As described earlier in this book, since the mid-twentieth century—when the Chinese assumed control of the former Uighur homeland of East Turkistan—China has oppressed the Sunni Muslim Uighurs and has designated the Uighurs as terrorists. Hakimjan believed that if he were returned to China, he would be judged a terrorist, and then tortured and killed.

Pakistan and China had close diplomatic ties, and China wanted him back. However, the US had offered bounties for alleged terrorists after the attacks on 9/11. The Pakistani officials apparently decided money spoke louder than diplomacy. They sold Hakimjan, along with other men allegedly aligned with al Qaeda or the Taliban, to the Americans. Hakimjan was transferred to Guantánamo, along with the twenty-one other Uighurs.

In 2006, Hakimjan was one of the first five Uighur Guantánamo detainees released from Guantánamo and sent to Albania. A year later, he received an invitation to a human rights conference in Stockholm, where his sister Kauvser Hakimjan lived.[1] She and her family had fled China for Pakistan after the Chinese government demanded that she abort her pregnancy when she was expecting her fourth child. The UN and the

Red Crescent assisted her family in gaining asylum in Sweden. When he arrived in Stockholm, Adil Hakimjan applied for asylum, specifying that he had family in the country.

At first, the Swedish government refused to grant him asylum. The government reasoned that he was not oppressed in Albania and could safely return. He and his lawyers appealed. Six months later, the government reversed its decision, acknowledging that Hakimjan had suffered great hardship as a Guantánamo detainee.

His first wife and child were still in China when he settled in Sweden. The Chinese authorities would not permit them to leave the country and reunite with him.[2] In adjusting to his new life in his adopted country, Hakimjan found a new wife and rebuilt his life. He now has a growing family. He works at two jobs, one as a delivery person for a postal company and the other as a taxi driver. Adil Hakimjan is moving into the middle class and on the path to Swedish citizenship.

CHAPTER 16

TIMMY

Alfred (Pete) Souza was never the same after his six-month tour as a hospital corpsman in Guantánamo. Souza observed a young detainee in his early twenties in a wheelchair with his head slumped on his chest. The clinic personnel called him "Timmy," the name of the disabled character in the animated show *South Park*.

The staff told Souza that Timmy had tried to commit suicide by hanging himself in his cell. Although prison guards were required to walk by the cells every five to ten minutes, by the time the guards found him and cut him down, Timmy had significant brain damage due to lack of oxygen. Timmy was carried to the detention clinic and shackled with handcuffs. He was fed through tubes that were pushed up through his nostrils and down into his stomach. Ensure and similar nutritional liquids were poured into the tubes at feeding times. Timmy had been in the clinic for more than a year when Souza arrived in July 2004.

Souza explained that he could understand why Timmy had tried to commit suicide. "If you thought that you would never go home and that this was going to be the rest of your life, why wouldn't you kill yourself?"

Souza felt honored to serve in the military and had previously enjoyed his work. But seeing Timmy was not what he had expected when he signed up to work at the base.

Nor was the sight of Timmy the only disturbing experience Souza had. Working at the Guantánamo clinic was a far cry from working at a humane medical facility, he explained to us. He described the mental health unit in the clinic as something that looked like a milking barn, with beds for mentally unstable detainees on either side of a walkway. It was also not what he had expected.

"It was like you have the central passage and then you got the cells on each side and each one is open—the crosshatch paneling, metal paneling. Very little room to move. And I just saw patient after patient just sitting huddled like this [leans forward], just staring off into space. I was like, 'Oh, dear, what the hell is going on here?'"

During the six months that he worked at the clinic, Souza never spoke with other corpsmen and prison guards about his discomfort and distress. When we asked him why he did not share his feelings with others on the base, he replied that the culture did not encourage such talk and that the men he knew did not communicate such things. What he understood was that military personnel went out each night and drank. Souza had quit drinking while in Guantánamo. At no time did he find someone at the base in whom he could confide his worries and his doubts about the mission.

On the day he was to leave Guantánamo for home, one of the newly arrived medical personnel asked his group whether they had any advice for the new arrivals. A female nurse spoke up: "Be true to yourself and don't let this place warp you."

Souza was surprised to hear these words from someone he knew. He wished he had voiced similar words. But he did not reach out to the nurse, who appeared to him to have an understanding and sensitivity similar to his. Even at the end of his tour, he could not bring himself to express to others how much pain he was feeling.

When he returned home, his parents took him out to dinner. They asked him about his mission and work in Guantánamo. Overcome with emotion, he replied, "It's bad, really not a good place." That was all he could say.

After he left the military, Pete Souza and his wife moved to a new city. He works in a hospital group.

F ormer prison guard Chris Arendt also mentioned Timmy in his interview with Witness to Guantánamo. Arendt confirmed that Timmy was hooked up to life support. But Arendt had a different version of the story.

Arendt had heard that Timmy was beaten so severely in one of the camps that he was rendered physically and mentally disabled. Arendt did not know personally whether the beating actually happened and, if so, when it happened. Arendt only knew that if it had happened, it was before he arrived at Guantánamo. Arendt considered it a "total rumor" and said there was no way to check on the story.

Arendt added that Timmy "was like a camp legend. He was just some detainee that was totally broken and we were just keeping him alive."

No one we interviewed told us anything else about Timmy—where he is or whether he is alive today. However, there was a Saudi detainee, Mishal Awad Sayaf Alhabiri, who attempted suicide by hanging in January 2003. He was cut down before he died, but suffered significant brain injury due to lack of oxygen. He was hospitalized for more than two years. Along with physical therapy, he was provided medications to control seizures and manage brain function. Designated as low risk due to his medical condition, he was transferred back to Saudi Arabia in July 2005.[1] Perhaps he was Timmy.

— CHAPTER 17 —

HALF-FULL

"I always look up at the sun, not down on the ground."

Abdul Aziz al-Swidi said these uplifting words to me.[1] He is a Yemeni citizen who was transferred to Montenegro in early 2016. I have been carrying his words with me ever since he spoke them. They are a testament to the indomitable human spirit that he and other men were able to maintain in Guantánamo in spite of their sufferings.

The men survived with a positive, sometimes soaring, life force and attitude. With resolve, sometimes even passion and the luck of temperament, they looked up at the sun.

In our interviews, we asked the former detainees what may appear to the reader as a surprising question: "Was there anything positive in your experience in Guantánamo?" The answers ranged from the expected to the startling to the heartwarming. Although there may be a melancholy tone of sadness underlying the words we hear, this chapter highlights the silver linings that some of the men experienced by living in Guantánamo. These men became more self-aware, found brotherhood, educated themselves, and wanted to share their experiences with others when released.

As could be expected, the men grew from their experiences. With so much time to themselves, they looked inward. They reflected on their lives and on their relationships with God, their families, and their brothers among them.

Being in the prison made UK citizen Ruhal Ahmed reflect on what makes a better person.

"No matter what you are, who you are, humans are humans. Human life is very valuable, very sacred, and just because you're a Christian or I'm a Muslim doesn't make me a better person than the other. What makes a better person is his behavior, his morals. That makes a person better."

As they looked inward, the men learned patience. Perhaps they had little choice. The authorities had informed them that they would be in Guantánamo forever. The men understood that if they lost patience, they could become unhinged. And, if they became unhinged and crazed, the Americans would win, they told each other.

The men counseled each other to maintain balance, to stay strong, calm, serene, and sane: Maintain a perspective that you can carry with you when you leave the prison. If possible, don't get demoralized. Work hard to fight depression and the sense of defeat.

The men bonded and worked together to withstand the psychological pressures of the prison. The comforting and supportive words of a brother helped, and often made the difference. Sometimes, while leading the men in prayer, a leader would counsel the men to be strong.

Necessarily, some men, in looking inward, also thought about death. Thinking about death gave them new perspectives on life.

"I think facing death, or at least thinking that you are facing death, prepares you for a lot. You start looking at life from a very, very different angle. Like, you know, your criteria change," British resident Bisher al Rawi explained.

Men who turned inward, also often turned to Allah. Several told us that they were not religious when they arrived. However, while in Guantánamo their Muslim faith grew. They began to observe Muslim rituals. They fasted during Ramadan. They prayed five times a day, facing Mecca. The military had painted arrows pointing toward Mecca on the floor of each cell. When they left Guantánamo, the men had become more religious, sometimes more so than their families.

With nothing else in their cells to read, the men read the Quran. And as they read it, they memorized a portion of it each day. Reading the Quran took them away from their surroundings and gave them a sense of serenity and peace. With Allah and the power of prayer, they knew they could endure and survive the sufferings required of them.

The men also understood that Allah, and not the Americans, determined their fates. That knowledge gave them strength. Life was a test, their religion taught them, and Guantánamo was a powerful test of faith.

Former detainee Feroz Ali Abbasi of the UK, whom I describe as smart and thoughtful in other parts of this book, struck me also as spiritual. When we sat down with him in London, he defined Guantánamo as the other side of paradise. Guantánamo had showed him the world as it truly is. In Guantánamo, Ali Abbasi learned to see "beyond the veil."

"Paradise is surrounded by hardship. And hellfire is surrounded by ease. Islam tries to instill in you that if you're going through hardship, you're actually going through a veil to paradise." He explained that he would never want to go to Guantánamo.

"But sometimes, God doesn't give us the choice. And the positive thing that comes out of Guantánamo [is that] the veil has been lifted off the world. I see what the world is. It is pain. It is suffering. Guantánamo is the real face of the world and life," he said.

The men in Guantánamo also found brotherhood. When they loved each other, they loved each other for the people they were, French detainee Khaled Ben Mustafa explained. They were not using another person for his money or "his sister." There was no self-interest, he said. The men were sincere in their friendships.

Sitting in their cells alone, the detainees were also reminded of their families on the outside. They learned what it means to lose family. One man promised himself that if and when he was released, he would "keep in touch with my mom as much as possible, my family, and my loved ones. . . . I promised myself I would not be angry with the ones I love."

The men sometimes described Guantánamo as a school. One man compared it to a four-year university. It was a place of learning. They learned from each other. They learned about Islam, about other cultures, and about other countries. A detainee who had known only his tiny village before he arrived in Guantánamo explained how his life became so much larger and grander after meeting people from more than forty nations. The men shared talk about their homes, their families, their villages, their cultures, and their lives. And in sharing their stories, everyone grew.

When the detainee from the tiny village left the prison, he knew that the world was a much more exciting, compelling, and fascinating place.

Today, he regularly watches the news, keeping up with events in the lands of his brothers.

The men learned new languages. Detainees from non-Arabic-speaking countries, such as Pakistan and Afghanistan, learned Arabic. Many men learned English. The men learned their new languages from neighbors who spoke the languages. They also learned English by listening to the guards, to medical personnel, and to other American soldiers at the base.

The men who had facility with languages became adept. Several detainees wanted to interview with us in English, even though English was not their first language. One man now dreams in English.

Several men explained that after living in Guantánamo, they now had stories that they wanted to share with the world. Murat Kurnaz told us that in having survived in the prison, he now talks to others about what he saw and experienced. Kurnaz, who lives in Germany and is of Turkish heritage, also told his story in an autobiography that he wrote after returning home.

Former detainee Moazzam Begg of the UK saw another benefit in having been held in Guantánamo, and now being able to share his story with the world. In telling of his experience, he could also advocate for prisoners.

"I look at it in a way that, had it not been for Guantánamo, then I wouldn't be sitting here talking to you, and people wouldn't have heard my voice in the way that they do now. And I couldn't have been the advocate for the prisoners that I am now." For years, Begg has been active in CAGE (formerly Cageprisoners), a London-based advocacy organization that works on behalf of prisoners.

Of the 780 detainees, one man was a journalist. Sudanese detainee Sami al Hajj was captured in December 2001 while working for Al Jazeera, a Qatari news and media company. At that time, Al Jazeera had just begun its news operations. Sami believed he was being held because the US wanted to interrogate him about Al Jazeera and whether it had any connections to the al Qaeda network and Osama bin Laden.

In 2018 al Hajj wrote about his life in Guantánamo in a memoir entitled *Prisoner 345*, published and hosted by Al Jazeera. He saw advantages in being the only journalist inside the prison. Living in the prison provided him with the unique opportunity to be among the detainees, to be able to talk to them, and to be able to observe the inner workings of the prison firsthand.

"The positive things—and this is also what gave me courage inside Guantánamo—I tell myself that I am a journalist and maybe I am lucky to be in place where there is no journalist except me. As you know, no journalist is allowed to come to Guantánamo." Journalists who visit the Guantánamo detention center are taken on strictly monitored tours of the prison. They must stay within defined boundaries, are shown only limited parts of the prison, and are not permitted to talk to the prisoners.

In listening to the thoughts of the detainees, I am reminded of comments that Clive Stafford Smith made when he sat down to interview with Witness to Guantánamo in August 2010.

Stafford Smith was one of the first lawyers to stand up on behalf of the detainees, joining forces with the Center for Constitutional Rights in December 2001. He is the founder of Reprieve, the London-based human rights organization. Initially, he knew little about Muslim culture. However, in working closely with the men and their families, everything changed. Today, he proudly stands "between Muslims and the people who hate them." Stafford Smith has become personal friends with the former detainees and their families. "And for that I am grateful," he told us.

— CHAPTER 18 —

BEING UP CLOSE TO TORTURE

As someone who has spoken for people on death row for more than twenty-five years, Bryan Stevenson is one of our angels. He has never represented Guantánamo detainees. But he has defended the young, the old, the innocent, and the guilty. In his book *Just Mercy* he writes that many of the people he has worked with were cruelly mistreated—abused and tortured—before they were executed in American prisons. His words express how his work with prisoners has affected him.

"Having tried to fix situations that were so fatally broken, [as well as] being close to suffering, death, executions, and cruel punishment, didn't just illuminate the brokenness of others; it also expressed my own brokenness."

At the moment that one of his clients was being put to death at Holman prison in Alabama, he recognized, "I do what I do because I'm broken, too."[1]

In speaking of his brokenness, Stevenson may be expressing a form of vicarious or secondary trauma. The experience can be described in many ways, and people may disagree on whether someone has actually experienced it. Nevertheless, people who work with trauma survivors may themselves become traumatized. Human rights workers in migrant camps in Southern Europe and North Africa, people assisting asylum seekers and their children along the US southern border, lawyers defending the accused, and volunteers supporting domestic violence survivors are examples of the kinds of people who may experience secondary trauma.

A number of people we interviewed seemed to have been vicariously traumatized by their experiences, although the expressions of their experiences and reactions differ. Readers may have already discerned that certain individuals profiled in this book appear to have suffered secondary trauma. Examples could include Gitanjali Gutierrez, the human rights lawyer who left the country, and Pete Souza, the hospital technician who witnessed nearly brain-dead "Timmy" each day, while working in the clinic.

There are many other instances where it appears that people working in Guantánamo may have experienced secondary trauma. Necessarily, people's reactions and coping mechanisms in working with survivors are different and complicated. Habeas lawyer Pardiss Kebriaei described how her meetings with survivors of torture deeply affected her.

"It was being up close to torture—not just hearing chilling stories but sitting in meeting rooms with clients and seeing the effects on human beings—for days and weeks at a time, years on end, that got to me," Kebriaei wrote.[2] She has been a lawyer for the Center for Constitutional Rights in New York for more than a decade. Nearly all her work in the early years was with Guantánamo clients. Several of her clients were held in solitary confinement, a form of psychological torture.

She told us of meeting a client who lived in a six-by-twelve-foot cell with no natural light. The only window was a sliver in the door facing into the hallway. She described how he was losing his vision after facing the whiteness of the walls for years. The stark whiteness of the walls was within feet, if not inches, of the detainee's eyes.

Kebriaei described another client, "a very, very young man who had been taken into custody when he was a teenager and who would just wail in these meetings."

There was no space or time to process what she was seeing and feeling in Guantánamo. However, when she returned home to New York, the observations, experiences, and interactions she had with clients in the prison hit her hard. She felt like she was emotionally breaking down because she "had never been up close to something like that before." When I asked what breaking down meant to her, she explained: "Crying. Yeah, really emotional. I mean just hearing—You're sitting across from people who were being actively tortured."

In those early years of her work, Kebriaei would feel guilty in seeing a movie or going to dinner. She thought about her clients all the time. "It's just constantly a split screen in my mind, of where I was and what I was doing and seeing them, thinking about them in Guantánamo."

Although feeling guilty and emotional over what she was experiencing, she had limited outlets for expressing her concerns. Much of what she heard in the prison was classified, and she was not able to discuss any part of it with people who were not privy to the same classified information. This included not only her friends and family, but also other attorneys in the office who worked on different cases. She could not share her experiences in the way that a therapist might encourage someone working with trauma victims to do.

In addition, because she could not share the details, her close friends and family could not fully understand what she was feeling when they were with her—no matter how much they wanted to be empathetic. Necessarily, this caused frustration on both sides.

"You know, the last thing you want is some response from someone that reflects that they don't really understand. I mean that just feels worse. So better just to not say anything," Kebriaei said.

She also understood that not being able to share her innermost thoughts with others could interfere with the balance necessary to be an effective advocate. Her clients were relying on her. Speaking openly to someone else would have helped her maintain that balance between her clients and her own needs. Speaking to others would constantly remind her that her role is that of the advocate, not the person in the prison.

"And I think it sounds strange to say this, but I've talked to more than one colleague where I think sometimes we feel like we're in there with [the detainees], and we're not. And it's important to remember that you're not because you have means and there are things that we can do on the outside and our clients are relying on us for that," she said.

Perhaps because she had observed the effects of secondary trauma on several other attorneys in her office, Kebriaei understood the importance of putting on the brakes to avoid burnout. She could see up ahead a "recipe for sort of crashing and burning and not being able to go on." Watching others caused her to reflect "a lot about sustainability and how to keep going, and what that takes, and what that really means.

Soldiers taking detainee to Camp X-Ray on opening day, January 11, 2002.

A soldier observes the processing of the first twenty Guantánamo detainees, January 11, 2002.

Military attorney Lieutenant Commander Matt Diaz believed families should know that their loved ones had been disappeared into Guantánamo.

Uighur interpreter Rushan Abbas became the voice of the Uighurs in Guantánamo.

JAG defense attorney Major Yvonne Bradley compared the legal system in Guantánamo to *Alice in Wonderland* and *The Twilight Zone*.

Habeas attorney Clive Stafford Smith was one of a handful of lawyers who challenged the government's detention policies following 9/11.

Correspondent Carol Rosenberg's uncompromising stories on Guantánamo are the first drafts of history.

Prison guard Private First Class Brandon Neely became Facebook friends with people he guarded at Guantánamo.

Guantánamo prosecutor Lieutenant Colonel Darrel Vandeveld left the naval base, entered a monastery, and asked a priest for advice about how to cope with his involvement with the prison camp.

Habeas attorney Gitanjali Gutierrez quit her job representing detainees and moved her family out of the United States.

Interrogator Jennifer Bryson was the first female team chief and the first civilian team chief in Guantánamo.

Former detainee and French citizen Mourad Benchellali changed his life after Guantánamo.

Former detainee and Uighur Adil Hakimjan said that Guantánamo saved his life.

Khalid al-Odah advocated on behalf of twelve Kuwaiti families, including his own, for the safe return of their sons from Guantánamo.

Australian wife and mother Maha Habib raised the children on her own while husband Mamdouh Habib was in Guantánamo.

Navy general counsel Alberto Mora tried to halt the torture of detainees at Guantánamo.

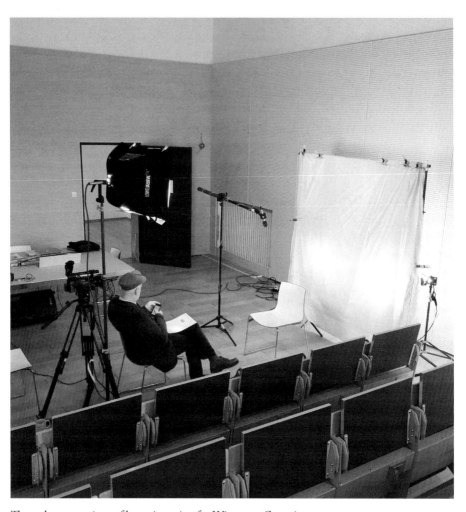

The author, preparing to film an interview for Witness to Guantánamo.

"That said, I was always grateful to leave the prison," she added. "I mean that's just honest. I would spend a week, two weeks down there. But when it was time to go I was just always so grateful. I mean the relief of leaving, it's really, it's one of the ugliest—it's sort of the ugliest side of human beings. And so oppressive in so many ways, and that's just honest—that getting on the plane was always a good feeling, with everything else. We think about the clients and we think about the cells and do the split screen back in New York. But I wouldn't be being honest if I weren't to say, yeah, it's just a relief to leave every time."

As the years passed, by paying attention to her own needs and sustainability, she "got better about self-care," she told us. Pardiss Kebriaei continues to perform effectively as her clients' counsel, and she inspires those who are fortunate to cross her path.

People who work with trauma victims and survivors are not always prepared or educated on the secondary effects on themselves before they begin their work. Even the organizations that work with survivors do not always provide their staffs with the essential ongoing counseling and support. CCR does provide such counseling to the attorneys in the office.

Habeas attorney Alka Pradhan has also been up close to torture. Her client Ammar al Baluchi is one of five men currently being prosecuted in a military commission for the attacks on 9/11. Al Baluchi had been tortured by the CIA before being transferred to Guantánamo. He is likely the model for the detainee named Ammar in the film *Zero Dark Thirty*. In the first twenty-five minutes of the film, the character Ammar is hung by his wrists, then later confined in a box.

When Pradhan sat down to interview with us, she read from al Baluchi's description of his torture. It was a lot more extreme and cruel than what the movie portrayed. For example, al Baluchi was not only suspended from the ceiling: he was naked, starved, and dehydrated at the time. In addition, his head was repeatedly smashed against the wall.

Pradhan is determined to tell the world what her client has suffered. We asked her how she copes in working with al Baluchi and hearing his stories. Similar to Pardiss Kebriaei, Pradhan welcomes the opportunities to go home. "How do I cope? That's always at the back of my head, that

I get to leave Guantánamo. I go home." She talked about watching television, taking a walk to the bookstore and buying a book or magazine.

But she also told us, "I am never not angry. I probably say that I am always angry. I'm always angry about all of this. And it never leaves you. . . . You can't tell [al Baluchi's story] without being angry." But, she said, "I've learned to smile."

Pradhan has an advantage that Kebriaei did not have. She can share many of her thoughts with the other attorneys, paralegals, and investigators on her defense team. Because Pradhan's team are all privy to the same classified information, the team not only works together but also helps her manage her work and her interactions with their client. "We lean on each other a lot," she said.

Lawyers were certainly not the only people who were seriously impacted by what they witnessed and experienced working in the prison. Prison guards also suffered from their observations of, and sometimes participation in, the mistreatment of prisoners. However, the guards had no authority to speak up to higher-ranked officers about their concerns. Consequently, in order to deal with their anguish and confusion as to what was right in this military setting, many of the guards would drink every night to escape their thoughts, prison guard Terry Holdbrooks told us.

"When you are doing a job you know is morally and ethically wrong . . . the easiest way to escape from those feelings of shame and grief and guilt is to drink it away. That's kind of the military solution, is to drink it away." He added, "I'd be a liar if I said drinking wasn't encouraged."

One guard told us that he did not drink. Rather, in dealing with the stress of seeing the prisoners mistreated, he would go running each day around the base. Another man turned inward. He removed himself from the daily activities at the base, limiting his conversations to superficial talk and keeping his thoughts and his words to himself. He did not think that others he knew would understand how troubled he was in Guantánamo.

Daniel Lakemacher was one of the few medical personnel we interviewed who worked in the Guantánamo detention clinic. He had grown up in a small town in Illinois and had married at nineteen. He was twenty-two when he enlisted in the navy, after attending a year of Bible school and college. As a self-described "patriotic guy," he wanted to do something that would make his family proud. That meant either joining the military or becoming a pastor. He chose the military and after training became a hospital corpsman, serving as a neuropsychiatric technician, also known as a mental health technician. He was assigned to the behavioral health unit at Guantánamo, a separate building behind the detention center hospital known as the prison's psychiatric ward.

Lakemacher told us that, initially, he was angry at the detainees for drawing him into their sufferings. They made his life complicated and miserable. He hated them. Like many others working in the prison, he did not see the detainees as human. He questioned why the US military was providing high-quality medical treatment to these "terrorists." He wondered, "Why am I going out and asking this terrorist how he feels?"

But as he observed the military's dehumanizing and brutal treatment of the detainees, especially during force-feeding sessions, he could not help but be conflicted in his feelings and even profoundly disturbed. To daily observe medical personnel bind a detainee's head, feet, and arms into a restraint chair and then push thick nasal tubes up his nostrils and down into his stomach in order to force-feed him was "like the most despicable thing." This was not the military culture Lakemacher knew as a child growing up in a "very pro-military" family.

His attitude toward religion, the other keystone in his life, also began to change. Lakemacher had been raised a fundamentalist Christian and evangelical. In Guantánamo, he found that the detainees were just as devout as, if not more devout than, the Christian people he had known. The detainees' belief in Allah was unshakable, perhaps even more powerful than his belief in Jesus. Observing the detainees' commitment to their faith had a profound effect on him.

As Lakemacher continued to think about his mixed emotions toward the detainees, he came to the realization that his anger and frustration were aimed at the wrong target. He should have been angry at the military, the government, and, most importantly, himself. In thinking about the lives of the detainees, Lakemacher began to think about his own life.

It was after his six-month tour ended and he had left Guantánamo that he realized how deeply Guantánamo, the prison clinic, and the treatment of the detainees had affected him. As is often the case, people cannot always comprehend the gravity of their situation until they are removed from it. When he returned home to his wife, Lakemacher knew that he was not himself. He saw himself as transforming into a different person.

Lakemacher and his wife decided to take immediate action to help him reflect and begin the healing process. They moved to a cabin in Oregon. They shared their innermost thoughts. They listened to each other as they examined their lives. As time went on, Lakemacher began to better understand himself and identify what it would take to rebuild his life. Finally, he was ready to look in the mirror.

"The last thing for me was accepting the fact that I was ultimately personally responsible for not having questioned things while I was down there. . . . The last piece of the puzzle was where it got really personal, and I had to admit that I personally bore responsibility for having helped to perpetrate what I view as rights violations."

After Daniel Lakemacher left the navy, he drifted from his fundamentalist evangelical upbringing and also became a conscientious objector.

CHAPTER 19

THE EMPTY CHAIR

A mother would leave her bed at night and sleep in her son's bed. A child crawled into himself, "to keep himself away from thinking." A brother quit his studies at the university to focus on how he could help his brother in Guantánamo. A mother and father experienced "very sleepless nights, because at night everything goes around and around and around your head."

The innocent victims—the parents, wives, children, and siblings of the people who were disappeared—suffered the worst thing imaginable: not knowing what happened to their loved ones. The parents lost contact with their sons, the wives with their husbands, the children with their fathers.

Little has been written about the effects on family members when their loved ones were disappeared into Guantánamo. The international law community has long recognized that families suffer torture or cruel treatment when their loved ones are disappeared. The suffering does not end when families learn the truth. Often it intensifies.

For families, gone are the predictable routines. Family holidays and family gatherings are no longer celebratory events. Emptiness fills the rooms where he once resided. Family members fear what would happen to them without the income and financial support. A wife would raise the children by herself. She would become both mother and father. In the process, she could lose her community support. Her neighbors could cease talking to her, branding her the wife of a "terrorist." Children would hear the comments, and sometimes taunts, of their classmates and teachers. But they could not always articulate their worries to their mother.

Yet, in interviewing family members, we also heard a few positive surprises. Some family members became proactive. They improved their own lives while advocating to bring their loved ones home. A mother returned to school to learn a new trade. A father traveled around his country sitting in a cage the size of his son's cell in Guantánamo. In their own ways, family members did their best to cope while waiting for the news that their loved one had returned home.

After Kuwaiti father Khalid al-Odah told us of his own heartbreak in missing his son Fawzi, who was in Guantánamo, we asked him how his wife was coping. We had not met her. Khalid told us this story.

"We have Fawzi's room the same—remain the same. Sometimes I wake up the middle of the night, I don't find [Sahad] my wife. It's—it's now I know where she goes, because when I wake up not finding her, I know that she went to his room to sleep on—on his bed, which hurts very much, very much."

Khalid al-Odah was the leader of a group of twelve families whose sons were in the prison. He believed that by working together, the families would be more successful. He learned that from the Americans, he told us. He had been trained as a fighter pilot in Texas in the early 1970s. As a Kuwaiti Air Force officer, he fought alongside American forces during the Persian Gulf War in the early 1990s. He knew English well, and interpreted for us when we interviewed four former detainees.

"I knew that if we get united, we will have more power, more convincing power. We have to sit together. I took that from the Americans themselves, you know. When they have a crisis or something, they get together as families and try to initiate some kind of campaign on that. And we did the right way of doing it."

When al-Odah heard that twelve Kuwaiti men had been taken to Guantánamo, he contacted the families of the eleven other Kuwaiti detainees. He organized the families to advocate for the release of their sons. Several had connections with the emir, and they asked him to assist. President Bush often responded to requests of leaders of countries supporting the US.

At the time we interviewed al-Odah, ten of the men had returned home, thanks in large part to his good work and the interactions between the emir and President Bush. However, al-Odah's son and another man were still in the prison. Al-Odah and others continued their efforts to release the two men remaining. Their efforts paid off. Fawzi al-Odah came home in November 2014. The other man was repatriated in 2016.[1]

Fawzi al-Odah now sleeps in his own bed, and his mother sleeps peacefully in hers.

Bev Hicks, mother of Australian detainee David Hicks, described how she and her husband Terry Hicks heard about their son's capture. A friend who had seen a newscast thought that the "Australian lad" described on the television was David Hicks. The friend contacted them. A few days later, the Australian authorities knocked on their door at nine o'clock at night.

Bev described the moment: "It was a very frightening experience to have bully men walking through the door with their piece of paper saying they can do whatever they like, search whatever they like, and you're frightened and intimidated, and you don't know what you're thinking because all thought stops. It's just—I can't do anything to make these people angry, or we know nothing, you know, do what you want, look at what you want—a very upsetting time. . . . Your heart pounds. It's fear I suppose, fear of the unknown. . . . Worried for everything. Worried for—what the hell is going on here? What the hell has he done that is so bad that people have to come to our house?"

The officials promised Bev and Terry Hicks that their names would not be released and no notices would be in the paper. Yet there was a "snippet" in the paper the next morning. They also received their first prank call early that morning. Then came the phone calls from news stations. "And then in the next breath, they were all hammering on the door, wanting to know all the details," she said.

Both parents had to leave for work. Bev phoned a friend for advice on how to escape the media when leaving her home. The advice did not work. The media followed her. "You know, the media were a pack of mongrels. Sorry, that's what they were, a pack of mongrels," she explained.

One reporter shoved her microphone in Terry Hick's face when he was getting into the car and said to him, "Well now, what do you think of your son as a terrorist?" Bev Hicks told us.

Both parents had countless "very sleepless nights, because at night everything goes around and around and around your head," she added.

Neither parent knew what Guantánamo really was. They would see television photos of the detainees arriving in Guantánamo in their orange jumpsuits, and also of the men standing in or next to their wire cages in Camp X-Ray. The Australian government was hardly ever in touch with the Hicks family. When it did contact them, it provided official documents and a photo of David Hicks in Guantánamo.

Over time, Terry Hicks found a constructive action that helped him manage his days. His lawyer, Stephen Kenny, had suggested that he sit in a cage that had the same dimensions as the one in which his son was held. At first, Terry Hicks was not fond of the idea. But Kenny convinced him that the publicity would help draw attention to his son's plight. And, although father and son had been estranged for years, the father wanted to do everything he could for his son. "So yes, I did it," he smiled.

Kenny cut up some galvanized iron to weld a cage. He brought the cage in a trailer to the convention center in their hometown of Adelaide. The Liberal Party was holding a convention at the center. Terry Hicks entered the cage, dressed up in an orange jumpsuit. Members of the government, as well as members of the media, passed by the cage.

The event attracted so much media attention that they were inspired to take the cage to the streets of New York City, where they repeated the event. Upon returning to Australia, Terry Hicks sat in his cage in the cities of Perth, Castlemaine, and Brisbane.[2] The publicity helped rouse the Australian public in supporting his son's release. Through negotiations, some of which has not been made public, David Hicks was transferred back home in 2007. In negotiating his release, he signed a plea agreement stating he was guilty of material support of terrorism—although it was not a war crime at the time he was arrested. Years later, his conviction was overturned.[3]

"I had to be a father and a mother. It's hard to be a father, you know," Maha Habib told us. Her husband, Mamdouh Habib, was disappeared into Egypt and brutally tortured in the CIA's extraordinary rendition program. He was then transferred to Guantánamo. While he was gone, Maha Habib took the role of both parents. Naturally, the children were affected by their father's absence.

One of their sons became aloof and remote, and retreated into himself. He worked and played music and "kept to himself, away from thinking." Another son saw a psychologist. He had issues with the police while he was underage.

As stressful as it was at home caring for her children, Maha Habib had to find work. She did not have a job or income to support the family. "They put me on single parent's pensioner and I hated that because I wasn't old enough to be pensioned. I didn't want it, to be on a pension, but there's no other choice." As time progressed, she came to take charge of her life.

When she sat down to interview with us, she described herself as quiet and reserved before her husband was taken. But forced to confront media allegations that her husband was a terrorist, she decided to redirect her suffering into a positive outlet. She became proactive and, in doing so, sought to transform herself. She became more outgoing, more media savvy, more vocal, and more self-assured. She initiated a campaign of "protesting and speaking out."

She then capitalized on her recently developed public speaking skills and looked to start a new career. "I had some experience of speaking out, [hence] why not have it as a qualification?" She went back to school, signing up for classes that would prepare her for a career in community welfare. Her pain and heartache led to her transformation into a career woman, at the same time she was raising her young children without their father.

Their daughter became her "shadow," spending all her time with her mother. The daughter quickly learned how to be comfortable talking to the media. "She sort of learned so much, she was really outspoken like me now," Maha Habib smiled. "I think she's become more mature, faster than her age." The daughter had taken a more proactive role in the family.

When Estela Lebron sat down with us to interview, she said that when she finally did get to see her son Jose Padilla, he was not the same person he was before. His personality was altered. "He is not going to react like me and you," she told us.

Padilla, an American citizen born in Brooklyn, returned from Pakistan in early 2002 and was taken to a New York prison cell. One month later, he was removed overnight to the military brig in South Carolina and designated an "enemy combatant." His mother and his lawyer were not aware of the move until after it happened. He was never charged with a crime while in the brig. Nor was he ever provided a due process hearing to determine whether he was rightfully held. Three and a half years later, he was relocated to a prison in Florida. Padilla was then tried and convicted of being part of a cell that supported jihadist causes overseas.

Padilla was not transferred from New York to Guantánamo, because he was an American citizen. Under American law, Guantánamo housed only foreign nationals. In the brig, Padilla was kept in total isolation, under conditions of severe sensory deprivation. His window was blackened. He saw no daylight. He had no clock, no mirror, no table, and no mattress. He slept on a steel frame. He always ate by himself, his meals on his lap. There was no one to talk to except his interrogators. He was alone all day and night, staring at his cell walls. Neither his mother nor his lawyers were permitted to visit him for more than three years.

Lebron was washing clothes in the condominium laundry room in her home in Florida. One of the neighbors said to her, "Why don't you go back to your country?"

"I said, 'Excuse me? Where are you from? Are you from Canada? I'm from America. I was born and raised here, so I guess you're the one that needs to go to your home.' So, it's like people, they judge you. . . . But it was like every single day, you see trucks, you see cameras everywhere."

Lebron continued to have a "lot of pain in my chest," she said. "Like right now I'm speaking to you, but I have pain inside of me. But you have to let it go. I mean, I have to be strong and think about that Jose is going to be fine. Even though that I know he's not going to be fine, but I was lucky they don't kill him. And as long as he's still here, I'm okay with that. But he was my everything, my baby. He was my first boy. And I don't know if you ever heard about a mom that says their boys are very close to the mom. He was one of those. He always used to touch my hair. 'Mom, are you okay?' I remember when they were little boys, little kids.

That's the reason why I cry. I cried a lot and I want to cry until the day I die, 'cause that's my son."

Mohamedou Ould Slahi was picked up at his family home by the Mauritanian secret police soon after 9/11. As mentioned earlier in this book, the police led the family to believe that he was being held in Mauritania. Although the police would not allow family members to see him, the officers accepted money, clean clothes, and food that his mother brought to the station house each week for her son.

Slahi's brother, Mahfoud Yahdih Ould Salahi, lived in Dusseldorf, Germany, at the time. (Because of the military's mistake, the brothers' last names are spelled differently. Several years after Mohamedou was released from Guantánamo, some people in the media referred to Mohamedou by his family name of Salahi. However, because he was known as Slahi in Guantánamo and wrote his memoir *Guantánamo Diary* under that name, we use Slahi when speaking of Mohamedou and Salahi when referring to Yahdih.) In fall 2002, Salahi read an article in the German magazine *Der Spiegel* saying that Mohamedou was being held in Guantánamo.

When Salahi phoned his family to tell them what he had read in the magazine, his family refused to believe him. They told him that the police had assured them that their son was in Mauritania. The family continued to want to believe that he was in Mauritania until they received a letter from their son in early 2003. The letter was dated August 8, 2002, and sent from the Guantánamo prison through the Red Cross/Red Crescent.

After the family received the letter, a government official came to their home and told them not to publicize that their son was in Guantánamo. If they did, they were told they "will have problems with the government."

When he first arrived in Germany, Salahi had no interest in politics. Soccer was his passion. But his life changed after he read *Der Spiegel*. Because the other members of his family lived in the repressive state of Mauritania, no one else in the family would be able to act on behalf of his brother. His family was fortunate that the members "could walk freely," yet they could not risk their freedom and their lives by challenging the state, even for their son.

Because he lived outside the country, "I was the only one who could do something," Salahi told us. He left his studies at the university in order to help his brother. He knew he had to begin by finding a lawyer.

Salahi turned to organizations and lawyers in Germany for help. The German attorneys advised him to find American counsel who would have access to Guantánamo and could better understand and navigate the American legal system.

Unfortunately, Salahi's English was not strong, and he could not afford a translator. Still, he did the best he could to find American lawyers, and later the American Civil Liberties Union, to assist. Salahi told himself that his brother was counting on him. The lawyers were able to persuade American authorities to allow the publication of Slahi's memoir, which he had written while in prison. The mounting publicity from the book, which sold well, may have helped Slahi's case. He was released in fall 2016, fifteen years after he was initially detained.

John Walker Lindh was captured in Afghanistan in December 2001 alongside Taliban soldiers. The media was quick to label Lindh "the American Taliban." Because he was an American citizen, he was not transferred to Guantánamo. Instead, he was tortured and subjected to sensory deprivation for fifty-four days. He was duct-taped to a stretcher while naked and confined in a closed metal shipping container in the middle of the Afghan winter. He was subsequently transported to the Washington, DC, area and initially charged with ten counts, including conspiracy to murder. He could have been sentenced to multiple life terms plus ninety years.

Apparently with Vice President Dick Cheney's consent, the government and Lindh agreed to a twenty-year sentence. Lindh pleaded to charges of violating economic sanctions imposed on the Taliban and carrying a firearm and grenade while serving with the Taliban. With time off for good behavior, Lindh was released from prison on May 23, 2019. His three-year probation imposed certain conditions: he is restricted on where he can live and travel; he needs permission to gain access to the internet; and he is required to undergo counseling.

His father, Frank Lindh, became an advocate for his son. In 2004 I invited Frank Lindh to speak to the University of San Francisco School of

Law community about his son. He prepared diligently for it. He wanted us to know what the US government had done to his son. It was an inspiring presentation, and it also inspired the father to carry on his work. For the next half-dozen years, Frank Lindh spoke to college and university communities throughout the country, telling his son's story. Frank Lindh had found a mission, and it helped him cope.

The message from international oversight and judicial bodies has been universally clear for more than three decades: When people are disappeared by the state, the family members suffer grievously, whether the suffering is described as torture or as cruel, inhuman, or degrading treatment. In recognition, international tribunals provide forums to hear the claims of victims' families.

However, the rules seem to be applied differently when it comes to the United States. The US has protected itself from accountability and lawsuits in both international tribunals and in American courts by family members for the disappearance of the detainees. The US either is not party to the treaties governing this conduct, or, if the US is a party, it does not accept the jurisdiction of the courts or oversight by bodies that enforce the treaties. The following is a brief summary:[4]

The International Convention for the Protection of All Persons from Enforced Disappearance protects people who have been disappeared by a state.[5] The US has not signed this treaty.

The Third Geneva Convention on prisoners of war obligates a state to provide notice to families and next of kin within one week or less of captured prisoners. On February 7, 2002, President Bush declared that the Geneva Conventions did not apply to Guantánamo detainees. In addition, although the Supreme Court held that Common Article 3 of the conventions applied to the men detained in Guantánamo, notice to families does not appear in the common articles.[6]

Additional Protocol I, Article 32, to the convention also emphasizes the "right of families to know the fate of their relatives."[7] The United States is not a signatory to the protocols.

American domestic laws on torture and cruel treatment bend when the US is the defendant. The US will provide a forum and a remedy for foreign nationals who have been tortured in other countries. In fact, the United States invites foreign nationals to pursue civil litigation in American courts against their alleged foreign torturers. However, when US personnel are accused of torture in these other countries, the rules in American courts are interpreted differently. The United States introduces roadblocks to assure that the claims do not succeed or even progress much beyond the filing stage.[8]

PART III

HUMAN RIGHTS FORSAKEN

French detainee Nizar Sassi told us he was horrified that the United States produced Guantánamo, saying that Guantánamo "is not the work of barbarians."

"What was done in Guantánamo was not done by ignorant [people]. On the contrary, they were thoughtful, well-educated people who have gone to the best schools, who have grown up in the greatest democracy in the world, in a well-educated nation, in a country that upholds human rights, where the word 'law' means something."

Sassi was not alone in being shocked that of all countries, the United States would engage in torture. The image of America before 9/11 was of a country that vouched for the rule of law and held other nations accountable for violations of human rights. Now those other nations were pointing at us. They pointed at Guantánamo. They pointed at the many CIA black sites, where men were disappeared and brutally tortured. They pointed at Abu Ghraib prison in Iraq—which was under the control of the American military—after photos were released of naked men in hoods standing on boxes and holding wires, naked men forced to lie on each other in a pile of bodies, and naked men in dog collars dragged around by leashes. And they pointed at waterboarding, an interrogation technique in which the captive experiences the sensation of drowning—a method that has come to exemplify the torture and brutality committed in the name of America's war on terror.

However, in sitting down to interview with us, detainees spoke of psychological torture, more so than physical torture, as having taken the most severe toll on them—although both kinds of torture occurred in Guantánamo.

It is not always easy to distinguish physical from psychological torture. The most common form of psychological torture is isolation. Other examples—which overlap with physical torture—include humiliation, hot and cold temperature manipulation, sleep deprivation, and removing comfort items, such as pillows, blankets, toothbrushes, and toilet paper. Part III describes how the military deliberately employed both psychological and physical torture in its treatment of detainees in Guantánamo. This part begins with the story of an American official who tried to stop the torture.

CHAPTER 20

BLINDSIDED

"**A**ctually, I thought, this is the best work I've ever done as a lawyer, best work I've ever done in government. This is the greatest service I've ever rendered for my country," US Navy General Counsel Alberto Mora told us.[1]

In alerting a high-level Bush administration official in late 2002 that torture was occurring in Guantánamo, Mora believed he had rendered "the greatest service" to his country. The high-level official, Mora assured himself, would put an end to the cruelty and torture. Unfortunately, Mora's trust in the system was not validated. Nothing changed. The torture and other cruel treatment in the detention center continued without interruption.

Mora's story begins in December 2002. David Brant, director of the US Naval Criminal Investigative Service (NCIS) at the time, brought Mora a portion of a military interrogation log describing the torture of Mohammed al-Qahtani, the twentieth hijacker of the 9/11 attacks. At the same time, Brant informed Mora that other detainees were being cruelly interrogated and tortured. Through another source, Mora obtained government memoranda allowing the abusive techniques. The memos were signed by Secretary of Defense Donald Rumsfeld.

Mora knew that the government had to shut down the abusive treatment immediately. He was worried that, if it continued, America would witness the destruction of our principles and values, and the abandonment of our Constitution.

He wanted Secretary Rumsfeld to understand the profound impact the torture and cruel treatment would have on our nation if the policies were not withdrawn. Because Rumsfeld had a crushing workload, he had overlooked the issues and their consequences, Mora believed. He was convinced that once the secretary was fully informed of the cruel policies, Rumsfeld would immediately end the abusive treatment. Rumsfeld would realize his mistake.

Mora made an appointment to meet with Jim Haynes, general counsel for Secretary Rumsfeld. Haynes reported directly to Rumsfeld. Mora showed Haynes the government memoranda supporting the abuse, and briefed Haynes on how the memoranda violated the Constitution and the Geneva Conventions. Haynes listened.

Mora further emphasized the impact that the abuse would have on our young American soldiers, who were instructed to participate in the cruelty. He was worried for the enlistees who had been trained in the Constitution and the Geneva Conventions, and were to be ordered to torture and otherwise abuse detainees.

"I must have employed half a dozen or ten arguments, including the argument: 'Jim, even if you wanted to do this, how could you ask an American soldier to do this?' We're trained as American citizens that you don't inflict pain. You don't apply cruel behavior," Mora told us.

Our constitutional standard is dictated by American values, he continued. It reflects our constitutional order, our jurisprudence, and our belief in human rights. Moreover, America's foreign policy is premised on the advancement of human rights, individual rights, and human dignity. Underlying all of these is the notion that every individual has the inalienable right to be free from cruelty.

Haynes appeared attentive during the meeting. He would look at Mora and, said Mora, "go, 'Uh-huh, uh-huh.'" Although Mora had no real sense of what Haynes was thinking, Mora assumed that his words were registering. When Mora ran out of words, the meeting ended.

When Mora sat down to interview with us in December 2010, he reflected back on the meeting with Haynes. He recalled that, for the entire hour of their meeting, "almost the only words [Haynes] said were: 'No, it wasn't torture.'"

After the meeting, Mora went home feeling relieved. He believed that Haynes would realize that it was a mistake, and that Haynes, "through overwork and just the volume of issues across his desk, had failed to exercise sufficient thought and sufficient imagination as to what could be the consequences" in allowing harsh interrogations.

Mora further believed that Haynes would do the right thing and advise Secretary Rumsfeld to shut down the abuse.

"I left that room confident that that's exactly what would happen. It never occurred to me that anything else would take place. We were starting to abuse one prisoner. It was a mistake. The fact that this was authorized at the highest level was a big mistake. But we caught it. You know—it's regrettable that this had happened. But, you know what? We caught it in time. Not going to happen again," Mora said.

Mora believed he had saved the US from going down the wrong path—a path that would have abandoned American values and its dedication to the rule of law.

Mora also believed that, with the immediate end of the torture, neither the public nor the media would ever know that America had embarked upon a course of torture and other cruel treatment in Guantánamo. Mora would keep the meeting with Haynes secret to his grave.

The next day, Mora, his wife, and son flew to Miami for Christmas. He was at his mother's house when David Brant called him a few days later.

"And Dave says . . . 'Sorry to bother you, you know, on your holidays, but we're still hearing that abuse is going on.'"

Mora's immediate thought was that it was a huge mistake to continue the torture. But now he knew that it was not inadvertent. "It was deliberate."[1]

CHAPTER 21

THE PAIN INSIDE

Former detainee Bisher al Rawi of the UK could not convince others that he had been tortured while in Guantánamo. There were no scars on his body. The torture he experienced was "not something you'll see. . . . I came out of Guantánamo and, physically, I could not show anything. But I have to tell you the pain I carry inside and the memories I have are really very great, and I have nothing to show."

Former detainee Nizar Sassi of France told us something similar. "Physical torture, whatever form it takes . . . at some point [it ends]. But psychological torture never ends. . . . Psychological torture remains forever inside you.

"If someone hurts your hand with a knife, as soon as the knife is being pulled off, you start to heal. But what is psychological is abstract, it is not physical, it is inside you, it destroys you and you have no control over it."

A "behavioral science consultation team" of medical doctors, psychiatrists, and psychologists participated in advising the military and its interrogators on the psychological torture techniques described in this chapter. The team was known as the BSCTs, or "biscuits."[1]

There are many examples of psychological torture in Guantánamo. Former detainees and human rights experts describe the techniques next.

"NO EXIT"/"NO HOPE"

The detainees were told that they would be in the prison until the war on terror ended. If it did not end, the men would never see their families again. Even when the detainees saw others going home, they did not know whether they would be next, or if they would become "forever" prisoners.

That sense of "no future" informed everything that a detainee experienced. It was the dark cloud that hung over the men every day. Officials said that hope did not matter. Their fates could never change. They would die there. There was no exit.

"The most precious commodity in any prison is hope. If you extinguish a prisoner's hope—hope for a better future, hope that this fate will end, hope that he'll be reunited with his family, hope that he will see his family again . . . if you extinguish that, the whole flame behind his eyes goes out," Joseph Margulies, one of the first attorneys to represent detainees, explained.

Margulies, who had been representing people on death row when 9/11 happened, said that he had never seen the kind of "deadness" that he saw in one of his clients in Guantánamo. As he described it, the entire purpose of the detention program was to create a sense of despair and desperation in the men so that they would give up their capacity to resist.

Perhaps that is why Sassi said to us, "They alternate between giving you some hope and then crushing that hope. That's why hope is a bad counsel."

Because nearly all the men were never charged with a crime, they were never tried and sentenced. And without a sentence, they could not see an end to their detention. They lived in limbo, day after day, week after week, month after month, year after year, and soon decade after decade. An interviewee told us that because the detainees did not see a light at the end of the tunnel, there was a sense of desperation in many of the men.[2]

Former chief prosecutor Colonel Morris Davis quit because he was pressured by his supervisor to convict. He did not believe the system was fair. Davis explained that a detainee who wanted to go home was better off being convicted in a trial and sentenced.

"I mean, kind of the running joke was, in order to win at Gitmo, you've got to lose. And you have to go to court and lose and be convicted as a war criminal, and you might get to go home. Or you can never face trial and be locked up indefinitely."

A forever prisoner does not know whether he will ever see his family again—his wife, his children, his parents, and other loved ones. Only the US government could change his situation and the government tells him nothing. Or what it tells him may be false. His lawyer wants to help. But the lawyer is also at the mercy of the government, because only the government can decide who will be released. Moreover, a detainee who protests his circumstances could be punished—likely with one or more of the techniques depicted in this chapter.

EMOTIONAL DEPRIVATION

Detainee Bisher al Rawi told us a story of how a Red Cross official brought a letter from a family member to a prisoner: "So, somebody who hasn't had any news of his family for many years now—the Red Cross approaches his cell, and he [the Red Cross official] says, 'Are you so and so?' You tell him yes. He tells you, 'I've got a letter for you from your family.' You are delighted, you are very, very happy. And then he gives you the letter. And you look at it. And the letter is all redacted—it is all in black. Nothing. Nothing. I don't know if you can imagine . . . how would that individual feel. Many people broke down because of things like this. I mean, from my eye, I could simply say, if the Red Cross had the decency—because the Red Cross [knows] what they are giving people, they see all the letters redacted—they could simply say to the person, 'Look, your family sent you a letter, and the officials blacked it all out, and there's nothing in it. But if you want, I can give it to you.' If the individual has been given that introduction, I think the situation would have been much simpler, another problem to deal with. But the way things were done, it was deliberately to destroy people." Australian detainee David Hicks's mother gave us another example of how letters were manipulated to cause psychological pain. While her son was in the prison, Bev Hicks sent a letter to him. The prison officials did not redact her entire letter, but they blacked out the word "love." I asked her why.

"Because they don't want people caring about you, do they? They don't want him to think, well, hang on a minute, someone at home does care about me enough to worry about me being in here. Why else would you block out a message of love? Love's all, isn't it?" The prison authorities were "playing with his mind."

PERSECUTING ISLAM

Detainees described military officials throwing the Quran, the holy book, into the toilet, tossing it on the floor, sitting on it, spitting on it, and tearing out pages. The disrespect caused great hurt to the men, who often had only the Quran to read and count on in their imprisoned lives. Many of these types of incidents were reported in the media. In addition, and according to habeas attorney David Remes, the military would sometimes paint the arrow supposedly pointing to Mecca in the wrong direction, or would inform the detainee of the wrong time for prayer.

There were also other, less-known religious abuses at the prison. James Yee, Muslim chaplain from November 2002 to September 2003, described an interrogation room with a large circle on the floor. Inside the circle "was a satanic circle, in which an interrogator would place the Muslim prisoner and attempt to force that prisoner to bow down and pray—like to prostrate in the form of the Islamic prayer." The interrogator would then scream at the prisoner, "Satan is your God now, not Allah."

Yee, a West Point graduate who had converted to Islam more than a decade before he arrived in Guantánamo, also told how the military would sometimes turn off the water before Muslim prayers, knowing that the Muslim practice required that the men wash before prayer. Other times, the guards would disturb the prayer time by "making noise, [and] throwing rocks at prisoners who were prostrating."

Ten months after he had arrived in Guantánamo, while serving as Muslim chaplain, Yee was arrested. The authorities held Yee in solitary confinement for seventy-six days at the naval brig in Charleston, South Carolina. He was accused of several charges, including espionage, aiding the enemy, and mishandling classified information. The military subsequently dismissed the charges.[3] After he was reinstated as a chaplain, Yee resigned his commission.

Kent Svendsen was a United Methodist minister. He worked as a Christian chaplain in the prison in 2004, the year after Yee left. The commander instructed Svendsen that "under no circumstances [was he to] have any kind of conversation with, or even a hello to, a detainee." This was in direct response to Yee's relationship with the detainees, Svendsen told us. Svendsen further said that no guard or service member ever reported having observed abuse or mistreatment of the detainees.

GOING HOME

Other psychological torture occurred when detainees were told they were going home. Over time, many detainees came to believe that "going home" was a ruse—an interrogation tactic to weaken the detainee's resistance. From the comments below, one can see how the concept of "going home" played cruelly on detainees' minds.

Detainee Mourad Benchellali described the process: "So, they would make them believe that they were going home. They would send them to Camp Four [which provides a communal-living and exercise space for compliant prisoners] and were given civilian clothes. They were told, 'It's okay, you are going back home.' And they stayed a few days, and then they would be sent straight to isolation. So there they would go crazy, completely, because they had thought they would go home, and then— only to start again from scratch."

When Benchellali and others heard that they would be going home, "we thought, better not to believe it. Then, when we would hear that a detainee had returned home, we thought they are making us believe that he went home, but he must be in a different camp, isolated from the others. We thought [that] when they tell us that someone is going back home, it means either that they are sending him to an isolation camp, or that maybe they are making him disappear in an American prison or even worse."

Mohamedou Slahi wrote of a similar "leaving" experience in his best-selling book, *Guantánamo Diary*. Military officials placed blackened goggles over his eyes, earmuffs on his ears, and a hood over his head as they dragged him from his cell onto a speedboat, pretending that they were moving him to another country.[4] After sailing around the Caribbean for three hours, they took him to shore, then tortured him by stuffing the space between his clothes and body from his neck to his feet with ice cubes and periodically smashing him in the face while he was blindfolded (he never knew when he would be punched again). They also threatened to take him to Egypt. Ultimately, they returned him to his cell in Guantánamo.

The Department of Justice inspector general's report described the interrogation plan designed for Slahi in 2003. The plan was for Slahi to be hooded and flown around Guantánamo Bay "for one or two hours in a helicopter to persuade him that he had been moved out of GTMO to a location where 'the rules have changed.'" The report indicated that the military interrogators used a boat instead of a helicopter—because the general in charge, General [Geoffrey D.] Miller, "decided that it was too difficult logistically to pull off."[5]

Murat Kurnaz of Germany also believed that the military authorities could be deceiving him when they informed him that he would be going home. They gave him a civilian T-shirt and jeans to wear.

"No, I didn't know if I'm going home or not. Because in many situations, even if people got told that they go home, they put them in the plane, they fly it around in Guantánamo a bit and came back down and said you are not authorized to leave Guantánamo because your government doesn't want you back. It was just psychological game. Guantánamo is not a prison. It's a torture camp."

Fortunately for Kurnaz, he went home.

An interviewee who wishes to remain anonymous told us that when he could bring word to detainees that they would be leaving, he was in tears. "That was a happy day, and sometimes you feel like your years of work haven't gone in vain. They can start their life and [for those who were sent to host countries] maybe eventually they'll be united with their families."

HUMILIATION TACTICS

JAG defense attorney David Frakt was supposed to meet his juvenile client Mohamed Jawad for the first time at nine one morning. Because of administrative delays, the meeting did not begin until ten thirty. When Frakt entered the meeting cell, he was told that there was a problem. Jawad had to pee.

"Then let him go pee," Frakt said.

The military official said that it was not that simple. Because Jawad had already peed that morning, he was subject to the "two-pee" rule.

"The two-pee rule?"

The official explained that if Jawad had to use the bathroom a second time, the interview will be canceled, and the session would be over. When Frakt went in to meet Jawad, he saw his client "hopping back and forth, doing the pee-pee dance," which "is not easy when the legs are shackled together," Frakt said. Consequently, Frakt introduced himself, then ended the meeting so Jawad could go to the bathroom.

Humiliation tactics caused prisoners to feel shame and lose their dignity. A typical humiliation practice was to have interrogators and guards shave detainees' beards and hair.

Other experiences included having a detainee stripped naked by a woman, having women take photographs of the naked men, and having women touch the men. These tactics violated Common Article 3 of the Geneva Conventions. Common Article 3 prohibits "outrages upon personal dignity, in particular, humiliating and degrading treatment."[6]

Mohammed al-Qahtani, the would-be twentieth hijacker, was forced to stand close to women, foreheads touching. Often a woman straddled him. In another instance, he was forced to wear a towel, in imitation of a burqa, and instructed to dance with the interrogator. For religious Muslim men, being forced to touch or interact with a woman who was not family was mental and psychological torture.

HARM TO FAMILY MEMBERS

Detainee Mohamedou Slahi was handed a letter, purportedly from the Department of Defense, saying that his mother would be detained and possibly transferred to Guantánamo if he did not cooperate. She would be the only woman in the prison.[7] There were suggestions that in the "all-male prison environment," she would be sexually assaulted, perhaps gang-raped.[8]

Interrogators told similar stories to detainees at Bagram and Kandahar bases in Afghanistan before the men were transferred to Guantánamo. At Bagram, detainees were informed that the military had captured their wives and/or mothers, and that the women were about to be raped in the adjoining room if the detainee did not reveal secrets he knew.[9]

When he was in Kandahar, UK detainee Moazzam Begg said he heard the sounds of a woman screaming next door. "It was suggested that my wife was next door being tortured," he told us.

Pictures of his children and family were waved in front of him. An American official held a phone in one hand, and the pictures in the other. According to Begg, the official said, "They're only a phone call away. Where do you think they are? What do you think happened to them the night we took you? Do you think you're going see your kids again? Where do you think your wife is?"

COMFORT ITEMS

Blankets, pillows, slippers, tissues, toilet paper, toothbrushes, cups, and hairbrushes were "comfort items" in Guantánamo. In fact, everything was a comfort item. The interrogators decided which items the detainees could have, and when. An uncooperative detainee suffered the loss of many or all comfort items, even toilet paper. And if the man was not clean, he could not pray. He could be required to sleep on a hard steel surface without a blanket or pillow. The guards could take away his pants, requiring him to wear only his shorts. He could not pray in his shorts.

Bisher al Rawi described to us the military's practice of denying comfort items: "People would be sort of deprived from decent food for long periods of time. They could simply switch off and disconnect the water supply, and you can't use the toilet. They could strip you, keep you naked, literally naked, or sometimes we just would be in our underpants." The prison officials would turn up the air-conditioning and take away the blankets. Or they would turn off the air-conditioning in the tropical heat of the day. Prison officials would also give a detainee someone else's blanket, which apparently also upset many of the detainees.

Detainees who were accommodating or compliant were given white prison uniforms to wear. These men were the most likely to receive comfort items. Men who were not as compliant as those who wore white, but who were considered somewhat amenable or obedient in their behavior toward the military authorities, were issued tan uniforms. The detainees who were identified by the authorities as uncooperative, defiant, or rebellious were required to wear orange uniforms. These men would not be issued comfort items or receive any privileges.

ISOLATION

Isolation was the most common form of psychological torture used in Guantánamo. It was employed both as an interrogation technique and as a form of punishment. Nearly every detainee suffered some form of isolation, often for minor infractions. Isolation is generally understood as a physical and environmental experience. However, a person can also be isolated linguistically. There are variations on what constitutes physical and environmental isolation, as well as linguistic isolation. Because nearly all the detainees suffered some form of isolation, the practice requires its own chapter, which follows.

SLEEP DEPRIVATION

There are many ways for abusers to keep their victims awake. One obvious approach is to shake, punch, or kick him, or throw water on him, every time he falls asleep. Prison officials can interrupt sleep by stripping a prisoner naked, by not providing blankets, and by adjusting the temperature in a cell to make it exceedingly cold. An overhead bright light might shine 24-7 in the cell.

Sleep deprivation is much more insidious than one may imagine. It is not merely a loss of one night of sleep, as parents of newborns experience. Sleep deprivation as a form of torture extends for days, weeks, or even months. It is devastating to the body and mind, resulting in cognitive impairment, hypertension, and cardiovascular disease.[10] Juan Mendez, a UN special rapporteur on torture and other cruel, inhuman, or degrading treatment or punishment, explained that sleep deprivation can be a form of mental or physical torture.

Jose Padilla, an American citizen accused of being an "enemy combatant," was held in isolation for nearly four years in the naval brig in South Carolina. His lawyers documented that he was kept awake by a huge roaring fan outside his cell and that he would often smell noxious odors.[11]

Some of the tactics similar to those to which Padilla was subjected have also been documented in Guantánamo in several government reports.[12] In June 2016, detainees in Camp Seven—where the "high-value" detainees are held—complained of intentional noises, vibrations, and odd smells. One detainee, Hassan Guleed of Somalia, claimed publicly that these disruptions had been present since 2009.[13]

"FREQUENT FLYER"

A prisoner is taken to a cell and locked up. Two hours later, the prison guards arrive to say that it is time to transfer to another cell. After the detainee is settled into his new cell and falls asleep, prison guards arrive to move him again. This "frequent flyer" program continues every two to three hours, for periods of two to four weeks. The purpose is either to soften up a prisoner to become a more compliant and cooperative interviewee in interrogations, or to punish him.

JAG defense counsel Major David Frakt did not expect that Jawad, his juvenile client from Afghanistan, would be subjected to frequent-flyer practices. Frakt described his surprise when Jawad told him that the military guards would repeatedly wake him and move him from cell to cell. Frakt did not understand what Jawad was telling him until Lieutenant

Colonel Darrel Vandeveld, the military prosecutor who was assigned to prosecute Jawad, gave Frakt Jawad's log. Such logs track everything that happens to an individual detainee, and Jawad's helped Frakt understand the gravity of the torture his client was enduring.

"[W]hat I found was that he had been moved back and forth from one cell to another 112 times in a fourteen-day period. So, on average, less than every three hours, like 24-7. And I'm like, what is this exactly? Why would they do that? There was a code for each entry. And of the 112 entries, 109 of them said 'special move,' or 'SM.' So that didn't tell me anything. But one of the entries said 'frequent flyer' and two said 'FF,'" Frakt told us.

In researching and investigating what was happening to his young client, Frakt was one of the first defense attorneys to identify the "frequent flyer" practice in Guantánamo. He also reported that the practice continued even after Jawad was determined to have no interrogation value. To Frakt, Jawad's frequent flyer treatment had been purely punitive.

SENSORY DEPRIVATION

Along with isolation and sleep deprivation, the government applied other sensory deprivation tools. The detainees were transported to Guantánamo wearing thick gloves, blackened goggles, sound-blocking earmuffs, and hoods, with their legs and arms shackled to a floor chain and a belly chain during their eighteen-hour plane ride.

In Guantánamo, the men were similarly sensory deprived. Feroz Ali Abbasi said that he did not see sunlight for a "long time." For recreation periods, the guards took him out at night. During the winter of 2002–2003, interrogators placed a hood over Mohammed al-Qahtani's head while torturing him.[14]

Although the following two examples did not take place in Guantánamo, they speak to the US government's practice of sensory deprivation. Bisher al Rawi and Jamal El-Bamma were seized in Gambia and flown to a location near Kabul, Afghanistan, where they were held in the notorious Dark Prison (also known as the Salt Pit) for two to four weeks. Given the circumstances, they could not be certain on the length of time.

The Dark Prison was absolute blackness—there was no light, natural or artificial. You could not see your hand, or anything else. The prison guards and the prisoners wore black clothes.

"The only time you'd see a little bit of light was when one of the guards would come to check on you—that you're dead or alive—and he'd open the bean-hole [the hole in the door to the cell], shine a torch, and look at you, and if you don't move, he'll sort of make some noise . . . [and] expect you to react to the noise," al Rawi said.

The men had to crawl around their tiny cells, bumping their heads and bodies against the walls and ceiling, while feeling their way for their food and their "honey buckets," or waste pails. Al Rawi knocked over his honey bucket. Manfred Nowak, a UN special rapporteur for torture and other cruel, inhuman, or degrading treatment or punishment from 2004 to 2010, described the Dark Prison as the worst of all CIA black sites. Al Rawi and El-Bamma were later transported to Guantánamo.

The military held American citizen and accused terrorist Jose Padilla for twenty-one months in solitary confinement and incommunicado detention in the naval brig in South Carolina.[15] He was not allowed any contact with his family or lawyers, whether via personal visits, letters, or phone calls. Nor was he permitted to visit with, or even see, other prisoners in the brig. His only human contacts were interrogators and guards.

Black paint covered the windows in his cell. There was no natural light. Padilla did not know whether it was day or night. He had no watch or timepiece to tell the time. He had no mirror to see how he looked or how he might be changing. The cells around him were all empty. There was no table in his cell. He sat on a metal bed with the meal tray balanced on his knees. The meals were passed through a bean hole in the door. He had no mattress or pillow. When he was taken to the shower or outside his cell for another purpose, he wore thick blackened goggles designed not only to block vision, but also to block out all light—natural and artificial—and conical headphones designed to lock out all sounds.[16]

Staff at the naval brig informed Padilla's lawyer that Padilla's behavior became like that of a "piece of furniture."[17] Padilla is now a changed person. He "is no longer the same person he was before," his mother Estela Lebron told us. Padilla is imprisoned in the facility known as Supermax, in Florence, Colorado.

DELTA BLOCK AND THE BEHAVIORAL HEALTH UNIT

Albert Shimkus, commanding officer at the naval hospital at Guantánamo until August 2003, created Delta Block, a facility for inpatient treatment of psychiatric illness. It was late 2002 or early 2003. The men were kept in separate cells, isolated from each other. Shimkus described the admitted patients as those who exhibited symptoms of "self-harm or harm to others." The patients would initially be held in individual rooms, then medicated and stabilized.

French detainee Nizar Sassi was in terror that he would be sent to Delta Block. To him, if you were sent to Delta Block it meant you had lost control of your thoughts and actions. Sassi had observed other men who had broken down, lost their mental firmness and steadiness, and been taken to Delta Block. Each day, he recalled, he awoke and "I would breathe in and tell myself, 'Lucky for me,' I still have all my senses." His goal each day was to be assured "that I still have my sanity."

The Behavioral Health Unit is currently the prison's psychiatric ward. It is not clear whether the BHU was initially the same as Delta Block or a separate unit. But it looks as if Delta Block was closed at the time that the BHU was opened in 2006.[18] Reporter Carol Rosenberg's "primer," published in 2016 in the *Miami Herald* on the facilities in Guantánamo, depicts Delta Block as a "communal lockup" where detainees are permitted to mix and mingle, rather than a mental health facility.[19] Rosenberg describes the BHU as the psychiatric ward. It appears, therefore, that the BHU is now the site's only mental health facility.

The BHU is a separate building located behind the detention center hospital. Detainees with mental illness, or detainees who tried to commit suicide or otherwise hurt themselves, were transferred to the BHU. There patients are held in single-occupancy cells.

"WORST" EXPERIENCES

We asked the detainees to tell us about their worst experiences. Many described experiences that did not directly affect them—such as being powerless to help others. The men said that they could suffer being physically beaten or abused. But a feeling of utter despair and helplessness would overcome them on seeing a detainee in a neighboring cell physically abused by the guards or otherwise in pain. They heard their brothers cry out and yet could do nothing. To the detainees, that was psychological torture.

French detainee Imad Kanouni said that the first three months—coming to Guantánamo and living in the open-air cell at Camp X-Ray—were the worst for him. He felt he was in a nightmare. He was isolated from the outside world and from his family. In addition, because no one knew that he and others were in Guantánamo, he wondered whether the Americans would "interrogate us and then execute everybody."

Kanouni ended his interview by telling us something he discovered in Guantánamo: "I learned that—which I didn't know before—there was so much injustice in the world." Before Guantánamo, "I lived my own life with the people close to me. I cared about my religion, my future, and I was not interested in anything else." In Guantánamo, he discovered another side, "an evil side of the world. Of mankind."

Abdul Nasser Khantumani and his son Muhammed Khantumani were both at the prison. Muhammed was seventeen or eighteen at the time he was seized. The military held them in separate buildings. They were not permitted to see or talk to each other, except the few times the military moved the father to a cell near his son as an interrogation technique. The military hoped the son would reveal actionable intelligence so that he could remain physically close to his father. In an article written by his lawyer, Pardiss Kebriaei, Kebriaei said that holding father and son together would have been considered a comfort item.[20]

Muhammed ultimately broke down from these experiences. He beat his head against the cell walls. He cut himself while in isolation and attempted to slash his wrists. When Muhammed's lawyer asked to have the son moved closer to his father, the government responded that the two men were not biologically father and son, but more like uncle and nephew. The lawyers never were permitted to see any alleged government paternity tests. The men have always maintained they are father and son.

Muhammed was transferred to Portugal in August 2009. Before the transfer, the military officials allowed father and son to meet for one hour. They were permitted to embrace once at the beginning and once at the end. They could not touch at any other time. During the meeting, Muhammed asked his father for his blessing. Abdul encouraged his son to leave, saying, "one of us in prison is better than two." Abdul was released the following year to Cape Verde.

Since that time, they have not met or otherwise seen each other, except through Skype. Although Kebriaei has never seen the terms of the agreement for their release, she believes the fact that the men requested numerous times, without success, to visit with each other suggests that part of the agreement was that they would remain apart.

TREATMENT OF JUVENILES

The treatment of juveniles who lived in Guantánamo is another distinct human rights violation. Although the treatment of juveniles is not an exact fit in this chapter, the topic deserves attention in this book.

Except for a few boys who were twelve to fourteen when brought to Guantánamo and kept in a separate camp, the juveniles in the detention center were held with the adult population and treated as the adults. In some situations, they may have suffered more, because they were more vulnerable to the pressures applied to detainees in the prison. For example, Mohamed Jawad, while a juvenile, was one of the first people in the prison to suffer the "frequent flyer" treatment.

Omar Khadr was one of the best-known juveniles in Guantánamo. He was brought to Afghanistan from Canada when he was six years old. His father had been a lieutenant to Osama bin Laden, and the family lived in bin Laden's compound, or nearby. After 9/11, when America bombed Afghanistan, young Khadr was captured in a firefight. Apparently, during the firefight, he had been blinded in one eye. He was accused of killing an American soldier, although there was no direct proof. Khadr was fifteen at the time of his capture.

He was first taken to Bagram in Afghanistan. His head was used as a mop to clean the floor, his Canadian lawyer, Dennis Edney, told us. Khadr was also hung by his wrists. Later, he was transported to Guantánamo.

Khadr spent a decade as an adolescent and young man in Guantánamo. There are videotapes of Canadian officials interviewing him at the prison. In the tapes, Khadr believes the Canadians are there to help him. He is seen crying several times. He asks for his mother. He pleads with the Canadian officials to protect him from the Americans. His story has been told in books and film by Canadian journalist Michelle Shephard and others.[21]

Khadr was transferred from Guantánamo to a Canadian prison in 2013 and released on bail two years later. Edney invited him to live in his home after he was released. Edney dedicated himself to Khadr and his case for more than a decade. He treated Khadr as a son.

In 2017, the Canadian government apologized to Khadr and agreed to a settlement of ten million Canadian dollars for its participation in Khadr's treatment. Khadr declined to interview with Witness to Guantánamo. The US has never acknowledged its mistreatment of him.

The US government used a different standard than the rest of the world in defining juveniles. The international community regards the age of eighteen as the time when juveniles become adults. In Guantánamo, the US determined that juveniles became adults at the age of sixteen.

Under two international law documents, a child is defined as someone under eighteen years old, who must be separated from the adult population. The US ratified one of these documents, the Optional Protocol to the Convention on the Involvement of Children in Armed Conflict. The US never ratified the other international agreement, the Convention on the Rights of the Child. The Optional Protocol should have restricted America's harsh treatment of the boys under eighteen, and certainly those under sixteen.[22] But the document did not. The boys were treated the same as the men.

There does not seem to be a resource on the exact number of juveniles who were in Guantánamo. Habeas lawyer Clive Stafford Smith issued a document indicating that fourteen juveniles were still being held in Guantánamo in 2006.[23]

Stafford Smith believed that the US military changed the definition of juvenile to include only "someone who is under the age of sixteen today, whereas legally the term juvenile as recognized by the United States Supreme Court and every international body in the world means that you were under eighteen [when] you committed whatever offense you [allegedly] committed."[24]

SUICIDES

In early 2002 Kristine Huskey joined the team that courageously represented the twelve Kuwaiti detainees in *Rasul v. Bush*. She continued to represent detainees for more than eight years. Huskey told us that a detainee had written out his will. He had asked her to give the will to his family "because I don't think I can go on." Huskey feared he would commit suicide before she returned. Knowing she could not make any promises, she tried to offer him hope. She asked him to give her more time. He waited. Fortunately, he was released a few months later.

As with the topic of the treatment of juveniles, the topic of suicides also does not fit neatly into this chapter. But it belongs in this part. There were six publicized suicides in Guantánamo.

Controversy surrounds the deaths of three men who allegedly committed suicide on the same evening, June 9, 2006. Sergeant Joseph Hickman, who was present the evening they died, alleged that their deaths were homicides, not suicides.[25] All three detainees were found with socks deep in their throats, and they died near each other. The NCIS issued a redacted report on the matter in 2009. To some people, the report raised more questions than it answered. A decade later, the deaths of these three men is still debated.

An undocumented number of men in Guantánamo attempted suicide but did not succeed.[26] The military believed that many of the men wanted to commit suicide to embarrass the US. It defined those kinds of suicides as asymmetric warfare.

Detainee Brahim Yadel of France described a man in the cell next to him tying a towel to the side wall of the cage, "near the top [but] not to the ceiling—we couldn't tie ourselves to the ceiling. . . . Then he tied a knot and he let go and lifted his legs up." Detainees who had observed the suicide attempt called the guards, who cut the man down and took him to the infirmary. The detainee recovered and was moved to another cell.

Many of the men would fake suicides to draw attention, Mourad Benchellali explained. But as time wore on, "there were a few who broke down. There were some who couldn't take it anymore. And so, those who couldn't take it anymore, well, they would do it for real."

However, as Benchellali explained, guards would show up in time to interrupt the attempt at suicide. If the guards saw that a detainee was mentally unstable, they would take away his sheets and his clothing to prevent him from using any article to hang himself. Benchellali added that some detainees "started to drink toothpaste, drink shampoo, to try to poison themselves. Some slit their veins with razors."

Because the Muslim religion forbids suicide, a Muslim who attempts suicide must be "in utter despair," detainee Imad Kanouni of France told us.

Uighur Khalil Mamut spent seven years in Guantánamo. He felt helpless and depressed after several detainees had allegedly committed suicide there. He could not understand how the men could have committed suicide when the guards were required to keep watch over them. He wondered whether the authorities had killed the detainees.

Mamut became so distraught that he asked the guards to bring him a paper to sign, authorizing the military to execute him. He was ready to die, he said. "So, bring pen and paper; I sign. Take me to beach and shoot me and throw me to the sea. I am OK." Fortunately, he survived the prison, and he was transferred to Bermuda.

— CHAPTER 22 —

ALONE

Detainee Moazzam Begg of the UK was held in solitary confinement in Guantánamo for twenty months, one of the longest periods of isolation at the prison. He was held separately, in a section known as Camp Echo. He lived in half of a converted shipping container separated at the center by a metal divider. A metal bed, toilet, and sink were on one side of the cell. A table was on the other side. Begg and his habeas attorney, Gita Gutierrez, would sit at the table. The military added a tiny opaque glass window and air-conditioning to his cell just before Gutierrez came for her first visit in September 2004. Prison guards sat outside the hut, watching him.

At one point during the years before Gutierrez was permitted to visit him, Begg was literally banging his head against the walls. He asked for human contact. In response, the military sent him a psychiatrist. Begg described to us his conversation with her: "She sat on the opposite side of my cell, and she said, 'Have you thought about hurting yourself?' I said, 'No, not in the way that you're suggesting.' And then she said, 'Have you thought about removing your trousers, threading your trousers with a sheet, putting the crotched part around your neck so you can make a strong noose, and then tying it to the top corner of your cell and jumping off to commit suicide?' I said 'No, not until you put that thought into my mind.'"

Feroz Ali Abbasi was held for twelve months in isolation as an interrogation tactic. His cell was on the other side of Moazzam Begg's metal container. Ali Abbasi was born in Uganda. At the age of eight, his family moved to the UK. Although he spoke some Arabic, his primary language was English.

At the beginning of his detention, he believed that he could "do with isolation better than others." He described himself as not a very talkative person who could be quiet for long periods of time. In his early days, he believed that he could hold out against his interrogators and maintain his sanity by being mindful of at least one of his actions each day.

For example, one day he might focus his attention on his footsteps. He would observe himself as he placed one foot before the other while pacing back and forth in his cell, or while walking to the shower. Other times, he would try to control or be mindful of the pain in his toes. Concentration, he believed, would keep him sane.

As the weeks and months wore on, Ali Abbasi began to develop panic attacks. He explained them as being "like something is attacking me and I have to defend myself." It was like having rational thoughts coextensively with less-rational thoughts. He tried to reason with himself—that nothing was there when he felt that something was attacking him. He could not convince himself. "I didn't have control over my body," he said.

During this time, the military medical personnel told him that they were giving him "immunization" shots. Ali Abbasi was not certain that they were inoculations. He believed that the inoculations contributed to his panic attacks. He did not want to admit this to a doctor, fearing that perhaps the doctors had actually given him "injections to unhinge my sanity." He was thinking, "I'm an innocent man. They want to save face and they are going to do it by taking away my sanity."

The panic attacks grew worse. He could not halt them. Finally, after one year, he said to the interrogators, "I've had enough. I want to go home." He agreed to talk to the authorities. "They broke me," he told us.

Sadly, even after being "broken," Ali Abbasi still did not feel better. Even though the panic attacks were largely gone, "for some reason, I just thought of drawing hearts and stupid stuff, girly stuff, in my letters. I didn't even understand what's going on. I can't make sense of this, so I don't understand what was happening. But there was the sense that—I could feel like there was this split personality in a way, that there was me and then there was something else in that regard. . . . And then there was a sense that there were maybe three people existing within me in a way.

It wasn't in a way that would impede my every day, but just a sense that it was happening. And it was very strange, like an old man, woman, and a child. I can't make sense of all of this. And then over time it just kind of dissipated."

Ali Abbasi remained at Camp Echo for another year before he was released. He believed his experiences in Guantánamo had a lasting effect on him. "I don't think I've really recovered from that situation. I can't make sense. I'm not a psychiatrist. I can't psychoanalyze myself. I don't think I really recovered from that situation. It's like, for instance, I don't feel the same. I don't feel the same."

He told us that it had taken him five years after he returned home to begin to process his experiences in the prison. When he returned home, he enrolled in college and worked for Cageprisoners—now known as CAGE—an advocacy organization working on behalf of prisoners. At the time he tried to bury and forget the experiences. When we met him, he said that he was unpacking his memories: "After five years, I'm opening the package now."

Canadian citizen and juvenile Omar Khadr was held for six-month periods in isolation. His military attorney, Colonel Colby Vokey, complained to the prison officials that the prison policy was limited to thirty days of isolation, followed by review. The prison officials responded that, because there was a slit at the bottom of Omar's cell—where he could attempt to yell out to other detainees nearby over the din of the prison—he was not in isolation.

Special rapporteur Juan Mendez explained that being able to yell through a slit in the door is a "ridiculous" argument. "You're still isolated. In fact, you yell because you are isolated." Vokey added that a huge fan roared next to Khadr's cell, essentially preventing him from being heard or hearing others.

Mendez has called for a ban on solitary confinement of any duration used against children under eighteen. Khadr was one of many juvenile detainees who was not treated differently from the adults in the prison. He lived with the adult population.

Isolation was the most common form of psychological torture in Guantánamo. It was used as both an interrogation technique and a form of punishment. Nearly every detainee suffered some form of isolation, often for minor infractions. The purpose of isolation in those instances was to have detainees understand that they were always vulnerable to harsh discipline.

Detainee Murat Kurnaz of Germany told us he would feed the iguanas and birds with bread that he had hidden. When his actions were discovered, officials "punished me with isolation." Similarly, when seen "doing martial arts inside my cell," he was taken to isolation. Men who were maced and harshly beaten in their cells by prison guards in riot gear for an (alleged) infraction of prison rules—a process known as ERFing, for emergency response force, or extreme reaction force—were often subsequently transferred to isolation.

At first, the military placed inmates in isolation for short periods. However, when the men tolerated the relatively short periods, the military ramped up the times to weeks and months. In 2011, special rapporteur on torture Juan Mendez officially recognized that isolation can amount to torture or cruel, inhuman, or degrading treatment or punishment.[1] He stated publicly that after only fifteen days of isolation—without meaningful social contact—a person might not fully recover to his previous self.[2]

Although Begg and Ali Abbasi were held separately in Camp Echo, most prisoners in isolation were held in what was called the isolation block inside Camp Delta, the primary prison. Prison guard Terry Holdbrooks described the circumstances prisoners experienced in the prison isolation block:

"They were just left in there, all day, all night. No recreation, no shower. Unless they were being served food, they had no contact with anybody. Generally, according to the SOP [standard operating procedure], they were only supposed to be in there for a number of days and then they'd be brought back out. Isolation blocks were used as punishment for actions, not for a lack of cooperation."

A NEW FORM OF ISOLATION: LINGUISTIC ISOLATION

In interviewing detainees, we met someone who described a very different and mostly unknown form of isolation in the prison. The man suffered linguistic isolation. He asked us to not reveal his name. He feared that if his community knew that he had been in Guantánamo, they would ask him to leave his mosque. He also feared that he would lose his job and no longer be able to support his family if his employer learned that he had been a prisoner in Guantánamo. We will call this man Sunnat.

The linguistic isolation Sunnat suffered is not a well-known punishment technique, and little has been written in the social science and law literature on the experiences and effects of linguistic isolation. But this form of isolation can be as tormenting and destructive as physical and environmental isolation.

Sunnat was sixteen years old when he was seized in Afghanistan following the attacks on September 11, 2001. He had come to Afghanistan from Uzbekistan. Uzbeks speak a language very similar to that of the Uighurs. When we met Sunnat, Uighur translator Rushan Abbas translated for us.

Sunnat was purchased by the Americans and transported to the detention center in Guantánamo in 2002. After interrogating him over a period of several months, the military understood that he was not a threat, but the US could not release him safely back home to Uzbekistan. Like many nations, Uzbekistan did not want any involvement with its citizens who were former Guantánamo detainees. According to Julia Hall, Amnesty International's expert on counterterrorism, "Uzbekistan is a place where torture is systematic, where people with a religious profile are routinely targeted." Sunnat waited eight years before the US found a safe country that would accept him.

While he waited to be released, he was placed in a cell in the general prison population. He was surrounded by prisoners who spoke Arabic or English, the two most common languages spoken among the prison population.

Sunnat could reach out and communicate with the other prisoners through eye contact, hand signs, and facial expressions. Over the eight years, he learned minimal Arabic and English. He told us that one of his goals was to greet—to "say hi" to—the men in close proximity.

Something important was missing from Sunnat's life in prison. All around him, the English- and Arabic-speaking prisoners conversed openly with each other and built a community. They learned about one another's lives, families and homes. Sunnat could sense the warm, communal contacts among his neighbors. But he could not join and meaningfully communicate with them in prison life.

Many of the detainees were able to learn English and Arabic while in the prison. However, Sunnat did not seem to have the skill to learn more than a rudimentary level of either language. Nonverbal communication forms, such as hand signs and facial expressions, did not substitute for meaningful conversations.

There were only a half-dozen Uzbek detainees in the prison, and they were never housed near him. Nor were any of the twenty-two Uighur detainees, who spoke a similar language to his, placed in neighboring cells. Sunnat lived inside the prison, but outside the prison community. For his eight years in Guantánamo, he lived alone.

Sunnat was not physically separated from other prisoners. He was not held in solitary confinement. Rather, he was socially isolated. He was denied meaningful conversations with others—conversations that would have allowed him to express his humanity. Imagine a stroke victim who sees the community of conversations around him but cannot participate. For eight years, although surrounded by people, Sunnat lived on his own island.

Because the United States government concluded that he was not a threat, Sunnat was not able to meet with a government interrogator or interpreter. Having access to an interpreter would have provided him with something approaching a regular conversation. In a cruel irony, he suffered further punishment because he was never charged with a crime. It was only in his later years, when he was represented by an attorney who brought along an interpreter, that he met anyone who spoke his language. Unfortunately, the attorney visits were infrequent.

When we asked him how he coped with his powerful sense of loneliness during those years in Guantánamo, he replied in his quiet and shy manner: "I cried, and then I felt better."

A prisoner who is linguistically isolated suffers beyond the absence of meaningful conversations and the feeling of always being alone. He can also suffer at the hands of the prison guards and officials because of his inability to speak and understand the prison language. As we would expect, guards sometimes become frustrated, angry, and even abusive with detainees who do not speak the language of the prison, and were thus unable to understand requests, inquiries, commands, and directions. This can be especially problematic in emergencies, such as hurricanes, fires, or earthquakes.

In addition, detainees who do not know the prison language might violate rules unknowingly, and consequently suffer further serious consequences, including beatings. If such prisoners are abused and beaten by guards, or even by other prisoners, they cannot verbally articulate in the prison language what happened. Nor can they describe any physical conditions resulting from the beatings and abuse, or any other medical issues.

Sunnat was finally released to Latvia in 2010. He spoke a broken Russian language, fortunately, and was able to meet people in his Russian Muslim community, find work, and begin building a family.

Sunnat was not the only detainee who was linguistically isolated. Two habeas attorneys described to us the linguistic isolation of several Pakistani detainees who spoke only Urdu. Center for Constitutional Rights attorney Gitanjali Gutierrez and habeas attorney David Remes told us how their Urdu-speaking clients were isolated when the military placed them in cells near only Arabic speakers.

Gutierrez believed that the isolation of the Urdu prisoners was purposeful. They were deliberately housed among speakers of only English and Arabic. "Language is a way to isolate someone," she explained. "They might as well be alone." I asked her to reconfirm that she thought it was deliberate.

"Absolutely. It is artfully manipulating their environment to be unable to communicate," she said.

Mohammed Jawad, a juvenile when he was captured in Afghanistan and transported to Guantánamo, was accused of throwing a grenade at an American military convoy in Afghanistan in December 2002. As mentioned previously, while in the detention center, Jawad had been subjected to the military's frequent-flyer treatment, in which detainees were moved from cell to cell every two to three hours for several weeks.

During Jawad's military commission hearing, David Frakt, his military defense counsel, asked witness Jason Orlich, an army major, about the sleep deprivation tactics used on Jawad. Among the questions Frakt asked was whether Jawad, who spoke Pashto, was also linguistically isolated.

Orlich admitted, "Linguistic segregation, yes—we divided the detainees up linguistically, which prevented them from communicating within the camp and organizing."[3]

When I asked Frakt to tell us more of this exchange at Jawad's hearing, he said, "I saw several documents in discovery in the Jawad case that referred to linguistic isolation. . . . I saw some documents that referred to efforts to linguistically isolate people. . . . From what I learned, linguistic isolation was done to increase dependence on the interrogator as the only person the detainee could talk to, but also to limit communications in an effort to maintain good order and discipline in the camps."

Frakt cited hunger strikes as a tactic the military wanted to prevent and said it would not want strike leaders to communicate with others who spoke the same language and thereby encourage them to join. Separating the leaders by language helped inhibit organizing among prisoners. To Frakt, linguistic isolation was a form of control as well as punishment.

When we met Sunnat, he did not seem to be a leader who could threaten the military's control of the prison population. Nor did Sunnat seem to be someone who would join a hunger strike and protest conditions in the detention center. In fact, the US quickly determined that he was not a threat.

It is possible that the military placed Sunnat and other detainees in whatever cells were available at the time, with no thought of the consequences regarding language and communication issues with other prisoners. But given what Orlich said to Frakt, it is difficult to imagine that the military did not act deliberately or was not fully aware of the effects and consequences of how detainees were housed.

Ayub Mohammed, who was separated from his Uighur countrymen in the prison, told us another story of coping in linguistic isolation. He had been housed among neighbors who did not speak his language or know of his unique culture as a Muslim in a country that had been seized by the Chinese government.

In the hope of being moved to a different cell, closer to his countrymen, Ayub Mohammed said that he deliberately caused a problem in his cell knowing that he would be "ERFed." ERFing, as described earlier, is a brutal cell-extraction procedure in which six guards storm a cell, mace the detainee, and severely beat him. Afterward the guards usually move the detainee to an isolation cell in another part of the camp. Mohammed hoped that when he was returned to the general prison population after isolation, officials might place him in a cell closer to other Uighurs. His plan worked.

— — —

solation by language differs with each individual. Someone who is able to learn languages with little effort will have an easier time in the prison. We interviewed a number of detainees who spoke no English when they arrived in Guantánamo but had the facility to learn English quickly.[4] In those situations, perhaps only some months or a year passed before a prisoner was able to have meaningful contacts with other inmates. Nevertheless, that inmate would have suffered linguistic isolation for some period of time. Future researchers will need to determine whether the time frame for long-term effects of linguistic isolation mirrors the time frame for long-term effects of physical isolation.[5]

Because it is a relatively new form of isolation, linguistic isolation warrants special attention and further study in the detention context. Linguistic isolation can be as pernicious as other types of isolation.[6] Human rights experts have recognized physical isolation as torture or cruel treatment.[7] Isolation by language should be similarly recognized.

COMMONLY KNOWN FORMS OF PHYSICAL ISOLATION

In addition to being sent to the isolation block, nearly every detainee suffered some form of isolation. The military would sometimes describe isolation as "single-cell operations." Although the word "isolation" is used in this chapter as a generic term, there are several distinct types of isolation in prison systems.

One is incommunicado detention, in which a prisoner may have contacts with prisoners inside the facility but not with those outside, such as family or lawyers. Another is administrative segregation, in which certain people—such as convicted child molesters and gang members— may be detained together, though separated from the prison population. Administrative segregation is also used for people belonging to vulnerable populations, such as LGBTQ inmates. Inmates held in isolation in US prisons are often described as being held in the "shoe," a reference to the acronym SHU, or special housing unit.[8]

The remainder of this chapter will focus on solitary confinement, the most pervasive form of isolation in Guantánamo.

In the early 1880s, prison reformers believed that if a prisoner lived his life alone in solitary confinement, he would have the time to reflect

on, and atone for, his misdeeds. The reflective inmate would then understand how to correct his behavior in the future. This reform program
was known as the "Philadelphia system."[9] The confinement would begin
with the inmate's solitary walk to his cell. He wore a hood so that he
could not see other inmates and other inmates could not see him. He
was beginning his inner journey. A new interior path of "redemption"
lay before him.

The Quakers and Anglicans developed this concept of solitary confinement as a compassionate form of penitence. It was also part of what they
believed was a humane reformation of the penal system. The term "pen-
itentiary" is derived from the word "penitence." Other countries adopted
this American practice of atonement through isolation a decade later.

Unfortunately, and not without irony, the practice did not work out
as planned. Taking the hooded prisoner to his isolated cell reminds one
today more of Guantánamo and its association with torture, than of
penitence. In the early Quaker and Anglican model, solitary confinement caused the inmate to further suffer. In some cases, he even became unhinged—severely undermining his rehabilitation.[10] In spite of
the apparent failure of the process, the solitary confinement method of
punishment in prisons was not abandoned. Rather, the US and other nations maintained it as a supposedly logical method of addressing pretrial
detention and breaches of prison discipline.

We might expect that in the two hundred years since the misguided
experiment with isolation was first attempted in 1820, the US would
have understood the perniciousness of isolation and abandoned it as a
form of punishment. Or, at minimum, the US would have regulated it to
prevent permanent damage to the individual. But these things did not
happen.

The practice of isolation in prisons has not been abandoned or even
seriously regulated. The military prison system, the federal prison system, and the prison systems of individual states do not consider isolation
a human rights issue. Instead, isolation in the penal system is considered
a matter of protection—the protection of the prison personnel or prison
population from the prisoner, or the protection of the prisoner from the
prison population.[11]

—   —   —

Solitary confinement involves locking someone in a single cell alone for twenty-two to twenty-four hours a day. Meaningful human contact is reduced to a minimum.[12] Solitary confinement has also been used as a substitute for proper medical or psychiatric care for mentally disordered individuals.[13] And it has been used as a coercive interrogation practice, as seen at Guantánamo.

In the years before 2009, when President Obama assumed office, most of the men at Guantánamo were held in solitary conditions. Their six-by-twelve-foot cells were windowless, except for a sliver of an opening facing the interior of the cell block. Guards looked into the sliver as they passed by. There was no natural light, and the detainee could not tell whether it was day or night. The detainee would eat alone in his cell, with the food delivered through a slit called a "bean hole." Sometimes, the detainee would be permitted to exercise in a single outdoor cell, with no other detainees nearby. Often the exercise would be at night.[14]

Michael Gelles, an NCIS psychologist, justified short-term isolation: "I don't think isolation's a bad thing. . . . If you are doing an investigation of someone, you need to form a relationship with him. [And] if I need to develop a relationship with you and you're going to talk with me, then why do I want you to have access to lots of other people who can support your being resistant? . . . If you're going to talk and you need to have a relationship, I want you to talk to me."

Interestingly, Center for Constitutional Rights habeas attorney Pardiss Kebriaei believed that even when President Obama released tensions a bit by opening up the prison doors and allowing the men in a prison block a more communal setting—that is, a communal area and recreation yard where they could eat and talk and move between cells— it was still a form of isolation. As she saw it, it was group isolation. It was still a group of twelve or eighteen people together all the time in a prison on an island. It may not be solitary, but it was still isolation.

There is currently no international consensus on whether or under what circumstances isolation constitutes torture or cruel treatment in violation of the Convention Against Torture. As mentioned previously, in 2011, Juan Mendez, the UN special rapporteur, recognized that isolation can amount to torture or cruel, inhuman, or degrading treatment, asserting that after only fifteen days of isolation, without meaningful social contact, a person might not fully recover to his previous self.[15]

The US has adopted a thirty-day, rather than a fifteen-day, cycle of re-view of a prisoner who is placed in isolation. The review does not neces-sarily lead to release from isolation. An inmate, although reviewed every thirty days, may continue in isolation for years.[16]

Alan Liotta, the director of the office of detainee policy at the Depart-ment of Defense, said that in the later years, he was informed that there was no isolation or solitary confinement at Guantánamo. He and Greg Craig, White House counsel for President Obama, flew to Guantánamo in 2009. When Craig asked to see the isolation cells, he was told there were none. Craig asked five different ways and received the same answer, Liotta told us.

As human rights physician Atul Gawande wrote, "Simply to exist as a normal human being requires interaction with other people."

— CHAPTER 23 —

WE TORTURED HIM

PHYSICAL TORTURE

"We tortured some folks," President Obama admitted in 2014, referring to the torture committed at CIA black sites.[1] The US also tortured in Guantánamo.

Although detainees described Guantánamo as a psychological prison, Guantánamo had its brutal physical terror programs too. But the raw, brutal physical torture that people sometimes associate with Guantánamo was actually more common in locations outside Guantánamo Bay, Cuba. Physical brutality was the norm at Bagram and Kandahar bases in Afghanistan, where most of the men were held before they were transported to Guantánamo.

Even more vicious violence was administered in the covert CIA black sites—as part of the CIA's extraordinary rendition program.[2] This program was designed to kidnap alleged terrorists and transport them to CIA black sites and to foreign prisons, where they were tortured. Prior to June 2004, Camp Echo in Guantánamo was also sometimes used to house detainees in the extraordinary rendition program.[3] Medical personnel oversaw the CIA torture program.

Alka Pradhan is a lawyer for Ammar al Baluchi, one of the men being prosecuted in a military tribunal in Guantánamo for the 9/11 attacks. In her interview with us, Pradhan read on camera a statement from al Baluchi, recording a small part of what he experienced in a CIA black site: "I wasn't just being suspended to the ceiling; I was naked, starved, dehydrated, cold, hooded, verbally threatened, in pain from the beating, and water drowning as my head smashed by hitting against the wall for dozens and dozens of times. My ears were exploding from the blasting harsh music, which is still stuck in my head. Sleep deprived for weeks, I was shaking and trembling. My legs barely supported my weight as my hands were pulled even higher above my head after I complained that the handcuffs were so tight as if cutting through my wrists. Then my legs start to swell as a result of long suspension; [I] started screaming. And then the doctor comes. The doctor came with a tape measure, wrapped it around my leg and to my utmost shock, the doctor told the interrogators, no, that wasn't enough. My leg should get more swollen."

Murat Kurnaz, who was born in Germany of Turkish descent, described a similar experience when he was held by American soldiers at the US base in Kandahar. He was hung by his wrists for five days. When he began to pass out after three days, the soldiers either gave him water or sprayed him with water to keep him awake. Twice they gave him an apple to eat, but "you can imagine in that situation we were not able to eat anything," he said. He was lowered twice a day, so that a doctor could check his vital signs.

"He checked my eyes and he checked my fingernails. He looked if everything is OK, if I can survive more or not. And if he said okay, then they pulled me just leg up and he said every time okay."

They also lowered him twice a day to ask him to sign papers saying he was a "terrorist." When Kurnaz refused, they lifted him back up. He described another man who was hanging in front of him: "There was another guy in front of me. He was hanging in front of me and he couldn't survive. He died. After he died they let him just hang over there and he was dead for a long time. The first day I could see him that he is moving and people going to him to talk to him or to try to talk to him. [But then he died.] He was just hanging twenty-four hours with no any breaks and he smelled of death of course. I could see it on his body, his face, everything was just—he was a dead man."

I asked him what he was thinking when he saw the dead man hanging in front of him. He replied that he could be the next one to die. "It was better for me to die than to sign those papers and to agree that I'm being a terrorist and I wouldn't want my family to think that I am a terrorist."

When I had dinner with Murat Kurnaz in Bremen, Germany, he told me that he had been on his motorcycle that day, driving 205 kilometers per hour on the Autobahn—which would be more than 125 miles per hour. First, I was shocked at his driving at that dangerous speed. Then, I thought to myself, "I wonder whether you drove so fast to prove to yourself that you are still alive."

Brahim Yadel, a former detainee from France, described how the military doctors at Bagram base operated on his back while he was only partially anesthetized. Then, during the surgery, and while suffering the pain of the surgery, he was interrogated. A detainee from the UK, Terek Dergoul, told a similar story of how the military operated on him in Kandahar. He, too, was interrogated during surgery, while semiconscious.

Mohammed al-Qahtani intended to be the fifth hijacker on the plane downed in the fields of Pennsylvania. However, in early August 2001, a customs agent in Orlando, Florida, refused him entry into the US. He was captured in Afghanistan in December 2001 and brought to Guantánamo two months later. When the government realized that he was likely the would-be twentieth hijacker, he was taken aside and severely physically and psychologically abused. He nearly died during one episode of unrelenting abuse. His heart rate dropped precipitously in the interrogation session, and he needed to be hospitalized. His eighty-four-page interrogation log, which a journalist for *Time* magazine uncovered, depicts much of his ordeal in detail.[4]

In 2009, senior Pentagon official Susan J. Crawford, who supervised the military tribunals, decided not to move al-Qahtani's case forward to a military tribunal in Guantánamo. Her reason was crystal clear.

"We tortured Qahtani," she said. "His treatment met the legal definition of torture. And that's why I did not refer the case for prosecution at a military commission."[5] Al-Qahtani will probably remain in the prison until he dies.

— — —

hapter 21 addressed psychological torture and noted that it is not always easy to distinguish physical from psychological torture. Sleep
deprivation and isolation, for example, include elements of both. The
men we interviewed describe Guantánamo a prison of psychological torture more than of physical brutality. And to many of the men, psychological torture is worse. Its effects last through the remainder of one's life,
until one dies. Yet physical torture existed in Guantánamo, and nearly
everyone experienced it in some form.

Of course, it is impossible to objectively evaluate whether physical
or psychological torture is worse. Both are horrible. And in the end it
depends on the person who suffers the torture. People are different and
experience torture, whether physical or psychological, differently. Per-
sonalities matter.

Dr. Vincent Iacopino, senior medical advisor to Physicians for Human Rights, believes that rape and other sexual abuse, in which the person suffers both physical and psychological torture, often have the most
lasting effect on people.[6] Sexual humiliation goes to the heart of the individual. He told of one man who never recovered from being "peed on"
while in the Abu Ghraib prison in Iraq. Other men in CIA black sites
were assaulted with anal instrumentation or subjected to "rectal feeding," where mashed food was inserted up the rectum.

THE TORTURE MEMOS

The Bush administration legally justified its torture and cruel interrogation techniques by relying on the infamous "torture memos." Many such
memos were written. But several of the most prominent ones were written by Deputy Assistant Attorney General John Yoo, including one in
August 2002 and another in 2003. His memos, which lacked rigorous legal analysis, defined torture very narrowly. The interrogation techniques
were not torture, the memos read, if the damage to the individual did
not rise to the level of organ failure or death. This definition gave CIA
personnel and military interrogators the license and legal cover to inflict
cruel treatment and torture, without naming it as torture.

Yoo served in the Department of Justice, Office of Legal Counsel,
during the early years of the Bush Administration. OLC has the rep-

utation of having the most academically skilled and bright attorneys. Often the lawyers are former Supreme Court clerks. Yoo had clerked for Supreme Court Justice Clarence Thomas and was a professor at the University of California, Berkeley, School of Law before he joined the administration. The work of attorneys in the OLC is highly respected, and their memos are deemed authoritative.

Yoo's supervisor at the OLC, Jay Bybee, signed the memos, which justified such abuse as slamming a head against a wall (known as "walling"), depriving people of sleep for extended periods, isolation, confining people in closed containers, and putting people in stress positions, such as prolonged standing without motion or prolonged squatting without support. Bybee sits on the Federal Court of Appeals in the Ninth Circuit.

The torture memos were not written specifically for Guantánamo. However, they are an important part of the story of the validation of harsh interrogation techniques after 9/11.[7] Neither John Yoo nor Jay Bybee agreed to interview with us.

SERE

In 2002, the CIA adopted a brutal interrogation program intended to torture detainees and induce a feeling of "learned helplessness" in them. The program was designed by two psychologists and based on a military project known as SERE—survival, evasion, resistance, escape. The SERE project had been created in the mid-twentieth century to train captured American soldiers to withstand torture, in its various forms.[8] Psychologists James Mitchell and Bruce Jessen were paid $81 million for their work in "reverse-engineering" the SERE project and constructing the CIA torture interrogation program.

In a rare instance of accountability, Mitchell and Jessen agreed to a settlement in 2017 with the families of three men tortured while held by the CIA.

WATERBOARDING AND WATER TORTURE

There are variations of this type of torture, but waterboarding generally involves strapping someone belly-up onto a tilted board with his head sloped downward. A piece of cloth covers his face and buckets of water are poured onto the cloth. The person experiences the sensation of drowning.

Another form of water torture is water-hosing. Detainee Khaled Ben Mustafa of France explained to us how he was water-hosed in Guantánamo. It happened when he and other detainees protested the treatment of the Quran by the guards in the prison. Mustafa had heard detainees were made to step on the Quran during interrogations. Other detainees had witnessed guards tossing the Quran into the toilet. The men protested the mistreatment of their holy book by refusing to return their plates after a meal.

"I took part in that protest. I didn't agree to go out to the shower or to return the plates, and so [the guards] intervened." Mustafa explained that he was ERFed—mentioned previously and described in more detail in the next section—and also water-hosed. This is how he described the ERFing and water-hosing treatment: "[The guards] spray the detainee with mace and then they open the door and come in, six or seven all at once, so you cannot move, it's over. They handcuff you, and they drag you out, supposedly to remove the gas off your face. They take a water hose—the hose is large—and they place it right here [into his nose and/or mouth]; you cannot breathe anymore. They say that they do this to remove the gas off your face. Actually, that's not true. They do it to drown you."

Although we were able to document that men in Guantánamo had been water-hosed, we have not been able to document that people in Guantánamo had been waterboarded. Nevertheless, it is possible that people were waterboarded at Guantánamo.

Several high-value detainees were held at Guantánamo in separate quarters controlled by the CIA from 2002 to 2003.[9] The government has acknowledged that two of the prisoners had been waterboarded. However, the government has not identified all the locations where they were waterboarded or whether they were waterboarded in more than one location. Abu Zubaydah was waterboarded 83 times; Khalid Sheikh Mohammed was waterboarded 183 times. It is possible that these men were waterboarded while they were held at the CIA section in Guantánamo, as well as in other CIA black site locations. As of August 2019, we still do not know.

ERFING

"We were just told there's five men on a team, and the first guy carries the riot shield, second guy gets left arm, third guy right arm, fourth guy left leg, fifth guy right leg, just pretty much take them down. That was pretty much the training," prison guard Private First Class Brandon Neely said in describing the ERFing process to us. The group in riot gear was called the ERF team.

The lead man would "go in with the shield and pin the detainee, or hit the detainee, and take him down or pin him against the cage, so, you know, just in case [there is] a weapon, or to get control of them," Neely said. When he entered the cell, the lead man—a lieutenant or sergeant first-class—would often mace the detainee in an S- or Z-shaped motion across the face.

As discussed earlier, the ERF team was known as the emergency response force, or extreme reaction force. (The ERF procedure was later renamed FCE, for forcible cell extraction.)

Prison guard Terry Holdbrooks also described the process to us: "You [would] have five angry men running in there and slamming you down, beating you down, making it difficult to breathe, putting in kicks and punches, using your head to open the door, et cetera. Yeah, there was certainly abuse that took place."

After the beating, the guards would sometimes take the detainee to the prison yard and shave his beard and hair. "It was the easiest way of cleaning up the [mace] spray," Holdbrooks told us. Sometimes the guards would carry the detainee to a cell in Delta Block, a psychiatric and isolation facility, for the men to be medicated and stabilized, or to another cell in the main prison population.

Often the guards did not provide an explanation to the detainee for ERFing him. Or they would offer a trivial or absurd reason—or an invented one. There were also legitimate reasons for cell extractions to move detainees to different locations, such as when a detainee threw feces or urine at a guard.

Detainees believed that the physical punishment of ERFing was applied with a randomness intended to keep detainees off balance. It was a method of prisoner control. The detainees could never be certain when they might next be ERFed. Uighur Ayub Mohammed was ERFed because the guards accused him of refusing to return a spoon at breakfast. He said that he was never given a spoon. A detainee who saved an apple from his lunch plate to eat as a snack later in the day was ERFed. No food was permitted in the cell, except at mealtimes.

Mohammed told us that it was sometimes worth being ERFed, because resisting the guards helped him cope with the system. Being resistant gave him reason to maintain and survive under the harsh conditions. The prison wanted "compliant" detainees. Mohammed and other detainees tossed body fluids, known as "cocktails," when they believed they were mistreated by the guards.

Holdbrooks recalled a time when he and another guard were escorting a detainee to an interrogation room, and the guard was mistreating the man. The detainee was not moving fast enough for Holdbrooks's partner, who said, "Come on, come on, move faster. Come on, you towel head. You stink. Move faster, move faster."

When the detainee still did not move fast enough, the guard "steps on [the detainee's] chain so it would cut his ankles and his feet, and keeps dragging him along. Eventually the detainee trips and falls. And he doesn't get up fast enough for my partner. My partner picks him up and just starts dragging him."

A few hours after Holdbrooks and his partner brought the man back to his cell, they returned to the same block. As Holdbrooks walked down the block, one of the detainees yelled at him to stop and stay where he was. Holdbrooks looked down the block and saw his partner get "covered with poop and pee from three different directions."

FORCE-FEEDING TREATMENT OF HUNGER STRIKERS

Sami al Hajj, the Al Jazeera reporter from Sudan who was captured and transferred to Guantánamo, was held in Guantánamo for nearly six years. Al Hajj went on a hunger strike after more than four years in the prison. He declared that he would not quit his strike until he was released. His strike continued for 480 days, ending on the day he was transferred back to Qatar, where Al Jazeera is based. Al Hajj was brutally force-fed and lost his sense of taste and smell. Now he only eats to "assuage" his hunger. "I eat eggs or I eat onions—to me they are all the same," he told us.

On February 27, 2002, six weeks after the prison at Guantánamo opened, 159 men refused to eat lunch, and 109 men refused to eat dinner.[10] They were protesting the actions of a guard who had pulled a turban off a man's head and, inadvertently or not, kicked his Quran. That was the first hunger strike. Since then, hunger strikes have continued at

Guantánamo. In the early years, the men were protesting primarily conditions and treatment at the camp. As the years passed and they saw no end in sight, the men went on hunger strikes to protest their indefinite detentions without charges.

As the years wore on, and more and more hunger strikes arose, the Department of Defense publicly depicted hunger strikers as participating in "asymmetric warfare." That is, the DOD tried to paint hunger strikes as acts of terrorism. The military argued that hunger strikers were bent on committing suicide, because that was the only power the men had for their voices to be heard.[11] The military claimed that it would force-feed the strikers in order to "protect, preserve, and promote life."[12]

A hunger striker's death would be a very undesirable and damaging reflection on Guantánamo, generating negative publicity the authorities do not want or need. The death could also encourage the protests of other hunger strikers, making it that much more difficult for the military to maintain discipline at the prison.

Consequently, when military medical personnel assessed that the health of a person on a hunger strike was jeopardized, they would force-feed him. Daily caloric intake, weight loss, and the number of meals that the detainee refused were factors in the decision. One interviewee told us that men who had weighed two hundred pounds would be down to ninety pounds after going on prolonged hunger strikes.[13]

In the early years, some men on hunger strikes agreed to accept oral fluids or IV rehydration outside the view of other hunger strikers.[14] However, as the years passed, the prison discontinued the IVs. Everyone on strike was subjected to the force-feeding protocol.

The process of force-feeding a detainee in Guantánamo follows this routine, as outlined previously: A man is strapped into a restraint chair manufactured specifically for force-feeding. His head, both hands, and both feet are tightly bound into the chair at five points, so that he cannot move. Medical personnel then thrust the man's head back and push thick plastic nasogastric tubes into his nostrils and down into his stomach. A medic pours Ensure or a similar nutritional liquid into the tubes.

The tubes usually are yanked out after each feeding. The removal is often as painful, if not more painful, than the insertion. Sometimes the tubes are left in all day. If the man throws up or dirties himself, he is compelled to sit in it. If a detainee refuses to leave his cell to be force-fed, he could be subject to the brutal forcible cell extractions described above. The force-feeding process is usually applied twice a day.

Some men quit their hunger strikes to avoid the further suffering of being brutally force-fed. Tom Wilner, one of the very first attorneys to represent detainees, told us that his Kuwaiti client ended his hunger strike when force-feeding was about to begin, because he did not want to be "tortured anymore." Wilner believed that "when they took away even his ability not to eat, it devastated him." The detainee became "emotionally broken."

Cori Crider, strategic director of the abuses and counterterrorism team for the London-based human rights charity Reprieve, described watching tapes filmed by prison personnel that showed the force-feeding of her clients. She was not permitted to reveal the images she saw on the tapes. But she explained that the men who chose to go on hunger strikes and were force-fed were "so desperate that they were willing to put themselves through unbelievable suffering just to remind the world that they still exist and that they're still human."

She added that hunger strikes take a toll not only on the prisoner; personnel required to participate, such as medical personnel and prison guards, are also damaged.

Daniel Lakemacher, a mental health technician at the prison's clinic, tried to keep from being present when detainees were being force-fed. He described the procedure as "far and away the most dehumanizing thing I've actually seen with my own eyes in my entire life."

In 2014, a federal district court required the public release of military tapes of men forcibly extracted from their cells and force-fed against their will.[15] The government argued against the release, saying that if people around the world saw the tapes, it would put America in a bad light and possibly lead to further dangers for our troops and Americans overseas. An appeals court agreed with the government and reversed the trial court's decision.

The participation of medical personnel in force-feeding and other hurtful treatment of detainees can be understood as violations of the universal medical obligation to "do no harm."[16] General Stephen Xenakis, who was an army psychiatrist before he retired in 1998, said that medical personnel are obligated to report on injurious treatment of the detainees and act to correct it. But junior and senior people in army medicine admitted that they would not get involved if and when mistreatment was reported to them. They were concerned about their careers, knowing that if they were not promoted, their military careers would come to an end.

Xenakis believed that a psychiatrist should examine the detainee to determine whether the detainee was undertaking the hunger strike as a political or military action, or if the man was on hunger strike because of a medical or psychiatric problem.

"You know, over the years I've watched patients go on hunger strikes who've been frankly psychotic. And, in fact, they weren't on hunger strikes. They just felt that everything that was given to them was poison. And you had to treat the psychosis in order to get them to eat," he said.

Although it is likely that several medical officials spoke up against the practice of force-feeding, only once did we hear of this. A medic in Guantánamo refused to participate in the force-feeding of a detainee. He was a navy nurse, and his name was never made public. His story began in 2014, when he was criminally charged with dereliction of duty. The navy intended to dismiss him from the military, after more than eighteen years of service. (At twenty years, he would be entitled to a full pension.)[17]

The American Nurses Association, the American Medical Association, and Physicians for Human Rights supported the nurse's refusal to participate in force-feeding. In 2015, the navy dismissed the charges against him, and he concluded his twenty-year career with an honorable discharge.[18] After he left the military, the Department of Defense Health Board—which advises on health practices—issued a report requiring that procedures be developed to allow objecting professionals to opt out of participation in force-feeding.[19] The nurse did not want to interview with Witness to Guantánamo.

MEDICAL CARE AT GUANTÁNAMO: A BRIEF REVIEW

Doctors and other medical personnel were present and complicit when men were tortured in CIA black sites. Alka Pradhan, the lawyer who told us at the start of this chapter of her client who was suspended from the ceiling while naked, starved, and dehydrated, explained that the doctors on site were not "doing no harm."

"The medical doctors who were on site were making decisions about how many and what techniques could be used, how they could be combined, and how—and really, kind of horrifyingly—how they could be combined in order to get information from these men," she said. She elaborated that the doctors were there not to ensure that nothing happened, but rather to actively participate in the torture.

Physicians, nurses, medical technicians, and other medical personnel present at the torture had taken oaths to "do no harm." Yet they supervised the torture of others, or neglected to notice when people were intentionally harmed. The medical personnel worked to keep the prisoners alive and "safe." They also participated in the collection of intelligence and in experimentation with techniques of torture.

Medical professionals would take care of ordinary conditions such as skin rashes. "But when it came to instances where there was intentional harm and people presented them with fractures, contusions, lacerations, nerve injuries—they never asked the question, 'How did this happen?'" Vincent Iacopino, senior medical advisor to Physicians for Human Rights, told us.

"It was stunning, the combination of direct involvement in the actual torture and the concealment of that involvement by the neglect of evidence of the clinicians who are supposed to take care of the detainees," he said.

Medical personnel who participated in the inhumane acts found moral justifications, such as needing to participate for national security, Iacopino added. In essence, these medical professionals morally disengaged and did not recognize the consequences of their actions. They would even blame the victim—the victims would not be in the situation if they were not "the worst of the worst."

Although we tried, we were not able to find a physician who worked at the detention center who was willing to talk to us.

Carol Rosenberg, the dean of Guantánamo reporters, told us that medical staff she met were proud of what they had accomplished. They believe that they saved lives and limbs, and improved the detainees' quality of life. She added that those she spoke to believe they performed professionally and honorably in their behavior toward the detainees. They believe that they have honored their Hippocratic oath.

Because medical care is a critical human rights issue, a discussion of medical participation in the torture of detainees deserves thoroughly researched reports and books. Physicians for Human Rights published a powerful report on the medical profession's participation in torture in 2009.[20] A decade later, in June 2019, the Center for Victims of Torture and Physicians for Human Rights released a major joint report on Guantánamo's broken medical care system. The report, *Deprivation and Despair: The Crisis of Medical Care at Guantánamo*, provides analyses from independent civilian physicians who had access to detainees, their medical records, and Guantánamo's medical care system.[21] More work on the medical and human rights issues at the prison is still needed. The comments below only very generally reveal the medical treatment at the prison.

As the first commanding medical officer of Guantánamo after 9/11, Albert Shimkus had intended to provide "the same quality of care" for the detainees as would be given to service members if held as prisoners of war under the Geneva Conventions. To Shimkus, it did not matter whether a detainee was "an enemy of the state." The profession demanded that he and his staff take care of each man and do "what's best for this human being."

At the time Guantánamo opened, there was a small clinic, also known as an infirmary, available for detainees in Camp X-Ray. When the indoor detention facility known as Camp Delta was constructed in late spring 2002, a new clinic and hospital were built alongside it. As Camp Delta expanded, at least one other clinic was added.[22] Shimkus said that detainees who were seriously ill or injured were taken to the ICU in the naval hospital on the base, outside the detention facilities.

Although Shimkus ran the medical facilities honorably, many of the detainees we interviewed believed that the medical care was just another miserable part of the abusive system they suffered under in Guantánamo. Several of the men said that they were given medications without explanation, and they believed they were guinea pigs for medical experiments.

Shimkus acknowledged that when the first groups of men arrived at the prison, the military did not have sufficient interpreters for the many languages spoken. Consequently, the medical staff could not always explain the medications everyone was required to take. One of the most common medications was for malaria. Shimkus did not tell us the name of the medication. But it may have had side effects that the detainees would not have anticipated, such as hallucinations.

It was not surprising that detainees did not trust medical personnel, Xenakis told us. He indicated that different cultural and ethnic backgrounds, along with the circumstances in which they were being held, would all contribute to explaining the detainees' attitudes.

"As the mission matured," the medical staff would not undertake surgical procedures without a signed consent form by the detainee, Shimkus said. He added that, although some detainees may have not wanted to be examined by a female physician, as far as he could recall no detainee resisted examination by a woman while he was at the base.

We heard from several detainees that if they had a problem with their teeth, the dentist assigned to them would likely pull the tooth, rather than try to save it. Shimkus responded that the dentists always cared for their patients and would not pull a tooth unless necessary. However, in cases where men did not have Western-style preventive dental care before they arrived at Guantánamo, their teeth sometimes could not be saved or restored, he noted.

Detainees indicated that if they needed medical care they had to access it through their interrogators.[23] If the detainee did not please the interrogator during an interview, the interrogator could, and often would, deny him access to medical care.

Interrogators had the authority to allow a detainee to meet with certain people, including medical personnel, explained Torin Nelson, a military interrogator in Guantánamo. It was "beneficial" to have that kind of authority, he said, because it gave him the appearance of being effective. As Nelson saw it, the detainees would understand that he "can get something done for [them]." Guards did not have that authority.

Sometimes the medical corpsman would tell a detainee who had a health issue to ask his interrogator for assistance, former detainee Djamel Ameziane of Algeria told me.[24] The medical corpsmen had no authority in these matters. Interrogators arranged detainees' medical appointments.

"During the first six or seven years, I didn't used to ask for medicine whenever I was sick. I would suffer for days until I get better, because if you ask for medicine they will tell you the famous answer, 'drink water,' or at most they will give you a painkiller, unless someone had a contagious disease like TB, for they were afraid the guards get the disease," Ameziane added. Several people told us that when detainees complained about not feeling well, the standard response of medical personnel would be to provide Motrin.

Shimkus did not agree that during his watch interrogators had the authority—perhaps exclusive authority—to determine who could see a medical doctor and who could not. He said that his staff had a policy of "eyes-on at least every day," and if there were a problem the staff would notice in eyeballing each detainee. Shimkus acknowledged that the process might have changed after he left his position in August 2003.

There was also the problem of interrogators' accessing the medical records of detainees, and learning their disabilities and vulnerabilities. "What were their fears, what would make them anxious, what their state of mind was, whether they're depressed," Xenakis told us, in describing the kinds of information that the interrogators would seek out in the medical records. Once, the interrogators had that information, they could use it to their advantage in future interrogations.

There was no policy for interrogators to access medical records and use them in interrogations, Shimkus said. However, he believed that there were times in the middle of the night when interrogators would come into the clinic and ask young corpsmen for a medical record of a detainee.

CHAPTER 24

CASTAWAYS

For many of the men, leaving Guantánamo was not the end of their suffering. The detainees told us that after leaving Guantánamo they were still "living in Guantánamo," or living in "Guantánamo Two." They were caught betwixt and between. They could not return to the life they had before Guantánamo, nor could they hope to begin a new chapter in their lives after their release. One detainee told a reporter that he wanted to return to Guantánamo, where he had stability, three solid meals, and good healthcare as he aged.[1]

Tariq al Sawah was born in Egypt. He was a member of the Muslim Brotherhood and imprisoned in 1981 as an explosives expert who associated with Islamic groups. Al Sawah moved to Bosnia during the Balkan wars in the early 1990s, served in the Bosnian army, married a Bosnian woman, and obtained Bosnian citizenship. He and his wife divorced before he left in 2000 for Afghanistan, where he joined the Taliban. He was seized after the attacks on 9/11 and taken to Guantánamo. He admitted to being a member of al Qaeda.

The US persuaded him to become a snitch. As a member of al Qaeda, he was a valuable asset. The military provided him with special privileges, including living quarters in a hut in Camp Echo, which was separated from the main cellblocks. He had access to a garden, special foods, books, television, and even pornography.[2] He could speak to his family on Skype every month. Al Sawah would have liked to live his life in

Guantánamo. He wanted the US to bring his wife and daughter to live with him. He would have been happy to work in a grocery store at the military base for the rest of his life.[3]

In Guantánamo, al Sawah's health deteriorated and his weight ballooned to more than four hundred pounds. After spending more than six years in Camp Echo, he was charged with providing material support for terrorism and conspiracy. The charges were dismissed in 2012. Subsequently, he became eligible for release. While al Sawah was in Guantánamo, Bosnia revoked his citizenship. He was never notified of the revocation.

Because of al Sawah's criminal record in Egypt, the US could not release him to his birthplace. Instead, the US transferred him back to Bosnia, although he was no longer a citizen. In the fifteen years he was absent, his wife had married another man and left the daughter behind. The daughter had to fend for herself at a young age. During part of her childhood, she lived with another family. Later, while still a juvenile, she lived alone.

When he arrived in Bosnia, al Sawah was taken to an immigration center and held for several months. After he was released, he was ordered to stay within the confines of Sarajevo.

When we met him in 2016, he was living with his daughter. He did not have a passport, travel documents, or a work permit. He had no legal status. Al Sawah could not find a job without the permit, and the Bosnian government did not provide money for food or rent. Moreover, some employers would not take a chance on him because he had been in Guantánamo. Being in the prison had given him a "bad reputation," he said. The "American media make us like we are going to eat the people," he told us.

He was trying to obtain refugee status, a difficult goal for many detainees. During our interview, he said: "I still live in Guantánamo."

Because the American government did not resettle any detainees in the US and could not return some men to their home countries, human rights organizations were grateful when other nations agreed to accept detainees. The hope was that, once free of Guantánamo and in a new environment, the men would have the opportunity to improve their lives. It has not always turned out that way.

THE RESETTLEMENT PROCESS: AN OVERVIEW

In the early years of the Bush administration, most of the men released were returned to their home countries. However, by the time President Obama assumed office in January 2009, a significant proportion of the remaining Guantánamo population could not be returned home. Their countries were unstable or at war, or the men would be tortured and even executed upon their return. After a man from Yemen attempted to detonate a bomb on a plane headed for Detroit on Christmas Day 2009, Obama banned all transfers to Yemen, which was at war and rapidly becoming a failed state.[4] Obama had to find third countries that would accept men who could not go home.

On his second day in office, President Obama announced that he would shut Guantánamo in one year.[5] There were approximately 241 detainees in Guantánamo at the time, and many countries wanted to help him close it. Nations agreed to become host countries and settle detainees. Leaders of these countries wanted to assist the new president and curry favor with him.[6]

"If they were going to [take detainees] this was the time to do it—where they have somebody who's going to be in office for the next four, perhaps eight years. So they get the credit with him, rather than with somebody who's on his way out the door," Clint Williamson, US ambassador-at-large for war crimes, told us. In addition, central European nations wanted to help resettle detainees to thank the US for standing by them in the 1990s—when they broke free from Russian dominance—and for helping them become members of NATO.

Daniel Fried, Obama's special envoy for Guantánamo closure, said he had argued to nations that were critical of our Guantánamo policy—such as Ireland and Portugal—that if they really believed Guantánamo should be closed, they should help by accepting detainees. Ireland and Portugal agreed to resettle detainees. However, the Scandinavian countries, the Netherlands, and Luxembourg, which were also critical of our Guantánamo policies, did not accept detainees.

In transferring detainees out of the prison, the US worked closely with nongovernmental agencies. International human rights organizations such as Human Rights Watch and Amnesty International had contacts with government officials in host countries and often communicated with detainees' family members.[7]

Obama did not shut down the prison in 2009, nor at any other time before he left office in January 2017. As confidence in Obama's declarations to close the detention center waned, fewer nations reached out to accept former detainees.[8]

In the later years of the Obama administration, countries that accepted detainees were less likely to be motivated by humanitarian policies or gaining the good graces of the president, but were driven more by economic advantages, military support, political favors, and diplomatic or trade considerations.[9] Uruguayan president José Mujica said that in exchange for Uruguay's acceptance of six detainees, the US agreed to open its markets to Uruguayan citrus fruit and pursue opening its relationship with Cuba.[10] Many countries, particularly Arab nations, were not interested in financial support but sought relationships with the US.[11]

The terms of the resettlements with the host countries were never made public. We have been told unofficially that the US paid several million dollars in exchange for acceptance by two countries of a number of detainees.[12] We heard very different numbers from Paul Lewis, DOD special envoy for Guantánamo closure. Countries had to submit a budget if they wanted funds to assist with the transition, Lewis said. The DOD or State Department would then submit the request to Congress. The amounts were usually about $80,000 per detainee for housing, training, and other essentials, although they could be increased for medical or security reasons.

Host countries may have supplemented US support. Local chapters of the International Committee of the Red Cross/Red Crescent (ICRC), as well as the Office of the UN High Commissioner for Refugees (UNHCR), may have added funding. The ICRC and UNHCR provided minimal services including healthcare, language classes, and transportation for the detainees.[13] The ICRC also assisted with family reunifications to the extent possible, when supported by the host country.

Security concerns were paramount to the Obama administration. Agreements required that the host countries surveil the detainees so that they did not "return to the battlefield." Lee Wolosky, the last US special envoy for Guantánamo closure under President Obama, explained that the standard for security was the "substantial mitigation of risks." He described the risk plan as having four elements: monitoring, restricting travel, sharing information with the US, and planning for integration.

The monitoring systems varied with the countries that agreed to re-settle detainees. One harsh example of surveillance occurred after several men were transferred to Kazakhstan, a country that has no tradition of welcoming refugees and an opaque government bureaucracy. The police came regularly to the apartments of the former detainees to monitor them. The men were apparently restricted to their apartments for weeks, if not months.

One of the men, Lofti Bin Ali, compared living in Kazakhstan to living in his former prison. "It's as if it's Guantánamo Two," he said.[14] Another man living in Kazakhstan, Sabri Mohammed Ebrahim al Qurashi, became a well-regarded painter while in Guantánamo. One of his paintings is of the Statue of Liberty wearing a hood. The hood is similar to that worn by victims of US torture and abuse at Abu Ghraib.

Apparently, the DOD and other agencies had their own security "assets on the ground" in these countries. These assets could, on their own, monitor the intelligence in the country. In addition, the DOD utilized local security agencies.[15]

Each country submitted an integration and security plan to the US for approval. Sometimes, the first time the US sent men to a country, the transfer would be considered a test case. If it looked like it was working, the US would transfer additional men, assuming the country was interested. For example, the US sent four men to Oman in January 2015, six more in June 2015, another ten in January 2016, and a final group of ten in January 2017.

Fortunately for President Obama, near the end of his tenure Arabic-speaking countries such as Saudi Arabia, Oman, and the United Arab Emirates stepped up to take more detainees. These countries often appealed to the men in Guantánamo, who sometimes had relatives there, likely knew the language, and were more familiar with the culture.

Transfer to a Muslim country was not necessarily without its problems. The stigma of having been in Guantánamo often followed the detainee. As one person explained, there were always people who believed that "there's no smoke without fire, and anyone who ended up [in Guantánamo] must have been a terrorist."[16]

When Donald Trump became president, in 2017, he dismantled the State Department Office of Guantánamo Closure. The office had assisted in finding homes for detainees after release and was responsible for monitoring released detainees. In the years following the closure of the office, the government has lost track of several men who had been released.[17] There is a fear that some may have returned to the "battlefield."

TRANSFERRING MEN TO HOST COUNTRIES

In the early years of the Bush administration, most of the men released were returned to their home countries. Before transferring the detainees, the US ostensibly asked for assurances that the detainees would not be tortured and would be treated humanely upon their return.[18] However, several Algerian detainees who said that they would be imprisoned and tortured upon their return were forcibly repatriated to Algeria.[19] There are credible reports that some detainees, including some men sent to Tajikistan, Tunisia, and Russia, were tortured, died in prison, or disappeared on their return home.

One of the first times detainees were not returned to their home countries occurred in 2006. As discussed earlier, five Uighurs were resettled in Albania rather than their home of East Turkistan in China. The Uighurs had been designated terrorists by the Chinese government, and if they had been returned to China, they would have been tortured and executed.[20] One Uzbek was also sent to Albania. The US believed that he, too, would have been tortured if he had been returned to his homeland.

Aside from expecting host nations to provide assurances on security issues, the US relied on the host nations to care for the men. All transferred detainees were usually provided substandard housing for two to three years and often received no more than fifteen dollars per day for food, clothing, and necessities. Counseling, as well as job and language training, were left to the host country.

Consequently, men transferred to countries with limited resources were trapped in foreign cultures with language barriers. They faced stigmatization and discrimination, lack of community, cultural and religious isolation, scarce economic opportunities, limited healthcare, and inadequate social and psychological services. The men had limited funds, struggled to find jobs, and lacked travel documents. Many also continued to suffer from PTSD.

After living in Guantánamo for years, the men often had difficulty training for work and adjusting to holding jobs. "It's not that the men don't want to work. They absolutely do. They want to be independent again and stand on their own two feet. And get married and have children," said Polly Rossdale, the first director of Reprieve's Life After Guantánamo Project.

It was not easy for many detainees to find jobs. Many of the host countries that resettled them—such as Palau, Albania, El Salvador, Portugal, Bermuda, Cape Verde, Slovakia, Uzbekistan, Latvia, Estonia, Georgia, and Uruguay—are poor. Julia Hall, Amnesty International's expert on counterterrorism, explained that finding work in these countries, whether as a former Guantánamo detainee or not, is trying. The detainees would sometimes be seen as people who "drain resources that should otherwise, in the public mind, be used on nationals of that country," she said.

The men were unfamiliar with the local language and culture, and although they might have been motivated to take language classes, learning a new language can be challenging. The ability to concentrate may be damaged when someone has experienced severe psychological and physical trauma. In addition, the language lessons provided are often limited in time and scope in many countries. The funds are not there, and the men are expected to learn quickly so that they can go out and manage on their own.

Although some men received "travel documents," the US asked the countries to restrict the men's travel for at least three years.[21] Sometimes, when that time passed, the men were still denied official travel documents and passports. Even men who were released to countries in the European Union were not always certain whether they had the right to travel to another country within the EU.

Legal status was another serious problem. Ideally, arriving detainees would have refugee status. However, it was not provided in many countries. Many of the men received a six-month renewable temporary residency permit, which is often interpreted as a "made-up category" and outside the law, Katherine Taylor, the coordinator of Reprieve's Life After Guantánamo Project, told us.[22] In addition, detainees were often given no guidance on how to get on the citizenship track.

One man who was living in an eastern European country was not provided any form of government status. He was deemed stateless. No country was home. He used a United Nations passport for travel. Moreover, because he was stateless, he stood at the very back of the line for a job. Anyone with a recognized status in the country had priority.

Dr. Sondra Crosby, an expert on the effects of torture, works with former detainees. She explained to us that, after being traumatized in Guantánamo, the men are often retraumatized in their host countries.

Many former detainees have described how they have lost the best years of their lives—the years of being a young man starting out in life, finding oneself, marrying, and embarking on a career.[23] One man described them as his "golden years." Several men said that they had "no future."[24]

ASSISTANCE AND OTHER PROBLEMS

When men return to their home countries, they usually have a family support system. Having family near, as emotional support, is the most important asset for a detainee. In the Muslim community, the family is everything. It is the "basic building block of Muslim society" and the "cornerstone of a healthy and balanced society."[25] It does not matter whether the family members are parents, wives, children, siblings, or others. They all provide the support the returning detainee requires.[26] In third countries, the men are often alone, without wives and other family members.

In addition to the ICRC, Reprieve tries to obtain minimal services for the men, especially in those countries where the men do not have family and are not familiar with the culture.[27] It does not act as a direct service provider. Although it cannot substitute for family members, Reprieve meets with the detainees and assesses their needs. It then reaches out to the local government and to other agencies in hope of facilitating and coordinating access to medical, psychological, social, and legal support.

To an outsider, the quality of life that the men have in their host countries may appear to be a significant improvement over what they suffered in Guantánamo. On the other hand, the culture shock in transferring, after a decade or more, from the detention center to an unfamiliar third country cannot be underestimated.

Detainees have little to no choice of country. They are interviewed by various interested countries, which then make a formal invitation if they are interested. The detainee knows that he can refuse to accept an invitation. If he refuses the invitation, he may have to wait for months or even years for another country to take him.

Yemeni Mohammed Ali Abdullah Bwazir was offered resettlement in Montenegro in January 2016. When he was about to board the flight from Guantánamo to Montenegro, Bwazir changed his mind. "I do not want to leave. I want to go back to my cell," he said.[28] He indicated that he wanted a transfer to a country where he had family. Fortunately, in January 2017, two weeks before the end of the Obama administration, Bwazir was transferred to Saudi Arabia.[29] It was one of three countries where he had family.

It is possible that the lives of detainees would have been no better economically had the detainees remained in their home countries. In fact, their previous lives could have even been economically worse. Yet they are not refugees in the same manner as those who choose to emigrate to another country. They do not really choose which country to adopt. Their choices are limited to the countries willing to accept them. And, often, no more than one country will.

RETURNING TO THEIR HOME COUNTRIES

Men who have returned to their home countries are not as likely to experience culture shock and a sense of isolation as those sent to third countries are. They have family to whom they can return, local mosques in which they are probably still welcome, and a culture that is familiar to them and embracing of them. It will be easier for these detainees to find wives and settle into familiar routines in their communities. They may continue to have problems, however, including stigmatization and difficulty in finding jobs. In addition, if the men live in a poor economy, or in a country with minimal social services, they will not receive the care and treatment that they require.

Three of the men we interviewed in Morocco did not settle back into their home country after returning from Guantánamo. They left to fight in Syria. One of the men, Brahim Benchakroun, told us that when he and several others arrived back in Morocco from Guantánamo, they were handed over to the police and held for eight months. When he and others were released, "there was no follow-up or care from the authorities. . . . But we started our life normally as any human being. I worked and I married and I have a son. I continue my normal life as the rest of the people." Apparently it did not stay that way.

One year after we sat down to an interview with Benchakroun and his Moroccan colleague Souleimane Laalami Mohamed, they were killed fighting in Syria with the al Qaeda affiliate Jabhat al-Nusra.[30] A third man we interviewed in Morocco, Mohammed Mazouz, had been fighting with the Syrian Harakat Sham rebels. We do not know whether he is still alive.

Bisher al Rawi described how he continued to suffer from his time in Guantánamo after returning home to London. However, four years after returning home, he began to "sense that I'm getting normal. . . . But now, I can sort of very slightly, I can sort of dare say, I am getting there."

FAMILY REUNIFICATIONS

Family reunifications are "one of the most difficult moments," Polly Rossdale explained to us. The expectations are huge, and the moment of reunification that has been longed for, for so long, brings fear on both sides that someone you have loved might have changed irreparably. Reuniting with someone with whom you have been intimate can be terrifying and overwhelming, especially when the person possibly brings back feelings of shame, mistrust, anger, deep sadness, depression, anxiety, and paranoia. You wonder if you will ever love again.

Many men, as well as their families, do not always want to acknowledge these complicated feelings. Rather, family members would like to think: Now that he is out, everything is okay. But everything is not always okay. And relationships do not always survive.

Upon returning home, a detainee found that his children did not want to bond with him. He was a stranger to them. Even more upsetting to him was the way that he did not feel a bond with, or even have feelings for, his children.

His relationship with his wife also suffered. She had grown and moved on while taking responsibility for raising the family. He was no longer certain what his role was in the family. His role was now fluid, not established by the culture, as when he left. He could not help but feel alienated, distant, and lonely. He was unable to find a way to return to what he desperately wanted. He did not know how to find some kind of normalcy. He would have likely benefited from counseling that the community provided. He refused counseling.

Although Witness to Guantánamo had never been able to enter Saudi Arabia to interview former detainees, articles have been written about the Saudi reintegration center, known as the Mohammed bin Nayef Center for Counseling and Care. Guantánamo prisoners and other former alleged terrorists have been directed to the center before reentering Saudi society.[31] The program provided religious education and psychological counseling.[32] Courses were taught by religious clerics and social scientists, and covered concepts such as jihad and the laws of Wahhabism, the very restrictive form of Islam in Saudi society.[33] The Saudi government assisted people in the program in finding jobs, cars, and housing. The government also paid for weddings.[34] Twelve percent of people sent through the program have relapsed and returned to terrorist activities, Saudi officials reported. [35]

AFTER GUANTÁNAMO: THREE SNAPSHOTS

Two Men in Australia

There were two Australian detainees in Guantánamo. Both were repatriated. David Hicks was prosecuted for "material support for terrorism." He was convicted after signing a plea agreement admitting to the crime. He told his lawyers that he would have signed anything to be released from Guantánamo.[36] In 2015, and to the surprise of many human rights advocates and attorneys, the US government admitted that MSOT had not been a war crime at the time Hicks was convicted, and his conviction was overturned.[37]

David Hicks's mother, Bev Hicks, told us that military officials at Guantánamo played with the minds of the detainees. She described how her son "is not sure of anything anymore. He is not sure on making decisions." She added that though she might not know much about Guantánamo and what goes on in there, "I know that something happened to him, with his mind."

Bev Hicks also confirmed something that was quite common among the released detainees, as it is among many soldiers. Many of the former detainees did not want to talk to their families about their experiences in the detention center. This was true of David Hicks too.

"David doesn't talk about it. And don't ask me why. We don't ask questions because we don't . . . want him going back thinking about what may have happened to him there. We sort of keep away from that area. And you sort of think to yourself, If he wants to tell you, he will tell you," Bev Hicks said to us.

We met David Hicks at his parents' home. We talked for about thirty minutes, but he would not go on record. David refused to go on camera, even to say why he would not talk. Before he left, he generously offered me copies of his autobiography. The US would not allow him or his publisher to sell the books in the US.

Maha Habib, the wife of the other detainee from Australia, Mamdouh Habib, described how her husband had become a changed man. Both of them confirmed that he did not recognize his wife when he first saw her on his return.

Mamdouh Habib was captured in October 2001 as he traveled by bus from Quetta to Karachi, Pakistan. He was held at a Pakistani military base and then transferred into Egyptian custody. For six months he was subjected to Egyptian interrogators and torture in a CIA black site. He was transported to Guantánamo in May 2002 and released nearly three years later, in January 2005.

It took Mamdouh about nine months to one year before he could actually believe that this was his family, his wife said. When the kids were not behaving properly, he would say, "There, you see, they're not my kids. You're not my family."

Men from Bosnia

In 2001, six Algerian men who were living in Bosnia were arrested for allegedly planning an attack on the US embassy in Sarajevo.[38] Manfred Nowak, a judge on the Human Rights Chamber in Bosnia-Herzegovina at the time (who later became UN special rapporteur on torture and other cruel, inhuman, or degrading treatment or punishment), indicated that the lower Bosnian court judges had asked the US for evidence to hold the men. The US responded that the evidence was classified. The Bosnian judges replied that under Bosnian law, without the evidence, the judges were compelled to release the men.

"General David Petraeus apparently went to the Bosnian police station, where the six were due to be released, with a money belt containing . . . $20,000, to pay off the jailers to turn over [the men] to our task force, who arranged for them to be spirited away," Guantánamo prosecutor Lieutenant Colonel Darrel Vandeveld told us.[39]

"In the dark of night, they were taken from the Bosnian jail directly to a C-130 that was waiting for them," Vandeveld continued. As he understood it, "they were apprehended and sent to Guantánamo on the flimsiest of information and evidence." These six men had never set foot in Afghanistan or Pakistan. They had been flown directly to Guantánamo.

When the men were released from Guantánamo, two of the men, al Haj Boudella and Mustafa Ait Idir, were allowed to return to Bosnia.

Lakhdar Boumediene was transferred to Nice, France, where he had family. Boumediene would be remembered as the petitioner in the pivotal 2008 Supreme Court case establishing the constitutional right to habeas corpus for Guantánamo detainees.[40]

Another Bosnian, Bensayah Belkacem, was transferred to Algeria against his wishes. He had feared persecution and possibly imprisonment if he were returned to Algeria. The US assured him and his attorney that he would be safe in Algeria.[41] He was detained briefly, in secret, upon his return home.[42]

Saber Lahmar, who lived in Bosnia and was of Algerian heritage, was transferred to Bordeaux, France, from Guantánamo. His wife continued to live in Bosnia. Lahmar seemed to be a sensitive, serious, and reflective person. He had been the head of a library in Bosnia. He was well traveled. He spoke five languages. When we sat down to interview with him, Saber described President Bush as an "imbecile," and said that Obama was more dangerous because he acted with intelligence.

The interview with Lahmar started out fine. He was intelligent and quite informative in his telling of his life. We were engaged in his interview when, suddenly, he switched into unforeseen and startling language. He began referring to psychologists as "magicians." He explained that these magicians performed magic on the detainees. When they performed their magic, he said, "You cannot do anything at all. You cannot eat, you cannot sleep, you cannot talk." He told us that he could not sleep for six months after the magicians appeared.

Lahmar continued by describing how the interrogators, including one named "Sarah," could make the devil enter into the body of a detainee. "Sometimes, the devil speaks and says, 'I didn't choose to go inside his body, but it is the interrogator, an interrogator named Sarah [who made me do it].'"

Lahmar explained that a detainee whose body the devil entered would then speak in a different voice and possibly tell "secrets." None of us knew what to make of his accounts.

In early summer 2017, he was arrested with several other people in France for helping to recruit men to join ISIS. This seemed out of character for the person we met. We could find only one short article on the arrest, and no further updates.

Rafiq al Hami from Tunisia

Rafiq al Hami, a Tunisian detainee, was cleared for release, but he could not return home. He had been sentenced to forty years in absentia under the Tunisian autocratic regime of Zine El Abidine Ben Ali.

Portugal was interested in taking him and interviewed him in Guantánamo. Al Hami told us that he was not comfortable with the officials' detailed questioning. Also, he had heard that two men who had been transferred to Portugal were not doing well there. Al Hami would not agree to be transferred to Portugal.

He understood that it was very unusual for men to turn down an opportunity to leave Guantánamo. He had been advised by his lawyers and cellmates to accept an offer from Portugal. Once out, he could always seek another country, they told him. He still refused.

Fortunately for him, an opportunity came six weeks later. Officials from Slovakia interviewed him. They had only two questions. First: could he live among Christians? He answered that he had lived among Christians before and that he had "no problem." They asked whether he would like to live in Slovakia. He replied, "Yes." The entire interview lasted fifteen minutes.

When he arrived in Slovakia, he lived in a repatriation center for six months. After that, he was provided with a passport and an ID card. "We enjoyed complete freedom. We were able to travel. I traveled outside Slovakia," he said. The Slovakian authorities also provided healthcare, a monthly stipend, classes in English and Slovak, and computer instruction.

After the Arab Spring, Ben Ali was deposed and Tunisia issued a constitutional amnesty. Al Hami wanted to return home to Tunisia. The Slovakian authorities assisted him. He returned on March 29, 2011. Soon after, he met a woman. They married in September 2011.

Although he was now home and married, he did not adapt well. "I was working with someone in commerce for five months, but for health reasons, I stopped. . . . For the last three months, I am using medication to pacify my nerves." He believed that living in Guantánamo was the cause of his nervous condition.

Sometime after our interview with him, he left Tunisia for Syria and joined the al Qaeda aligned faction Jabhat al-Nusra. Rafiq al Hami died fighting for Jabhat al-Nusra in late 2015.[43]

CHAPTER 25

DRONES

A nwar al-Awlaki was an American citizen and imam living in Yemen. From his hideout, he motivated al Qaeda recruits to plan and execute terrorist attacks on US operations and on American citizens. He was well protected in the mountainous region where he lived. The American military feared too many civilian losses if it sought him out for capture. On September 30, 2011, al-Awlaki was targeted and killed by a drone strike authorized by President Obama. Another American citizen, Samir Khan, was killed with him. Al-Awlaki's sixteen-year-old son, Abdulrahman al-Awlaki, was targeted and killed in a similarly authorized drone strike two weeks later.[1] He was also an American citizen.

Several people we interviewed expressed concerns about President Obama's use of drones to target and kill people, including Americans— rather than capturing and detaining them, as the Bush administration had done. In some situations, the drones sent by the Obama administration extinguished the lives of innocent civilians along with suspected terrorists.

Several interviewees compared President Obama's drone policy to President Bush's detention policy. As they saw it, Bush's policy of capturing and detaining people was arguably more humane and a moral alternative to Obama's policy of killing people with drones.

"One thing that people forget about our detention and capturing people is that the alternative is to kill them," Alan Liotta, the director of the office of detainee policy, told me. Under the Obama administration, "we have many more people killed by drones that possibly could have been captured and held in detention. If we had captured them and held them in detention, is that more of a human rights violation than killing them with a drone?" he asked.

John Bellinger, legal advisor for Secretary of State Condoleezza Rice during the Bush administration, had similar comments. He noted that Obama did not promote the Bush detention policy but instead "dramatically ramped up the use of drones. . . . Obama's preference [was] to simply kill senior al Qaeda leaders, as opposed to attempting to detain them."

Bellinger added, "One might imagine that they saw what happened to the Bush administration with respect to detention and they decided that trying to detain suspected terrorists is an unsuccessful policy. The problem with drone strikes, though, is that it results in killing not only the people you're targeting but also civilians. And it's not transparent. At least the people in Guantánamo—we know who they are. We can argue whether they ought to be there or not," he emphasized.

Under the Geneva Conventions, prisoners can be held until the end of hostilities. As people like Bellinger and Liotta might argue, even if there was no clear termination to the hostilities in the war on terror, most of the people in Guantánamo finally saw an end to their detentions. Yes, many were held in the prison for years, even for more than a decade without charges. Yes, life was miserable, brutal, and deadening inside the prison. Moreover, returning to a life outside the prison was often challenging for those released. Nevertheless, when they were released, the men had an opportunity to embark on a new life. They had not been killed by a drone.

To his credit, President Obama took full responsibility for the drone strikes. Government white papers were written to justify the drone strikes, including the targeting and killing of American citizens.[2] But there was no rule of law system in place for those targeted, including American citizens. It is possible that the killings were justified under American or international law. However, the United States never held public hearings on the issues before the killings occurred. The drone policies and justifications for the killings were created in secret.

LOOKING FORWARD AND LOOKING BACK

"Guantánamo Bay, I think, is going to be seen as the significant start of the fall of American democracy. . . . And I think that Guantánamo Bay will stand out as a beacon of when things really started to go bad. I hope that never comes to pass, but I really fear it."

These prophetic words were spoken by Australian lawyer Stephen Kenny on January 1, 2012. He was one of the first lawyers to visit Guantánamo.

President Obama said we should look forward, not back. If we do not look back, will Kenny's prophecy become a reality? No American official has been held accountable for the damage to our Constitution, the rule of law, and human rights after 9/11. How will we learn to do better if we shut our eyes to the past?

Part IV looks at accountability, and how we could do better to keep America safe and uphold our principles and values.

— CHAPTER 26 —

RISING ABOVE

"In our darkest hour, that's when we really need to remind ourselves who we are and what we claim to be. . . . The thing that has made this nation singular are those difficult and indefinable goals that cause people to try to be better than their human nature would normally cause them to be," Major General Michael Lehnert said to us.[1]

Lehnert was the first commander of the Guantánamo detention center. He came to work each day with a sincere belief that military and elected leadership should apply the highest moral standards.

Six weeks after Guantánamo opened, the detainees went on a hunger strike. The men were protesting their indefinite fate. One of their leaders was at that moment very concerned about his pregnant wife in the UK. Did she have the baby and was everyone fine? The man was despondent and had not eaten in a couple weeks. He only drank water.

Not wanting the detainee to die, and also thinking that the man might help end the strike, Lehnert called England. The man's wife had delivered the baby, and everything was fine.

"I made the decision to tell [the detainee]. He didn't believe us. So we allowed him to make a monitored cell phone call. We got her on the line, let her talk, let them talk for thirty seconds or so. And ultimately, that broke that first hunger strike," Lehnert said.

"And I will tell you that was not a popular thing that I did. . . . There was actual discussion about me aiding and abetting the enemy."

Although there were people in the military and the Bush administration who were irate with Lehnert's actions, he believed that he was acting consistently with the Geneva Conventions.

"I mean, you're allowed to have communication, and even though there weren't cell phones back in World War II, it seemed to me to be a reasonable thing to do and a fair thing to do. . . . If we treat them [the alleged terrorists] like they would treat us, we become them."

Every nation in the world had signed the Geneva Conventions. Yet, in February 2002, President Bush issued a memorandum stating that the conventions would not apply to the men in Guantánamo.[2]

Soon after the hunger strike ended, General Lehnert redeployed and was replaced by more compliant leadership. The treatment of the detainees deteriorated. And Guantánamo became a rallying cry and recruitment tool for terrorist organizations.

Many of the men we held in Guantánamo believed that before they were brought to Guantánamo, America was exceptional—that we stood steadfastly for human rights and the rule of law. We were the gold standard. The Statue of Liberty meant something to many of the men we held. Yet, as French detainee Nizar Sassi saw it, Guantánamo was not the work of barbarians or people who were ignorant. He believed that some of America's best educated and brightest people created the hell that is Guantánamo. To Sassi's shock and disbelief, Guantánamo was created in the greatest democracy in the world, where human rights and the rule of law mean something.

"People like us [former detainees] don't have access to the US anymore, which means that we won't be able to speak to Americans directly to tell them exactly what happened and who we were," Sassi said. He explained that Americans cannot meet him and other former detainees and hear their stories firsthand, because former detainees are banned from traveling to the US. He is not able to "bear witness" to the American people, "who have the right to know what happened over there."

When I asked him whether America owes him anything, he answered, "I don't know. What was taken from me—thirty months of humiliation, degradation, physical and psychological torture—that's not something that can be returned."

Many detainees believe that they are entitled to some form of reparations for their treatment. The type of restitution sought varies among the detainees. One man asked for financial compensation to allow him to manage in his later years. He had spent nearly fifteen years in Guantánamo and was released at the age of fifty-nine. Others would like assistance in resettling and reintegrating into their new homes. Some men simply seek an apology.

"I feel that I am owed—well, I should receive reparations. Reparations, explanations, an apology? I don't know. But I want something to happen," French detainee Mourad Benchellali told us.

For the most part, requests from detainees have been quite modest. Generally, they would like to lead productive lives, although, as described earlier, returning to a productive life from Guantánamo is not always simple. Nearly all the men released from the prison, whether returning to their homeland or transferring to a third, host country, needed jobs, financial assistance, adequate healthcare, and counseling. They had to adjust to their return to society.

In addition, the men transferred to host countries often were challenged by unfamiliar cultures, languages, and religions. Usually, they arrived without family members and a support system.

In making lives for themselves, former detainees needed to find gainful employment. But finding employment was not easy—even in their home countries. Moroccan detainees explained how, upon returning home, they could not find work; the economy was not strong, and they were stigmatized by having been in Guantánamo.

Uighur detainees from China who were resettled in Albania said that employers would not hire them because they had been in Guantánamo. An Uzbek detainee in Latvia asked us not to reveal his name for fear that his employer would fire him. Men transferred to poorer countries— where the economies cannot support jobs for all those who want them— were often placed at the bottom rung of the hiring ladder. Those without refugee status were assigned to stand last in line for jobs, while their status remained undetermined.

Some detainees who returned to their homelands requested assistance and counseling to readjust to family life. After being gone for years, the men found it difficult adapting to families that have grown and evolved. The children may not know their father when he returned. And, the wives had taken over the role of father as well as mother.

Understanding both the profound familial changes that occurred while the men were gone and the task of finding one's place in the new

and often unfamiliar family and community structures requires professional counseling. This is something that not all countries recognize or
can afford to offer. America can.

Many of the men have asked for an apology from the US government.
An apology would be the best "reparations" for many. An apology would
be an important signal that America understands the wrongs we have
committed. The men also hope that through an apology the US would
become more mindful of its deeds and prevent another Guantánamo
from happening in the future.

Because an apology admits wrongdoing, it would have a momentous
impact not only on the detainees, but also on the global stage. People
would admire us for standing up and acknowledging our wrongs. But
an apology could possibly make us financially liable in future lawsuits,
something the US might not welcome. If history and the present are any
indication, an apology from the US will be a long time coming.

Lee Wolosky was the last State Department special envoy for Guantánamo closure under the Obama administration. He did not see the
need to apologize to the detainees who were captured in Afghanistan
and Pakistan and had been staying in al Qaeda safe houses, or who had
been part of the Taliban. "We never make apologies. We don't make
apologies for the detention of any of the people who we ended up releasing," Wolosky told us.

But he did make one concession: people who were essentially innocent and had been swept up after 9/11—for example, people caught up in
cases of mistaken identity—"are deserving of apology."

AMERICAN LAW AND THE COURTS: AN OVERVIEW

Ordinarily, an individual can turn to the law and the courts for monetary
remedies for mistreatment by government officials. But it is not the same
for Guantánamo detainees and other victims of the US's detention and
torture policies. Lawsuits against the president, high-ranking government officials, government agencies, and CIA personnel under various
statutory and Constitutional theories have failed. Except for two actions
against CIA contractors, the law and the courts have closed their doors
to the detainees.

Several federal statutes either deny detainees the right to sue, or grant
government officials immunity. An example is the Military Commissions

Act (MCA) passed by Congress in 2006.[3] One provision explicitly bars federal courts from hearing lawsuits brought by detainees for the detention, treatment, or conditions that they suffered while in the prison.[4] Subsequently, several claims brought by former detainees against government officials were, without further action, dismissed.

REVISING THE WAR CRIMES ACT

Congress also adopted legislation in 2006 to shield federal officials from prosecution for violating certain provisions of the Geneva Conventions. The legislation was in response to a decision by Justice John Paul Stevens in the Supreme Court case of *Hamdan v. Rumsfeld*, a 2006 case holding that Common Article 3 of the Geneva Conventions applied to al Qaeda detainees in Guantánamo. Common Article 3 requires that all prisoners shall be treated humanely. Cruel treatment and torture are forbidden, and so is humiliating and degrading treatment. People also must be tried and sentenced in a "regularly constituted court."

Justice Stevens's ruling refuted President Bush's 2002 declaration that the Geneva Conventions did not apply to the detainees. The War Crimes Act of 1996 had made it a war crime to violate provisions of Common Article 3.

Fearing that high-ranking government officials could now be prosecuted, convicted, and sentenced to prison for violating provisions of Common Article 3 of the Geneva Conventions, Congress, at the urging of the Bush administration, rewrote the 1996 War Crimes Act, specifically addressing two provisions of Common Article 3.[5]

The first was the provision forbidding "humiliating and degrading treatment." The other was the provision requiring that trials be held in "regularly constituted courts affording all the judicial guarantees which are recognized as indispensable by civilized peoples." Human rights advocates have argued that the courts envisioned by this provision would be similar to the military's courts-martial or the federal civilian courts, and not the military commissions that try cases of the "high-value" detainees in Guantánamo.

Under the new War Crimes Act that was passed by Congress, American officials could no longer be convicted of a war crime if they violate these two provisions. That is, the Common Article 3 provisions on humiliating and degrading treatment, and on providing regularly constituted courts, were no longer recognized and protected under the 2006 War Crimes Act. In rewriting the act, Congress effectively granted immunity to government officials who had authorized mistreatment of the detainees or required that detainees be tried in a less than fair and just trial.

To further protect the officials, Congress made the 2006 War Crimes Act retroactive to 1996. Thus, any actions in violation of the Common Article 3 provisions committed by government officials after September 11, 2001, but before passage of the act in 2006, would also no longer be deemed a war crime. Accordingly, it has become nearly impossible to successfully prosecute and punish government officials for certain war crimes articulated in the Geneva Conventions, because they are no longer identified as war crimes under American law.

There are a number of relevant statutes in American law that seemingly would assist in supporting detainee lawsuits. Yet, for various reasons, they are not applicable to the detainees. For example, the Torture Victim Protections Act (TVPA), which by its name should apply to the treatment of detainees, does not. The act requires that claims can be brought only against individuals acting "under actual or apparent authority, or color of law, of any foreign nation."[6] Courts have interpreted this language to mean that the torturer must have been acting under the authority of another country, and not under US authority. A federal court explained that "the 'under foreign color of law' requirement was understood to serve as an important limitation of the Act that would preclude its application to United States operations abroad."[7]

In addition, if a court decides that the detainee only suffered something less than torture, such as cruel mistreatment, the TVPA would also not apply. The act speaks exclusively to torture.[8]

The international Convention Against Torture and Cruel, Inhuman or Degrading Treatment, known as CAT, has been signed and ratified by the US. It would also appear to apply. But it, too, is unhelpful. The language requires that torture or cruel, inhuman, or degrading treatment or punishment be "intentionally inflicted on a person." The government has maintained that even if torture or cruel mistreatment was inflicted on the detainees, it was not intentional.

John Yoo was deputy assistant US attorney general of the OLC in the Bush administration and the author of several of the "torture memos" that justified the cruel mistreatment of the detainees. He has written that, even though an interrogator may have tortured a detainee, the intent of that official may have been to interrogate the detainee, rather than to torture him. Thus, to the extent that there was torture, Yoo argued that the torture was incidental to the interrogation and was not intended.[9] Because it was written by someone in the OLC, the legal opinion shielded CIA agents and other government officials who participated in torture. They could rely on this Justice Department opinion to legally justify their actions.

If a detainee sues for mental or psychological torture, rather than physical torture, the requirement necessary to prevail is similarly difficult to meet. For an act to be considered mental torture under CAT, the actor must also "specifically intend" to inflict severe physical or mental pain.[10] Moreover, courts have not been able to agree on a definition of torture.[11]

Even if a court cannot conclude that torture occurred, the court could rule that, at minimum, US treatment of the detainees constituted cruel, inhuman, or degrading treatment. This kind of treatment is also covered by CAT. However, as with torture, there is no precise definition of what exactly constitutes this treatment. Additionally, the detainee again faces the difficulty of proving intent.

Moreover, when a detainee argues that he was subjected to cruel, inhuman, or degrading treatment, he must also prove that the act violated the Constitution or a federal statute. The government has argued, and courts have accepted the argument, that certain harsh acts done to detainees do not violate the Constitution because "enemy combatants" do not have the same Constitutional rights as Americans outside the US.[12]

Detainees have also brought claims under a Supreme Court-created Constitutional right to a remedy, known as a "Bivens" claim.[13] The claim is available when government officials violate people's core Constitutional rights, such as depriving someone of liberty without due process. These claims have been rejected in the terrorism context. The courts have ruled that the political branches, particularly Congress and not the courts, should decide whether detainees have a Bivens remedy.[14]

NATIONAL SECURITY ISSUES

The government has also blocked detainees from pursuing their claims in court by raising a "state secrets" or "national security" defense. The government has argued that the cases should not proceed in court because litigation would involve the release of privileged and classified information that could be harmful to US interests or personnel. Additionally, the government has argued that the president, as the executive and commander in chief, is best informed on the most current information. Thus, courts should not interfere with the president's prosecution of the war. Judges rarely challenge the government's position when the executive raises a national security defense.

However, there were conflicts within the federal government itself as to what constituted national security interests, US District Court Judge Ricardo Urbina explained to us: "Homeland Security, CIA, and Department of Justice all had different interpretations of what should be top secret or not, what should [or could] be shared or not."

These conflicts would lead to frustration among some judges, he added. One agency would agree to release certain information and then a second agency would deny the release based on national security.

Because of national security concerns, federal judges have sometimes declined to make decisions that would result in the release of an alleged terrorist. Senior Judge Laurence H. Silberman, a member of the court of appeals for the District of Columbia circuit, the second highest court in the land, said as much when he wrote:

> When we are dealing with detainees, candor obliges me to admit that one cannot help but be conscious of the infinitely greater downside risk to our country, and its people, of an order releasing a detainee who is likely to return to terrorism. . . . I doubt any of my colleagues will vote to grant a petition [for habeas] if he or she believes that it is somewhat likely that the petitioner is an al Qaeda adherent or an active supporter.[15]

On the other hand, Judge Urbina told us that he does not allow the thought that someone before him may be an alleged terrorist to color his actions. As a judge, he follows the law and decides whether there is sufficient evidence to hold the detainee. If the evidence is deficient, the man should be released: "If the country needs protection, it has to do something itself."

Except for a lawsuit brought in early 2016 against CIA contractors— psychologists James Mitchell and Bruce Jessen—who created an interrogation program intended to induce a feeling of "learned helplessness," and another lawsuit brought in 2008 against CACI, a private military contractor that provided interrogators for Abu Ghraib, the federal courts have unwaveringly accepted the government's arguments. Because the court allowed the lawsuit against them to progress, Mitchell and Jessen agreed, in 2017, to a settlement with the families of three men tortured while held by the CIA. Other than these two suits against the government contractors, the federal courts have dismissed or rejected every action filed.[16]

INTERNATIONAL JURISDICTION AND UNIVERSAL SHAMING

As powerful as the United States is, it is not immune to criticism of its reputation. Consequently, even when there are few or no sanctions available against the government's behavior, publicly identifying the US as a violator of human rights and the rule of law may have an effect on curbing its unlawful actions.

However, the United States will not subject itself to the jurisdiction of international oversight bodies. This is so even though none of the bodies, except for the Inter-American Court of Human Rights (a body of the Organization of American States) and the International Court of Justice, have enforcement mechanisms. They issue only nonbinding recommendations.

The Inter-American Commission on Human Rights is the only international body that can hear a case against the United States on the issue of detainee treatment. Although the commission can issue only an unenforceable decision or nonbinding recommendation, a decision from the commission could shame the US in the eyes of the international community.

TRUTH AND RECONCILIATION COMMISSION

In a truth and reconciliation commission, survivors of major human rights violations generally give statements about their experiences in the hope that justice will be served. Justice may be served. The perpetrators may be prosecuted and punished. Or the perpetrators may admit to their wrongdoing and be shamed. Although most truth commissions have been initiated and conducted by government bodies, there are a few instances in which local communities and nongovernmental organizations have established such commissions. Local archbishops and the World Council of Churches have undertaken investigations.[17] For a short time, President Obama's staff considered a truth commission, but it did not come to pass.

JAPANESE AMERICANS IN WWII

Sixty years passed before the US publicly acknowledged that it had unlawfully held 115,000 Japanese Americans in internment camps. Many of those internees were US citizens. When the government finally recognized the harm, it compensated each person with a $20,000 payment. Congress passed the Civil Liberties Act of 1988, which included an official apology acknowledging that "a grave injustice [had been] done to both citizens and permanent residents of Japanese ancestry." Might Congress do the same today for the detainees?

Of course, for generations people have advocated for reparations for slavery, to no avail.[18] Nor has Congress offered reparations to American Indians. Even if advocacy of reparations for detainees appears to be another lost cause, many view the effort as important and worth pursuing.

The concept of reparations and financial assistance as a viable option for the detainees is not as extreme as one might expect. In 2015 former Supreme Court justice Stevens suggested that the US provide reparations to Guantánamo "detainees who have been deemed not to be a security threat to the United States and have thereafter remained in custody for years."[19] He was specifically referring to the detainees who had been cleared for release yet were still being held at the prison. Stevens compared his suggested compensation plan to the Civil Liberties Act of 1988.

DECISIONS BY OTHER NATIONS

Other governments and international tribunals have not raised the same self-protective responses as those raised by the US. Several countries have admitted errors and have made payments to Guantánamo detainees they had mistreated after 9/11. The UK has distributed sixteen million British pounds to the seventeen resident and citizen detainees in a settlement agreement.[20] Canada agreed to pay more than ten million Canadian dollars to Canadian citizen Omar Khadr. He was a fifteen-year-old juvenile when captured and taken to Guantánamo, where he was kept with the adult population. Canadian authorities did nothing for him while he was in the prison. Khadr was held for a decade in Guantánamo. Canada also paid ten million dollars to Canadian citizen Maher Arar, who had been seized at Kennedy Airport in New York while in transit back home to Canada. Arar was transported to Syria, where he was tortured under the CIA's extraordinary rendition program.[21]

In other examples, Sweden issued an apology to two men it had handed over to US officials, who were then imprisoned and tortured in Egypt. The European Court of Human Rights required that countries pay reparations to two men who are still in Guantánamo who were subjected to America's CIA extraordinary rendition program, Abu Zubaydah and Abd al-Rahim al-Nashiri.

The European Court also ordered Macedonia to compensate a Lebanese German man, Khalid el-Masri, who had been seized in Macedonia on erroneous suspicion of terrorist ties. He was rendered to Egypt, where he was tortured.[22] Julia Hall, Amnesty International's counterterrorism expert, told an audience at the Human Rights Council in Geneva that all el-Masri wanted was an apology.

During our first summer interviewing detainees, in 2009, I asked Ayub Mohammed, a Uighur who was transferred to Albania in 2006, what he would like America to do. Mohammed answered that the question should not be addressed to him, but rather to the American people.

"Now, if you want America to be safer or Britain to be safer, there's a simple solution, and the solution is to behave decently. It really is true that effective enforcement of human rights is the greatest antiterrorism weapon in our arsenal, because if you behave well, fewer people want to kill you, more people want to help you, and the few nutters who are always going to be out there are going to find themselves very isolated. If you behave badly you're going to achieve exactly the opposite goal. And that's just true. That's just the way the world is." Clive Stafford Smith said these words to us when we sat down to interview him in summer 2010. Founder of the UK-based human rights organization Reprieve, he was one of the handful of lawyers who challenged the government's Guantánamo policy in the early days after 9/11. A friend and human rights activist describes Stafford Smith as a "rock star."

In our interviews, several people told us that America's policies after 9/11 did not make Americans safer. They made things worse. "In reality, for every Guantánamo detainee, probably hundreds [of] newly recruited terrorists went to the so-called battlefield. . . . I think Guantánamo created many more terrorists than they actually brought to justice," Manfred Nowak, UN special rapporteur for torture, said.

FBI special agent Ali Soufan, who first determined that Osama bin Laden was behind the 9/11 attacks, told us that the idea of Guantánamo made sense at the start. It was, to him and many public officials, a safe place outside the Afghanistan war zone, where the US could process the people captured and release those who were nobodies. However, Guantánamo became part of a bureaucratic process that had no end in sight. Soufan believed that we held people "who were not involved in radical activities" for too long. Although Guantánamo may have "started with good intentions," he said, "the road to hell is paved with good intentions."

CHAPTER 27

KUWAITI ESCORTS

I n January 2011, our Witness to Guantánamo crew flew to Kuwait to interview four released detainees and Khalid al-Odah, the father of a detainee who was still in Guantánamo. Al-Odah kindly let us use his home for the interviews. Because he spoke English, he also generously offered to interpret for us.

Each evening, al-Odah sent one of the former detainees to pick us up from our hotel and bring us to his home. Like many people in Kuwait, the detainee drove an American-make SUV. We had lots of room for ourselves and our film equipment.

On the third night, the car had another passenger sitting up front. Neither the detainee nor the passenger spoke English. But they managed to explain that the passenger was a friend of the detainee's, a police officer. The officer showed us his identity card. The two talked between themselves while my wife, Mary Louise Zernicke; our filmmaker Johnny Symons; and I sat quietly in the back seat.

About fifteen minutes into the ride, the detainee stopped the car, turned around, and said something in Arabic to us. He then hopped out of the vehicle, leaving us with the police officer.

It was evening, and pitch-black outside. We could see nothing from our windows. Where were we? Although we were told that the police officer did not speak English and would not understand us, the three of us did not converse. We sat there in silence.

Americans are advised to check in with the local United States embassy when traveling to foreign countries. We never informed the US embassy in Kuwait of our presence. It would take days, perhaps a week, before someone figured out that we were missing. Our children knew we were traveling, but they were not following our schedules.

Why did he leave us with the officer? Were we being arrested? Kidnapped? Worse? Each of us thought of leaping out of the car and running. But where would we run? Besides, we would look odd, if not crazy, running helter-skelter in some unknown neighborhood of Kuwait in the black of night. We continued to sit in the back seat. I was feeling like sheep to the slaughter. Time passed.

Although it seemed like an eternity, the former detainee returned about fifteen minutes after he left. When he opened the door, we noticed he was carrying three shopping bags. He smiled and handed each of us a bag. The bags were filled with dates, nuts, and other local delicacies. Khalid al-Odah had asked him to purchase a gift bag for each of us to take home to America.

AFTERWORD

A few weeks before I completed *A Place Outside the Law*, I heard Audra McDonald sing the show tune "I'll Be Here."* A young couple accidentally meet in New York City on a cold wintry day. He asks to see her again. I'll be here, he says. She is intrigued. She goes to the meeting place. As the courtship unfolds over the following months, they go to dinner, kiss, see a show, drink hot chocolate. Their charmed romance blossoms into marriage.

On their first anniversary, they plan to spend the day together. It is September 11, 2001. He needs to stop at his office that morning. The planes hit the towers. He realizes he will not be returning. He leaves her a voice message encouraging her to move on and not let life pass her by. After a time, she remarries and starts anew. I'll be here, she says, and her memories of him will be here too.

What else is there to do? The towers fell. Memories linger. New towers are built.

"You realize—or at least for me, I realize—to be much more thankful and appreciative of anything that I have. It's life, you know," an anonymous interviewee said to us.

This afterword has been the most difficult part of the book to write. I started to write it many times. No matter the theme, nothing flowed onto the computer screen before me. If I forced myself to write something, the words would appear ridiculous and the sentences meaningless.

---

* The song is by composer Adam Gwon and was written for the off-Broadway show *Ordinary Days*.

But hearing Audra McDonald's heavenly voice sing of carrying on our lives impelled me back to this computer. I typed the words about the song you are reading today. When I finished the song, this afterword began to roll off the keyboard and onto the screen. The lessons and legacy of Guantánamo found a home on this page.

The rule of law was broken in Guantánamo. The Witness to Guantánamo testimonies remind us of the responsibility we all shared. Our fears after the attacks on 9/11 trumped the better part of ourselves. Our humanity, our American character, and our Constitution failed to disrupt the horrors of Guantánamo.

The rule of law continues to be broken today—in Guantánamo and in the culture of the current administration. Pursuing the Muslim ban; blocking families from lawfully applying for asylum; separating children from parents at the southern border and holding them in unsafe, overcrowded, and unsanitary conditions; banning transgender people from serving in the military; directing illegal campaign payments; lying habitually; suggesting political opponents be jailed; unilaterally withdrawing from treaties; ridiculing federal judges; and pursuing policies that enrich the president and his family's business reflect an abuse of power and indicate that the president is not committed to guaranteeing that the Constitution and the laws of the United States will be faithfully executed, as he solemnly swore under oath.

Our leaders, blinded by hubris and with little self-reflection, led us astray after 9/11 and into Guantánamo. Today, our leaders similarly appear to act without thoughtful examination of their conduct and the consequences of their actions. Yet their conduct affects us all. These elected officials will continue to lead us, if we let them. We have allowed meanness and unpleasantness to trump ethics and morality. Who speaks truth to power today?

To begin a renewed hope and a return to civility and the rule of law, we must recognize how our actions in Guantánamo caused great damage to America's principles and values. Let us send our message to the world that we are, once again, committed to the rule of law and human rights. We hold ourselves accountable. We pledge that the current administration and every administration that follows will faithfully execute the laws and Constitution of the United States.

In the Muslim religion, it is important to plant a tree for the next generation. The 158 people who told their stories to Witness to Guantánamo planted trees as an act of hope. The seasons will wax and wane, as the stories are passed down from one generation to the next. And because the stories are to be shared, each story implies a future reader.

You may forget some of the voices and stories in this book. Other voices and stories will sit on your shoulder and linger in your memory. They will whisper of our humanity. They will be mirrors into ourselves.

Memorial Day, 2019

TIMELINE

US NAVAL BASE, GUANTÁNAMO BAY, CUBA

THE LATE NINETEENTH CENTURY

1898: The United States enters Guantánamo Bay, Cuba, during the Spanish-American War.

THE TWENTIETH CENTURY

1900–2000: Guantánamo is used as a coaling station, a repository for fuel to service naval vessels.

1903: The United States and Cuba sign a lease guaranteeing that the US shall exercise jurisdiction and control over forty-five square miles of land and water along the southeast coast of Cuba, housing the Guantánamo Bay Naval Base.

1934: A revised treaty requires that both the US and Cuba agree to termination of the lease. The annual rent is set at $2,000 in gold coin.

1990S: Guantánamo Bay is used to house both Cuban and Haitian refugees.

THE GEORGE W. BUSH PRESIDENCY

JANUARY 2001: George W. Bush takes office as the forty-third president of the United States.

SEPTEMBER 11, 2001: Nineteen al Qaeda terrorists hijack four American planes and attack the World Trade Center in New York City and the

Pentagon in Washington, DC. More than three thousand people die that day as a result.

SEPTEMBER 16, 2001: Vice President Dick Cheney tells the audience on *Meet the Press* that America would "have to work sort of the dark side."

SEPTEMBER 17, 2001: President Bush issues a secret directive authorizing the CIA to detain alleged terrorists in foreign countries and CIA "black sites." The kidnapped captives are disappeared and tortured under a practice known as "extraordinary rendition."

SEPTEMBER 18, 2001: President Bush signs the Authorization for Use of Military Force (AUMF), giving the military the authority to attack the Taliban and al Qaeda in Afghanistan.

OCTOBER 2001: The US military begins bombing Afghanistan. The US also drops leaflets over Afghanistan and Pakistan offering thousands of dollars in bounties for alleged al Qaeda and Taliban fighters.

NOVEMBER 2001: Guantánamo is chosen as the site to hold captured detainees. Officials believe that because Guantánamo is offshore, the detainees would be barred from filing habeas petitions challenging their detentions in federal court.

NOVEMBER 13, 2001: President Bush issues an executive order creating military tribunals to charge and try captured fighters.

DECEMBER 2001: The American military purchases men from Afghan and Pakistani soldiers for bounty, and holds the men in Kandahar and Bagram bases in Afghanistan. The men are brutally interrogated and tortured. Defense Secretary Donald Rumsfeld advises interrogators to "take the gloves off."

DECEMBER 2001: The US captures "American Taliban" John Walker Lindh in Afghanistan. After fifty-four days of isolation and torture, he is transferred to the US and ultimately agrees to a twenty-year sentence.

DECEMBER 2001: Mohammed al-Qahtani, the twentieth hijacker, is captured in Afghanistan and later transferred to Guantánamo, where he is physically and psychologically tortured.

DECEMBER 2001: The Center for Constitutional Rights (CCR) in New York, along with a handful of courageous lawyers from around the country and the world, agrees to represent captured detainees in order to uphold the rule of law and the Constitution.

JANUARY 11, 2002: The first planeload of twenty detainees arrives in Guantánamo Bay, Cuba, from Afghanistan. The men wear blackened goggles, earmuffs, mittens, woolen caps, and orange jumpsuits, and their legs and arms are shackled. When they arrive, they are housed in Camp X-Ray, a patchwork of outdoor eight-by-eight wire-mesh cells.

JANUARY 20, 2002: Nine days after Guantánamo opens, dean and law professor Erwin Chemerinsky and attorney Steve Yagman file the first case on behalf of the detainees in Guantánamo, *Coalition of Clergy v. Bush*, in federal district court in California.

FEBRUARY 7, 2002: President Bush issues a memorandum declaring that the Geneva Conventions, which the US and all nations have signed, do not apply to the detainees in Guantánamo.

FEBRUARY 19, 2002: CCR in New York, along with a handful of attorneys from the US, Australia, and the United Kingdom, file *Rasul v. Bush* in federal district court in Washington, DC, to challenge the detention of the detainees.

MARCH 21, 2002: The first day that members of the Bush administration officially refer to the captured detainees as "enemy combatants," a generic descriptor that has no legal meaning under American or international law.

SPRING 2002: The US completes construction of Camp Delta, consisting of four camps of indoor housing for Guantánamo detainees. Camps 1, 2, and 3 house prisoners in individual cells. Camp 4 provides a communal living space for compliant prisoners. Camps 5 and 6, which become more permanent facilities, are constructed later.

MAY 8, 2002: American citizen Jose Padilla is arrested at Chicago's O'Hare Airport. He is accused of planning to detonate a dirty (radioactive) bomb. One month later, he is labeled an enemy combatant and held for nearly four years in a naval brig in South Carolina. While in the brig, he is denied a due process hearing. For nearly all his time in the brig, Padilla is held in stark isolation and is subjected to severe sensory deprivation.

JULY 8, 2002: Washington, DC, attorney Tom Wilner files *Odah v. United States* on behalf of twelve Kuwaiti detainees housed in Guantánamo. The case is consolidated with *Rasul v. Bush* later in the month. The joined cases, filed under the name *Rasul v. Bush*, make their way to the US Supreme Court.

JANUARY 2002–JUNE 2004: The detainees are isolated from the outside world, with no access to lawyers or family. They suffer intense interrogations, severe isolation, sleep deprivation, and other cruel physical and psychological torture during these years. Very few men are charged with crimes.

AUGUST 1, 2002: The first of many "torture memos" justifying the torture of detainees is issued by Deputy Assistant US Attorney General John Yoo and signed by his supervisor, Jay Bybee. Both men work in the Department of Justice, Office of Legal Counsel.

MARCH 1, 2003: The suspected mastermind of 9/11, Khalid Sheikh Mohammed, is captured in Rawalpindi, Pakistan.

MARCH 19, 2003: The United States invades Iraq. The Iraqi government was not involved in the 9/11 al Qaeda attack on the United States.

APRIL 2004: CBS News publishes graphic photos of American soldiers committing violence, torture, and sexual abuse against detainees in Abu Ghraib prison in Iraq.

JUNE 28, 2004: The Supreme Court rules in *Rasul v. Bush* that the detainees have the statutory right to bring habeas corpus petitions challenging their detentions, and the right to retain attorneys. Guantánamo is not beyond the reach of US federal courts.

JUNE–JULY 2004: Approximately four hundred to five hundred attorneys from around the US volunteer to represent Guantánamo detainees in habeas hearings. The Center for Constitutional Rights acts as clearinghouse for the lawyers and trains them in handling habeas hearings.

FALL 2004: The Bush administration creates Combatant Status Review Tribunals—administrative proceedings that the government intends as substitutes for habeas hearings in federal courts.

SEPTEMBER 2004: Center for Constitutional Rights attorney Gitanjali Gutierrez is the first habeas attorney to fly to Guantánamo to represent detainees.

NOVEMBER 2004: President Bush is elected to a second term in office.

DECEMBER 30, 2005: Congress passes the Detainee Treatment Act, designed to strip federal courts of jurisdiction to hear habeas petitions from the detainees.

FEBRUARY 2006: A study released by professor Mark Denbeaux of Seton Hall University Law School concludes that no more than 5 percent of the detainees had been captured by US forces. In addition, only 8 percent of men captured were considered al Qaeda fighters. Fifty-five percent of the captives never committed any hostile act against the US. They were not "on the battlefield."

MAY 2006: The United States officially releases the names of the prisoners in Guantánamo, more than four years after the first planeload of detainees arrived at the base.

JUNE 29, 2006: The Supreme Court rules in *Hamdan v. Rumsfeld* that (1) the president did not have the authority to establish military commissions in November 2001, (2) pending habeas petitions filed by detainees may go forward in federal court, and (3) the Geneva Conventions apply to al Qaeda members in Guantánamo.

SEPTEMBER 2006: President Bush reveals that fourteen "high-level" detainees were transferred to Guantánamo from CIA black sites, part of the CIA's extraordinary rendition program. Among the prisoners is alleged mastermind of the 9/11 attacks Khalid Sheikh Mohammed. The men are held in Camp 7, a camp not publicly known before.

OCTOBER 2006: Congress passes the Military Commissions Act, creating new military commissions and stripping federal district courts of jurisdiction to hear habeas petitions from detainees. The act also rewrites the War Crimes Act in order to protect US government officials from liability for cruel, inhuman, or degrading acts that they committed after 9/11. The new War Crimes Act is made retroactive to 1996, the date of the original act.

MARCH 2008: The last man is brought to Guantánamo, increasing the number of total detainees to 780.

JUNE 12, 2008: The Supreme Court issues its third and most sweeping Guantánamo decision, *Boumediene v. Bush*. It upholds the constitutional right to habeas for all detainees, and establishes that Guantánamo is not beyond the reach of the Constitution.

DECEMBER 2008: As President Bush leaves office, 539 men have been transferred out of the prison. The number includes five deaths.

THE BARACK OBAMA PRESIDENCY

JANUARY 2009: Barack Obama takes office as the forty-fourth president of the United States. On his second day in office, he pledges to close Guantánamo in one year.

JANUARY 2009: The Pentagon decides not to move Mohammed al-Qahtani's case forward to a military tribunal because senior Pentagon official Susan J. Crawford, who supervised the military tribunals, admitted that "we tortured Qahtani." The military had previously dismissed charges against al-Qahtani, the twentieth hijacker, in May 2008.

DECEMBER 25, 2009: A man on a flight from Yemen attempts to down a plane over Detroit. Obama issues an executive order barring the eighty-six Yemeni detainees in Guantánamo from being repatriated to Yemen.

JANUARY 2010: One year after Obama's pledge to close the prison, Guantánamo remains open. Although Obama pledges three more times throughout his presidency to shut the prison, Guantánamo remains open throughout his tenure.

FEBRUARY 2011: The first of consecutive National Defense Authorization acts is passed by Congress. The acts are intended to block President Obama's ability to close the prison.

MARCH 2011: President Obama establishes the Periodic Review Board to consider the status of remaining detainees and determine whether they should be cleared for release.

MAY 2011: US SEAL Team 6 enters Osama bin Laden's home in Abbottabad, Pakistan, kills him, and buries him at sea.

OCTOBER 2012: The Obama administration authorizes the federal government to purchase the Thomson Correctional Center in Illinois to possibly house Guantánamo detainees. After congressional opposition is voiced, the plan is abandoned.

NOVEMBER 2012: President Obama is elected to a second term in office.

FEBRUARY 2013: More than a hundred detainees go on a massive hunger strike, catching the administration by surprise and causing it again to focus on closing the prison. Obama lifts the ban on transferring men back to Yemen and reopens the State Department office in charge of transfers out of Guantánamo. More prisoners are transferred out of the prison over the next year.

DECEMBER 2016: At the end of President Obama's tenure, two hundred detainees have been transferred out of the prison, a figure that includes four people who died. Forty-one detainees remain. Seven men are in military commission proceedings. An eighth man has been convicted and will be sentenced in 2019.

THE DONALD TRUMP PRESIDENCY

JANUARY 2017: Donald Trump becomes the forty-fifth president of the United States.

SPRING 2017: President Trump dismantles the State Department office of Guantánamo closure. The office had been involved in finding homes for detainees after release and was responsible for monitoring released detainees.

MAY 2018: One detainee is transferred to Saudi Arabia under a plea agreement made by the Obama administration. Forty men remain in the prison.

FEBRUARY 2019: The US State Department offers a $1 million reward for information on Hamza bin Laden, Osama bin Laden's son.[1] The State Department says that Hamza had threatened attacks against the US to avenge the killing of his father. Reportedly, Hamza married the daughter of Mohamed Atta in fall 2018.[2] Atta was the lead hijacker and terrorist pilot for American 11, the flight that crashed into the North Tower.

APRIL 2019: The US Court of Appeals throws out more than three of years of pre-trial orders and rulings in the Guantánamo military commission case of Abd al-Rahim al-Nashiri. Al-Nishiri is accused of masterminding the bombing of the USS *Cole* in 2000 off the coast of Yemen, where seventeen sailors died.

The commander of the Guantánamo detention center admits that hospice or end-of-life care will eventually become necessary, as the detainees continue to age. There is no current plan to close the prison.

JUNE 2019: Congress is considering whether to allow the military to move prisoners who need acute emergency or complicated medical care to the US. The Pentagon has asked Congress for more than $88 million to build a wheelchair-accessible detention facility with hospice care.[4]

Supreme Court justice Stephen Breyer wrote a dissenting opinion to a Guantánamo case that the majority of the court refused to hear. In his opinion, Breyer argued that it is time to confront the question of whether it is lawful to hold a person in perpetual detention without charges until he dies, decades after his capture, in a war that has no end.[5]

JULY 2019: Supreme Court Justice John Paul Stevens, who authored the *Rasul v Bush* and *Hamdan v Rumsfeld* decisions and was instrumental in deciding the *Boumediene v Bush* decision, died at the age of ninety-nine.

It was reported that Hamza bin Laden, the son of Osama bin Laden, had been killed sometime during the two years of the Trump administration. Details as to where and when were not revealed.

AUGUST 2019: Forty men remain in Guantánamo. Twenty-six of the forty men are considered "forever prisoners."[3] They cannot be tried because the evidence against them is either insufficient or unreliable—having been obtained through torture. However, these men are also considered too dangerous to be released. They are likely to die in Guantánamo, never charged, never tried, and never convicted.

Of the fourteen men who are not designated forever prisoners, seven are being tried in military commissions. Preliminary proceedings have been ongoing for these men for more than a dozen years. There is no assurance these seven suspects will ever have a trial. Five other men were cleared for release during Obama's tenure but were not released before he left office. President Trump shows no interest in releasing them. Two men have been convicted. One is serving his sentence; the other is waiting to be sentenced.

During the past seventeen years of Guantánamo, only eight people have been convicted in military commissions. Six of those people were convicted through plea bargains. In three of the plea-bargain cases, the convictions were overturned on appeal. A fourth plea-bargain conviction survived an appeal, although two of the three charges against the detainee were thrown out.

It is still not clear whether President Trump intends to deliver any new people—such as captured Islamic State, or ISIS, fighters—to the Guantánamo detention center.

REFLECTIONS AND EVOLUTION OF WITNESS TO GUANTÁNAMO

In November 2008, when Barack Obama was elected president, I completed *Our Nation Unhinged*, a book on the war on terror. I examined human rights and rule-of-law violations post-9/11, at home and abroad, in five parts. One part was on Guantánamo. The book was a natural complement to my articles, blog pieces, and classes on terrorism, national security, international law, and human rights. It also chronicled my visit to Guantánamo in May 2007.

Once *Our Nation Unhinged* was published, my friends thought I would move on to other issues. The attacks on 9/11 and America's response were fading in the sunlight of the new, inspiring president. But I was still restless.

In those early days of Obama's presidency, many of us believed that his administration, elected on a theme of hope and change, would return our nation to its former position as the defender of human rights and the rule of law. During his campaign, President Obama had advocated for closing the Guantánamo prison camp. And on his second day in office he said he would close the prison within a year.

We believed that America's policies of torture, cruel interrogation, and indefinite detention would come to an end. We would return to our core values and principles. Under President Obama, the world would again recognize America's exceptionalism and its position as the shining light to the world.

However, the post-9/11 issues I had been studying and writing about were still unresolved. And I was afraid that our newly elected president would not fully address and resolve them.

During Obama's transition to the office, when we were all optimistic, I was reminded of how my parents had escaped from the Nazis at the last moment possible. My Jewish parents were born and raised in a small town in Austria. When they married, they moved to Vienna. In 1939, my father received two notices from the Austrian authorities to appear at the train station to be taken to a concentration camp. He ignored them. The authorities sent a third notice instructing him to appear at the train station the next morning. If he did not show up, the Nazi officers wrote, they would seize him and take him directly to the station. That same day, he and my mother received visas to America.

The University of Southern California Shoah Foundation interviewed my father about his experiences in Austria. The Shoah Foundation was established to document the Holocaust, as well as to reply to Holocaust deniers. My father was one of more than forty-eight thousand survivors whose stories were told on camera to the foundation.

The work of the Shoah Foundation was my inspiration. Witness to Guantánamo was born. Even if President Obama closed Guantánamo, the stories of the people who lived and worked at the Guantánamo Bay, Cuba, detention center needed to be filmed and documented for history.

It was not the Holocaust, of course. But Guantánamo was a shameful moment in the history of America. The stories we would film would be there for future generations. Unlike renowned film director and producer Steven Spielberg, who was behind the creation of the Shoah Foundation, I had neither filmmaking nor interviewing experience. But no one else was documenting the first-person narratives of Guantánamo detainees on film. And the work had to be done before the memories faded and the voices disappeared.

A student in one of my classes had connections to a local family foundation. Through the student's contact, the director of the foundation generously financed the germination of the project. With the seed money, we were able to travel to five countries and interview sixteen former detainees during the first summer of our work, in 2009. Those interviews gave us credibility. We then could apply to larger foundations for continued funding.

Like Spielberg's videos of Holocaust survivors, the interviews recorded for Witness to Guantánamo will be here long after we are gone.

After Obama was elected in November 2008, a member of the Obama transition team informed me that Obama would create a truth commission and that I did not need to undertake my proposed Witness to Guantánamo project. I replied that I hoped the president would establish the commission, because he had the resources and the connections. I added that I was not convinced he would do it. But if he did, I would discontinue my work immediately. I was still interviewing people for Witness to Guantánamo after President Obama left office.

Throughout the years, people have asked about our work: how we found and encouraged people to interview and why we use film as the medium. They also ask about the interview process and our funding, and about several other issues. This appendix addresses some of the questions people have asked.

GROWTH AND EXPANSION OF WITNESS TO GUANTÁNAMO

Witness to Guantánamo has always consisted of a small number of very committed individuals. We have never had full-time staff. Our core consisted of Johnny Symons, filmmaker; Eva Moss, creative director, editor, and website designer; Adriana Puente, director of development and audience engagement; Wendy Betts and Alaina Piland, senior researchers; Mary Louise Zernicke, producer; Joe Hoffman, website designer; and board members Virginia Anderson, Laura Truffaut, and Gary Alexander. (Laura Poitras filmed summer 2009; Theo Rigby filmed summer 2010; Alexa Koenig served as development director during our first year.) I am its founder, director, and interviewer.

Initially, our objective was to interview only detainees. As often happens, necessity became the mother of invention. In winter 2010, we were in the tiny Pacific island nation of Palau, near Guam. Six Uighur detainees had been transferred from Guantánamo to Palau in October 2009. We traveled to Palau with Rushan Abbas, our interpreter and a Uighur, to meet the men.

When we arrived in Palau, we learned that only three of the men agreed to interview. Four had originally consented. Because of the high costs in undertaking the trip, we decided to turn the camera on Abbas. In the early days of Guantánamo, she lived and worked as an interpreter at the military base for nearly a year. After interviewing Abbas, we decided to expand our interview pool to include others who had lived or worked in Guantánamo.

As the years went by and we told people what we were doing, we would sometimes get the response, "But isn't Guantánamo closed?" In fact, several habeas attorneys told us that they had similar reactions when they told people that they were working on Guantánamo issues.

I am not sure why people believed it was closed. I am guessing that when President Obama announced on his second day in office that he would close Guantánamo, many people assumed that he had accomplished his mission.

FINDING AND ENCOURAGING PEOPLE TO INTERVIEW

It was not always easy to find and encourage people to interview with the project. However, we did find people who wanted to tell their stories. There were former detainees who wanted the world to know about violations and abuses in Guantánamo. Many went public, some writing books. They were glad to also tell us their stories on camera. A number of the men wanted to interview in the hope that the publicity would help their brothers to be released from the prison.

Moroccan former detainee Souleimane Laalami Mohamed had never spoken publicly before. When he sat down with us to interview, he said that he did not like Americans. But he agreed to speak to us in the hope that it would make a difference for the men still in Guantánamo.

"I asked the brothers and consulted them about the objective behind this interview, and they said that, first, this interview might influence the situation of the brothers who remain over there . . . and they said that because you are a university professor, those things will be documented so that those violations will not happen to human beings who might come after and this will, God willing, be a good thing," he said.

Sami al Hajj, from Sudan, works for the news service Al Jazeera in Qatar. He explained that he was interviewing because of his "search for justice [and for the] sake of history—so this inhuman situation never gets repeated in the future." To al Hajj, "Guantánamo was not a crime committed against one thousand detainees. Rather, it was a crime against all of humanity."

We explained to the detainees that we were not journalists looking for sound bites. Rather, we were filming their stories for history and for the purpose of creating a public record. We emphasized that we had no agenda. The men were free to tell their stories in their own words for as long or short as they wanted. One detainee spoke for six hours over two days. Another spoke for twenty minutes. The average was two hours.

We were at first worried that by telling their stories the men could be retraumatized. Fortunately, the opposite occurred. Many of the former detainees expressed relief at the end of the interviews. They found the interview experience therapeutic. They thanked us for the opportunity.

When we reached out to Americans who had lived and worked in Guantánamo, many also welcomed the opportunity to tell their stories and document the historical record. They were patriotic Americans who had become disillusioned and wanted to speak out against the injustices they had observed. They wanted the world to know that although some people in America strayed from honor, there were many more people who did the right thing. And they did it with humility. Because most of the people we interviewed had worked for the Bush administration, we interviewed many more Republicans than Democrats.

Colonel Lawrence Wilkerson was chief of staff to Secretary of State Colin Powell in the Bush administration. He told us that his plan was to "go to the grave with what I know. My plan was not to speak out." His plans changed for two reasons. The first was Iraq, where he "didn't see any prospect of there being a change in it."

The other issue was the accumulation of executive power. "No president will surrender power willingly. So I am looking at this being perpetuated. . . . That's dangerous for the republic. We look as much like a tyranny as we have ever looked in our history, and that worries me. And that was enough to persuade me to begin to speak out." He spoke to us in 2011.[1]

Some of the interviewees had more personal motivations in speaking to us. Several may have had misgivings about what they had done and wanted to counsel others for the future. Others spoke to explain their actions, memorialize their decisions, augment their legacies for history, or refute what others had said of them. Tom Berg, staff judge advocate for detainee operations, said he wanted his son to know that he did the right thing. And then there were people who told us that they were inspired by Witness to Guantánamo and honored to be part of the work.

I was very fortunate in knowing people who assisted in connecting us to potential interviewees. While researching my book *Our Nation Unhinged*, I had made contacts with lawyers who represented detainees. I also made contacts with key personnel in organizations that represented and worked on behalf of the detainees—organizations such as the Center for Constitutional Rights in New York, Reprieve in London, the American Civil Liberties Union, and Amnesty International, especially in Belgium.

Clive Stafford Smith, habeas attorney and founder of Reprieve, and I had met through my research. He was one of the earliest supporters of Witness to Guantánamo. He opened doors for us when we were raising funds. I am forever grateful to him and inspired by him.

Shayana Kadidal at CCR linked us with Rushan Abbas, the interpreter for the Uighurs, and with several of the lawyers who represented former detainees. Kadidal's assistance and connections were invaluable that first summer of 2009.

Abbas's close contacts with the Uighurs helped us secure interviews with thirteen of the twenty-two Uighurs who were held in the prison.

In addition, we reached out to private lawyers who worked pro bono in representing detainees. Stephen Oleskey in Boston represented the men in Bosnia, William Bourdon represented French detainees, and Bernhard Docke represented Murat Kurnaz in Germany. All three were very helpful in providing us with contacts for their clients during that first summer.

In subsequent years, many other attorneys generously assisted us. David Remes was one. He had been a partner at a prestigious firm in Washington, DC. In 2008, four years after he began representing detainees pro bono, he left the firm and founded Appeal for Justice, an organization for representing detainees. A decade later, in 2018, Remes closed down his Guantánamo work and returned to private practice.

In the early years of our work, a woman named Maryam Hassan assisted us in interviewing former detainees in the UK. She had been referred to us by Andy Worthington, a Guantánamo blogger in the UK for more than a decade. He is also the author of *The Guantánamo Files*, which tells the individual stories of the men in Guantánamo. He told us that Hassan was involved in creating Cageprisoners (now CAGE), an advocacy group formed to assist former UK detainees. Worthington had met Hassan at several events, but she always wore a veil covering her face.

We communicated with Hassan through emails. Sometimes she provided us with contact information for the detainees. More often, she contacted detainees in the UK on our behalf. One UK detainee described her as the "mysterious Maryam." He had never met her. He said that people believed she was Pakistani and may not have been a lawful UK resident. Another theory was that she worked undercover because she could have been deported if discovered. Later, a lawyer in the UK said she was Saudi. We knew nothing more about her.

Hassan continued to email us until March 2012. After that, we never heard from her again.

One person led us to another. Many of the interviewees provided us with names of other people who would be interested in interviewing. As our reputation grew, knowledge of Witness to Guantánamo circulated both through word of mouth and social media. Doors opened. Several detainees spoke to us because they had heard from their brothers that we were the only organization in the world that would provide a forum for detainees to tell their stories in their own words. "What the former GTMO detainees on the project said about it being the first time anybody has listened is true," Feroz Ali Abbasi wrote.[2]

They could trust us, they said. (Writing this reminds me of a former student who once told me that I had "street cred" with the detainees. That made me laugh.) Sometimes, family members of the detainees agreed to speak with us.

Several detainees were advised by their attorneys not to interview. The men were either suing the US for the mistreatment they had received or to clear their records after release. Their attorneys did not want the men to say anything that could possibly backfire with their lawsuits. I offered to keep the interviews confidential, not revealing that we had spoken until some later date. But that did not persuade the lawyers.

We also had the assistance of University of San Francisco's brilliant law librarian, Lee Ryan. Ryan found contact information for many of our interviewees when no one else could find the information. And the dozens of law students who graciously volunteered to work for the project were tenacious in reaching out to the interviewees and explaining why they should interview with Witness to Guantánamo. Often, I think the interviewees did not want to say no to a hardworking, passionate law student.

Finding and interviewing Americans who lived or worked in Guantánamo raised another issue. We knew the names of many of the high-ranking military and government officials. However, personnel such as prison guards, medical technicians, and interrogators were more difficult to identify, unless they had already gone public on their own. Again, personal contacts made the difference.

In locating interviewees, we kept our eyes on windows of opportunity. We learned that often people were more likely to speak immediately after they left Guantánamo or government service. Other people surfaced later on.

Guantánamo interrogator Jennifer Bryson agreed to speak when Osama bin Laden was killed in 2011. She wanted to set the record straight because former vice president Dick Cheney had asserted that in torturing an al Qaeda courier, the US had obtained the information that led to the killing of bin Laden. She believed that torture did not lead to the information.

Former detainee Feroz Ali Abbasi was beginning to work on a book after five years of hibernating. Fortunately for us, he made himself available for a brief period of time.

We asked all the people we interviewed to sign consent forms. Most signed without any objections or modifications. Some of the interviewees asked for modifications, restrictions, or limitations on the use of their interviews.

For example, one detainee asked us not to post his name on our website. He explained that he would lose his job and possibly be asked to leave his mosque if it were was known that he had been in Guantánamo. Others had requested that we not make their interview available until a certain period of time passed. Still others had placed restrictions on the use of their interviews, such as limiting access to scholars and educators only, and not allowing them to be used for commercial purposes. A few of the interviewees asked to be interviewed in silhouette. Sometimes they asked that their faces be shadowed after the interview. We always honored the requests.

A few of the detainees would not sign the consent form. Several explained that they had been compelled to sign documents at Guantánamo. Now that they were out of prison, they would no longer sign any documents. Most of these people agreed to give consent on camera. A couple of the men would not consent on camera, noting that by the mere fact that they were talking to us on camera meant that they had agreed to the interview.

Inevitably, a number of people refused to interview with us. Several former detainees wanted to move on with their lives and not relive the memories. Several high-ranking government and military officials were unreachable, ignored our emails, or declined. A few interrogators and prison guards were afraid of the consequences of going public.

THE INTERVIEW PROCESS

People, especially archivists, have asked me to explain my interview process. I am certain that I made an infinite number of mistakes not only at the start, but throughout. I would like to think that I learned on the job and became better over time. Fortunately, my first set of interviews was of the Uighurs in Tirana, Albania. We brought along Uighur interpreter Rushan Abbas. Abbas knew the Uighurs and their stories very well, having met them as a government interpreter in Guantánamo in 2002 and then working as an interpreter and advisor with their lawyers later. Although I had a suggested list of questions, Abbas guided me along. Under her lead, I began to see how the process worked and what to expect.

My questions were based both on my knowledge of Guantánamo and on research regarding the particular individual. Because Witness to Guantánamo was a rule-of-law project, we were concerned with how the detainees were treated when they were in custody and whether the Constitution was observed. Hence, we began our interviews by focusing on when the detainees were first captured. Of course, if the detainees wanted to provide personal background and discuss earlier points in their lives, we welcomed everything they told us.

I was fortunate to have very competent law students research for us throughout the decade of our work. When people we were interviewing had spoken elsewhere to journalists and the media, I tried to include questions that had not been covered in those interviews.

Over time, I learned that when interviewees stopped talking, they might still have more to say. Slow down and wait before asking the next question, I was advised. The interviewee might fill the silence. Still, because I was engaged in their stories, I sometimes stepped in too soon. Our filmmaker, Johnny Symons, would gently remind me to step back.

I have also been told by several filmmakers to let interviewees be emotional on the screen. Let them cry. It makes for a powerful visual. That did not always work for me. There were times when I could not watch an interviewee tear up. I would upend the moment to ask whether they would like to take a break.

My ideal interview is to encourage the interviewee to talk as much as possible, and for me to say as little as possible—unless the interviewee veers off course and loses focus. Although I keep a list of issues/subjects that I would like to cover, I try to ask open-ended questions and encourage spontaneity. Because of the nature of open-ended questions, people would sometimes surprise me with their answers, and I would often find myself moving in directions that I had not anticipated. That organic approach suited me, although I did try to address certain concerns regarding each interviewee.

Unfortunately, even when I asked open-ended questions, there were times when people answered in brief words or short sentences. That required me to ask too many questions, which would possibly disrupt the cadence of storytelling and narrative.

I also learned an important lesson when I shared a meal with an interviewee before the interview. It happened that first summer of 2009. At the dinner, the person told me things that I wanted on tape. When I interviewed him the next morning, he reminded me that he had already told me the story. He then summarized it without the emotion and sentiment he had expressed the first time I heard it. After that incident, I never again had a meal with an interviewee before the interview. However, to be certain that the interviewee would be relaxed and hopefully trust me, I would meet the interviewee briefly and make small talk before we went on camera.

Every person has an interesting and unique story. Our job was to encourage the person to share that story with us. Scratch the surface of any person and you will often be amazed at the stories that lie below. Most people are waiting for the opportunity and encouragement to tell their stories.

Naturally, sometimes people do not tell the "truth." People's memories differ and suffer. Sometimes people may believe in what they are saying. Or they may simply embellish the story to make themselves appear in a better light. Other times, it is a deliberate misstatement.

In one instance, someone who observed one of our interviews of a former detainee said to me after the interview that the interviewee had lied. The observer "knew" this because the observer had been there when a particular event described by the former detainee had occurred. When I mentioned this incident to a friend, the friend said that even if the interviewee had lied, the interview still had validity. This is how the former detainee coped with his experiences. And maybe he really remembered it this way. Maybe the observer got it wrong. In fact, aren't most people telling their own personal versions when they tell stories, or write memoirs?

We were fortunate to hire Rushan Abbas as our Uighur and Uzbek interpreter, and Ashraf Michael—who had worked for more than a decade in Guantánamo—as an Arabic interpreter. When we went to France, I brought along a student who spoke French and who—as our researcher—was also familiar with the issues and understood where I was heading with certain questions. When these interpreters were not available, or when the cost was too high to bring them with us, we hired local interpreters. The local interpreters were not always well informed on the issues. And we did not have the time to educate them sufficiently.

Because the interpreters did not simultaneously translate—it would have been too distracting—I counted on each interpreter to catch the key phrases and issues. I explained this as best I could to the local interpreter before the interview began. When we returned home and the interview was translated by someone else, we sometimes found problems. The interpreter sometimes overlooked key words and statements that would have caused me to ask different, and likely more important, follow-up questions.

In one particular situation, the local interpreter seemed infatuated with the person we were interviewing. The former detainee was recently transferred and in the news. The interpreter, gratuitously and off-topic, asked questions and pursued personal conversations with him during the interview.

Although there may have been one or two instances where a Witness to Guantánamo interpreter favored a certain detainee during an interview, we always used someone other than the interpreter to translate the interview. Thus, no matter what an interpreter told us, the translator would accurately transcribe the words of the interviewee.

Many detainees either knew some English or learned it while in Guantánamo. There were detainees who knew English well enough to understand my questions but were more comfortable answering in their own languages. Sometimes detainees corrected the interpreter after he or she interpreted the detainee's response. In one instance, Souleimane Laalami Mohamed, a Moroccan detainee who spoke in Arabic, told me after the interview that he knew English perfectly, but refused to speak the language of his captors.

Former detainee Mosa Zemmouri of Belgium said he wanted to interview in English, the language he had learned in Guantánamo. He dreams in English, he explained.

During our first summer, one of the detainees was hesitant to talk to us. He was not working and needed money, he said. A professor at Berkeley Law School informed me that it was acceptable to give each man a stipend for his time and expenses. We contacted an ethnologist, who also approved of the stipend. Finally, we confirmed with the Institutional Review Board (IRB) at the University of San Francisco. The IRB is an ethics committee that monitors behavioral research conducted by university professors. The IRB approved the stipends.

Beginning that first summer, we gave each of the detainees a hundred dollars after the interview for time and expenses. In a few instances, we gave more if the men had additional expenses. For example, one man needed to cover his childcare. On the other hand, an interviewee asked for more money because he had never told his story to anyone else. We turned down his request. A few men, instead of accepting the money, asked that we use the hundred dollars for our work. Some of the men donated the funds to charitable organizations.

There is a power in sharing one's story and experiences. At the end of the interviews, former detainees and others would often express a sense of relief. They were grateful for the opportunity. Telling their story assisted in their healing. Many revealed that they had never told their full story before, even to their family members. Perhaps the family members did not want to hear the details or did not want the teller to relive those moments again. On one occasion, a former detainee brought his wife along to hear his story.

TRAUMATIC EFFECTS

When I returned home after our first summer of interviews, my personal physician diagnosed me as having secondary trauma. I had not expected that diagnosis. I had gone to see her for a torn Achilles tendon.

During the first summer of our work, in 2009, when we interviewed sixteen detainees in five countries, I did not really know what to expect. Reading and learning about detainees' lives is one thing. Meeting them, and listening to their compelling and often heartbreaking stories is something very different. No one had prepared me for what I would hear in the interviews. Probably that was just as well. Had I known how difficult it was to listen to the detainees' stories, I might not have rushed into this project.

Our first city was Tirana, Albania. A larger than life statue of Mother Teresa—whose parents were of Albanian descent—greeted us as we walked out of the airport. For some reason, it reassured me about the work we were about to undertake.

The next morning, we met Rushan Abbas, our Uighur interpreter, at our hotel. She had arranged for us to interview four Uighurs and an Uzbek. She asked Uighur Abubakir Qasem to be our first interviewee. Qasem is very personable and wanted to tell his story. Because I had no experience in interviewing former detainees, I feared that I would say something awkward or offensive without even knowing it. In addition, I was anxious that the questions could trigger unwanted flashbacks.

Thankfully, Abbas guided my questions and translated any awkward phrases I might have said into gracious inquiries. She knew that Qasem would be a perfect first interviewee, and what particular questions to ask him. She understood how to make my first interview less stressful. Abbas carried me along.

Among the stories Qasem told us was one about how, when he and the other Uighurs were captured by Pakistani soldiers, the Uighurs changed their names to Afghan-sounding names. They did not want the Pakistanis to know they were Uighurs. The Uighurs feared that the Pakistanis would send them back to their homeland in China, where they would be tortured and executed. Pakistan and China had strong diplomatic ties.

Our second interviewee was Ayub Mohammed. He was sixteen when captured, and on his way to Turkey. His long-term plans were to make his way into the US from Turkey. When Mohammed was released, he immediately phoned his mother in China. She cried the entire time they were on the phone. She thought he was dead, he told us.

As we moved on to other cities, the stories became more intense and disturbing. We met one man who spoke in a tone and manner that made us think he was chronically depressed. Another man told how he had a red sticker on his cell in the mental clinic because he was a "danger detainee and a danger mental patient." No one else mentioned the red stickers in the decade that followed.

An interviewee described how he was interrogated while undergoing surgery for his back. During the procedure, he was only partially anesthetized. Another man said he had been hung by his wrists for five days, and had watched another man die hanging in front of him. He thought he would be the next person to die.

A man told us how a military psychiatrist asked him whether he had ever thought of committing suicide. The psychiatrist then described a method for the detainee to kill himself, using his pants as a noose. In another incident told to us, a guard forced a man to lie down on the gravel, and then the guard kneed his face. One side of the detainee's face became partially paralyzed for weeks.

It never got easier, even when one of the former detainees who had a great sense of humor made me laugh.

After each interview, we hurriedly packed up our gear and rushed to the airport to fly to our next destination. When we arrived at the baggage counters, we were frequently informed that our luggage was overweight and we would be charged an extra seven to ten euros per kilo.

Drained and exhausted, hurrying to the next city and still thinking of the stories I had heard the detainees tell, I was not particularly easygoing when the airlines insisted on the extra costs. We were on a very limited budget, and I was worried that we would run out of funds. I tried to convince the airline personnel to give us a break because we were a nonprofit organization dedicated to human rights. But, except in one instance, that argument made no difference. In my mood, I could not stay calm.

When we were in Germany, someone who was present when we interviewed former detainee Murat Kurnaz took me aside to say that not all Germans were former Nazis, or were all bad. He also wanted me to know that America should not think too highly of itself, given the blackened image of Guantánamo. I thanked him for his thoughts and interest in our project.

I did not tell him that my parents barely escaped from the Nazis in 1939. I was in no mood to engage in a conversation. He was a stranger, and because of my work I was beginning to feel vulnerable.

Near the end of this whirlwind and frenzied trip of interviewing, I tore my Achilles tendon. I am not certain how it happened, but I am guessing that carrying the overweight luggage, running to catch planes, listening to the detainees' raw stories, and possibly even the arguments at the airports all contributed. I dragged my inflamed foot for the remainder of the trip. I barely made it to the gate in time for my flight home.

When I arrived home, I made an appointment with my doctor to address the pain. Dr. Denise Davis asked what I had been doing that summer. I told her. Did I have nightmares? she asked. Yes. Any flashbacks? Yes. We do not need to worry about your Achilles tendon, she said. It will take care of itself. Instead, we need to work on your nightmares and flashbacks.

She wrote a prescription listing as her diagnosis "vicarious traumatization." She jotted down a list of remedies: cultivating emotional closeness with colleagues, debriefing, checking in, talking about moments stuck in memory, examining what feelings come up, and expressing appreciation. She required that I phone all my friends and ask each of them to have lunch with me, so that I could describe my experiences that summer. Dr. Davis restored more than my tendon.

This was not the only time I experienced secondary trauma. After returning home from interviewing detainees in Morocco and Tunisia, I had ongoing dreams of feeling trapped. I had the sense that not only was I not home, but that I would never be able to return home. Each time, I woke up disoriented and in sweats. Fortunately, I recalled my conversation with Dr. Davis and phoned my friends again.

During one of the conversations I had when I returned home that first summer, a friend asked what I was getting from my work. Without hesitation, I blurted out "humanity." I may have torn my Achilles tendon.

I may have suffered secondary trauma. But that "aha" moment inspired me. I realized that I had embarked on a journey that would open my heart to humanity and make me a better person. We were all in this together. Those thoughts accompanying the compelling stories carried me forward.

FILM AS THE MEDIUM

At the time we began, the filming of oral history interviews was not as commonplace as I had thought. Rather, oral history projects frequently relied on the old-fashioned tape recorder, a medium significantly less expensive than film. To us, filming was worth the cost. Filming reveals layers beneath the voice. We see the person's mannerisms, grimaces, smiles, and movements. In their expressions, the interviewees may sometimes be telling another story, different and even inconsistent with the words we hear.

The man is seemingly laughing in the interview, but his sadness filters through. Another man calls himself a joker but is near tears. The storyteller's affect may be flat and without emotion as he tells of being abused or tortured. Or his affect may reveal pain, anguish, and sadness as he relates his story in a monotone. The interviewee's eyes may turn away from the camera as he talks. The person's sorrow and grief may peek out from beneath that seemingly bright smile.

The interviewee may lunge toward the camera to make a point. Or he may recede to the corner of the chair when uncomfortable and upset. If he finds that telling his story is therapeutic, his eyes, and even his entire face, may light up and express the satisfaction and release. Or he may tear up in exhaustion and relief. Film captures the body and facial language. The viewer knows more than what is being said.

We used the same background of white-layered fabric for all the interviews. We wanted consistency and decided that backgrounds could be distracting. We were not making a movie, but filming people's stories for history. It was an oral history project, not a documentary.

ARCHIVING THE INTERVIEWS

The full interviews will be housed in perpetuity at the Duke University Human Rights Archive. Duke will post most of them on the internet. The university will also preserve and update the interviews as the technology evolves. Duke will monitor any restrictions requested by the interviewees. Because of restrictions, a few interviews will be available only on a dedicated computer at Duke. Unfortunately, a few people refused to allow their interviews to be shown to anyone. Those interviews will likely be destroyed and lost to history. Over the years, we have posted video clips of many of our interviews on our website: WitnesstoGuantánamo. com. Those video clips are still accessible.

In 2017, to accommodate the movement to hand-held devices, we redesigned our website. The earlier version showed thirty to forty faces on the homepage. The images transformed each time a person logged into the site. It was a powerful visual, with randomly selected photos of former detainees and others side-by-side. When people gravitated to their phones and handheld devices to access the internet, we updated the design.

We would like to create a permanent home and museum that tells the story of Guantánamo. Ideally, it would be in Washington, DC. We are actively working on creating an exhibit for Duke University in summer 2020. We hope to transform that show into a traveling exhibit. Our goal is for the US government to recognize the need to house the work in a permanent location in our nation's capital.

We are the only people in the world who documented the stories of 158 people of Guantánamo in more than three hundred hours of film. We traveled to twenty countries to find their stories. No one else has done this work. Without Witness to Guantánamo, many people would never have told their stories on film. Their stories would have been lost from history forever.

FUNDING

Witness to Guantánamo would not have been able to film its first round of interviews in summer 2009 if not for Angela Fitzsimons, a former student in my "Legal Issues of Terrorism" class. Although she had graduated by the time I began the project, we had stayed in touch. When I told her about my creation of Witness to Guantánamo, she mentioned her friend Scott Handleman. Handleman had gone to Berkeley Law School and worked as a public interest lawyer. His family foundation had supported social justice causes in the past. I asked her whether he would be interested in providing seed money. Handleman agreed immediately and gave us a very generous grant. We were remarkably fortunate.

Once we had completed the sixteen interviews that first summer, we had a measure of credibility. We were able to obtain additional generous grants from the Handleman Foundation, and then repeated grants from the Levinson Foundation, the Samuel Rubin Foundation, and the LEF Foundation. Two major foundations in the UK, the Sigrid Rausing Trust and the Anita Roddick Foundation, became interested in our tiny organization with its huge mission. A friend said that it was "divine intervention" that we received such generous funding so quickly. In making exceptions for us, the Handleman Foundation supported us for eight years, Sigrid Rausing for seven, and Anita Roddick for six.

Several people expressed surprise that we were awarded larger grants from foundations in the UK than from US foundations. (In later years, we had received funding from two other major UK foundations, the Oak Foundation and Revolution in Kindness.) Perhaps from a distance, it was easier for people in other countries to acknowledge the grave human rights and rule of law violations caused by Guantánamo.

After President Obama was elected in 2008, American funders reassessed priorities and moved away from Guantánamo issues. They believed that Obama would shut down the prison. Nevertheless, we received significant funding from George Soros's Open Society Foundation in later years.

Largely because of consistent funding and incredible multiyear support, we raised more than $1.7 million between 2009 and 2018. We are forever grateful to all our generous supporters.

Thank you.

ACKNOWLEDGMENTS

Neither Witness to Guantánamo nor *A Place Outside the Law* would have succeeded without the skilled contributions and thoughtful guidance from many friends and colleagues. I am very fortunate and honored. Thank you! In thanking people below, I have omitted those who have asked to remain anonymous. Some people belong in both groups. You know who you are.

For Witness to Guantánamo: Mary Louise Zernicke, Johnny Symons, Eva Moss, Laura Truffaut, Lee Ryan, Alaina Piland, Joe Hoffman (RIP), Angie Fitzsimons, Scott Handleman, Rushan Abbas, Stefani Pellinen-Chavez, Julie Nice, Richard Sakai, Susan Freiwald; Jeffrey Brand, Talia MacMath, Sebastian Letheule, the interpreters and translators, and the dedicated University of San Francisco law student researchers.

For *A Place Outside the Law*: Wendy Betts, Virginia Anderson, Gary Alexander, Adriana Puente, Rakia Clark, Felicia Eth, Diana Burden, Alan Levy, Lianne Voelm, Tristin Green, Steven Shatz, Lara Bazelon, Naomi Epel, Dorothy Wall, Susan Lumenello, John Shafer, Elizabeth Farnsworth, and Sam Farnsworth.

Thank you to the people who believed in the mission of Witness to Guantánamo and very generously supported our work through their foundations: the Sigrid Rausing Trust, the Anita Roddick Foundation, the Left Tilt Fund, Open Society Foundation, the Levinson Foundation, the Lynn Handleman Charitable Foundation, the Oak Foundation, the Body Shop Foundation, the Samuel Rubin Foundation, the Uplands Foundation, LEF Foundation, and the Jesuit Foundation.

And a special thank-you to Christopher Honigsberg, Liam Honigsberg, Colleen Honigsberg, Karlene Navarro, Nadia Alam, Tanner Wilcher, and their families.

NOTES

INTRODUCTION: WHEN THE PLANES HIT

1. Ed Vulliamy, "'Let's Roll …,'" *Guardian*, December 1, 2001, https://www
.theguardian.com/world/2001/dec/02/september11.terrorism1.

2. Sarah Larimer, "Three Firefighters Who Responded to Ground Zero Died
on the Same Day. They All Suffered from Cancer," *Washington Post*, September 26,
2014.

3. J. Freedom du Lac, "The Photo of the Doomed 9/11 'Dust Lady' Still Haunts
Us After All These Years," *Washington Post*, September 11, 2018. Her name was
Marcy Borders.

4. Lawrence Wright, *The Looming Tower: Al-Qaeda and the Road to 9/11* (New
York: Knopf, 2006), 365–67. Soufan also explained to Witness to Guantánamo how
he came to identify the hijackers.

5. Patrick E. Tyler, "A Nation Challenged: The Family; Fearing Harm, Bin Laden
Kin Fled from U.S.," *New York Times*, September 30, 2001.

6. 9/11 Commission, *Final Report of the National Commission on Terrorist
Attacks Upon the United States (The 9/11 Commission Report)* (Washington, DC:
July 2, 2004), 330, 557n28.

7. Cheney interview, NBC's *Meet the Press*, transcript, September 16, 2001.

8. US Department of Justice, Office of the Inspector General, *The September 11
Detainees: A Review of the Treatment of Aliens Held on Immigration Charges in Con-
nection with the Investigation of the September 11 Attacks*, no. 11 (June 2003).

9. Peter Jan Honigsberg, *Our Nation Unhinged: The Human Consequences of the
War on Terror* (Oakland: University of California Press, 2009), 63–70.

10. Honigsberg, *Our Nation Unhinged*, 63–70.

11. His remarks are available from the Office of the Press Secretary, White
House, September 17, 2001, https://georgewbushwhitehouse.archives.gov/news
/releases/2001/09/20010917-11.html.

12. Katharine Q. Seelye, "Threats and Responses: The Detainees; Some Guantánamo Prisoners Will Be Freed, Rumsfeld Says," *New York Times*, October 23, 2002.

13. In March 2019, military prosecutors revealed that they have tapes of
intercepted telephone calls between Khalid Sheikh Mohammed and three accused
coconspirators discussing the intended attacks months before 9/11. Carol Rosenberg, "U.S. Said to Have Tapes of Alleged 9/11 Mastermind Plotting with Co-
Conspirators," *New York Times*, March 25, 2019. Mohammed has refused to be

questioned as to what he does or does not know about Saudi Arabia's role in the 9/11 attacks, as long as his Guantánamo trial continues to have the death penalty on the table. Carol Rosenberg, "Lawyers Say 9/11 Confessions Given to FBI Are Tainted," *New York Times*, July 30, 2019.

14. "Guantánamo Periodic Review Guide," *Miami Herald*, updated March 23, 2018, https://www.miamiherald.com/news/nation-world/world/americas /guantanamo/article68333292.html; *Miami Herald* Staff, "Who's Still Held at Guantánamo," *Miami Herald*, August 24, 2016, https://www.miamiherald.com /news/nation-world/world/americas/guantanamo/article2203501.html.

PART I: A PLACE OUTSIDE THE LAW

1. Tom Wilner's case, *Al-Odah v. United States*, was joined with *Rasul v. Bush*.

2. Appendix I describes the administrative proceedings—known as Combatant Status Review Tribunals—and the various pieces of new legislation designed to replace or suspend habeas hearings.

CHAPTER 1: COMING TO AMERICA

1. Honigsberg, *Our Nation Unhinged*, 78–79.

2. "Guantanamo Inmates Say They Were 'Sold,'" AP, May 31, 2005, on NBCNews .com; Honigsberg, *Our Nation Unhinged*.

3. See Honigsberg, *Our Nation Unhinged*, 77–78.

4. Emile Nakhleh, CIA analyst, interview with Witness to Guantánamo in San Francisco, April 10, 2013.

5. *Uighur* is also sometimes spelled *Uyghur*.

6. Seelye, "Threats and Responses."

7. Mark Denbeaux and Joshua Denbeaux, "Report on Guantánamo Detainees: A Profile of 517 Detainees Through Analysis of Department of Defense Data," Seton Hall Public Law Research Paper No. 46, February, 2006, https://papers.ssrn .com/sol3/papers.cfm?abstract_id=885659; Bob Drogin, "No Leaders of Al Qaeda Found in Guantánamo Bay, Cuba," *Los Angeles Times*, August 18, 2002.

8. American officials believed, based on Johnson v. Eisentrager, 339 U.S. 763 (1950), a World War II–era Supreme Court decision, that detainees held offshore would not be entitled to the constitutional right of habeas to challenge their detentions in federal court.

9. Katharine Q. Seelye, "A Nation Challenged: The Detention Camp; U.S. to Hold Taliban Detainees in 'the Least Worst Place,'" *New York Times*, December 28, 2001.

10. "Agreement Between the United States and Cuba for the Lease of Lands for Coaling and Naval Stations; February 23, 1903," available at Avalon Project, Yale Law School, http://avalon.law.yale.edu/20th_century/dip_cuba002.asp, accessed May 21, 2019.

11. Honigsberg, *Our Nation Unhinged*, 76.

12. The third man from Tipton was Asif Iqbal.

13. Honigsberg, *Our Nation Unhinged*, 77.

CHAPTER 2: RIGHT SIDE OF THINGS

1. William Glaberson, "Red Cross Monitors Barred from Guantánamo," *New York Times*, November 16, 2007.

2. Memorandum from President George W. Bush to Vice President, Secretary of State, et al., on Humane Treatment of al Qaeda and Taliban Detainees (February 7, 2002), https://www.pegc.us/archive/White_House/bush_memo_20020207_ed.pdf.

3. *In re Diaz*, 288 P.3d 486, 490 (2012).

4. *In re Diaz*.

5. "Pentagon Hands Over List of All Guantánamo Bay Detainees at AP Request," Associated Press, May 16, 2006.

CHAPTER 3: CHINA'S SHADOW

1. John Pomfret, "China: Go West, Young Han," *Washington Post*, September 15, 2000.

2. Erick Eckholm, "U.S. Labeling of Group in China as Terrorist Is Criticized," *New York Times*, September 13, 2002.

3. Terrorist Exclusion List (TEL), Office of the Coordinator for Counterterrorism, US Department of State, Dec. 29, 2004 [citing to Section 411 of the USA PATRIOT ACT of 2001 (8 U.S.C. § 1182)], https://www.state.gov/j/ct/rls/other/des/123086.html.

4. Amy Gardner, "Candidates Cautious or Concerned About Possible Relocation of Detainees to Va.," *Washington Post*, May 15, 2009.

5. Gardner, "Candidates Cautious or Concerned About Possible Relocation of Detainees to Va."

6. In re Guantánamo Bay Detainee Litigation, 581 F. Supp. 2d 33 (D.D.C. 2008).

7. Kiyemba v. Obama, 555 F.3d 1022 (D.C. Cir. 2009).

8. Since 2014, Dostum has been vice president of Afghanistan.

9. See Honigsberg, *Our Nation Unhinged*, 197–214.

10. Paul Lewis, US Department of Defense special envoy for Guantánamo closure.

11. Denial of writ of certiorari, Kiyemba v. Obama, 130 S. Ct. 1880 (2010).

12. Nick Cumming-Bruce, "U.S. Steps Up Criticism of China for Detentions in Xinjiang," *New York Times*, March 13, 2019.

13. Nick Cumming-Bruce, "U.N. Panel Confronts China Over Reports That It Holds a Million Uighurs in Camps." See also Darren Byler, "China's Government Has Ordered a Million Citizens to Occupy Uighur Homes. Here's What They Think They're Doing," *China File*, October 24, 2018.

14. Chris Buckley and Paul Mozur, "How China Uses High-Tech Surveillance to Subdue Minorities," May 23, 2019, *New York Times*.

15. Edward Wong, "Uighur Americans Speak Against China's Internment Camps. Their Relatives Disappear," *New York Times*, October 18, 2018.

16. Carol Rosenberg, "Uighur Sent to Palau Not Missing After All," *Miami Herald*, February 20, 2013.

17. Alan Liotta, director, Office of Detainee Policy, US Department of Defense, confirmed that they had gone to Turkey.

18. Owain Johnston-Barnes, "Resettled Uighur Is Desperate for Work," *Royal Gazette*, October 2, 2012.

19. Post Staff Report, "Three Years After Gitmo, Uighur Prisoners in Paradise," *New York Post*, September 30, 2012.

20. Tom Leonard, "British Anger Over Bermuda Decision to Take Guantánamo Detainees," *Telegraph*, June 11, 2009.

21. Rushan Abbas to author, January 1, 2019.

22. Abbas to author.

23. Conversation with Rushan Abbas, March 6, 2019.

24. Conversation with Rushan Abbas, March 6, 2019.

25. "The Guantánamo Docket," *New York Times*, last updated May 2, 2018, https://www.nytimes.com/interactive/projects/guantanamo.

26. Meeting with president of Palau, Johnson Toribiong, January 6, 2010.

CHAPTER 4: LAWLESSNESS

1. Coalition of Clergy v. Bush, 189 F. Supp. 2d 1036 (C.D. Cal. 2002), filed Martin Luther King weekend, 2002.

2. UK resident Binyam Mohamed's case is very disturbing. When he was captured, the CIA flew him under its extraordinary rendition program to a Moroccan prison. The UK *Guardian* published extracts from his diary as to what happened after: "One of them took my penis in his hand and began to make cuts. He did it once, and they stood still for maybe a minute, watching my reaction. I was in agony. They must have done this 20 to 30 times, in maybe two hours. There was blood all over. . . . I suffered the razor treatment about once a month for the remaining time I was in Morocco, even after I'd agreed to confess to whatever they wanted to hear. It became like a routine." "One of Them Made Cuts to My Penis, I Was in Agony," *Guardian*, August 1, 2005. Binyam was released in 2009.

3. Ali v. Obama, 741 F. Supp. 2d 19 (D.C.C. 2011).

4. The six people who resigned or requested reassignment were Lieutenant Colonel Darrel Vandeveld, Colonel Morris Davis (chief prosecutor), Lieutenant Colonel Stuart Couch, Major Robert Preston, Captain John Carr, and Captain Carrie Wolf. Colonel Fred Borch (chief prosecutor) also resigned. However, he resigned because of criticism from others—he was not opposed to management of the cases. "Justice: Guantánamo Prosecutors vs. the System," *Newsweek*, May 17, 2008; see also "Guantánamo Prosecutor Steps Down," BBC News, September 25, 2008.

5. Omar Khadr's age at capture was confirmed by his civilian attorney, Dennis Edney, in an email to the author, May 13, 2019.

6. Anna Junker, "Judge Rules in Favour of Omar Khadr's Request to End Remaining Sentence," *Edmonton Journal*, March 25, 2019.

CHAPTER 5: UNDERMINING HEROES

1. Peter Finn, "At Guantánamo, Microphones Hidden in Attorney-Client Meeting Rooms," *Washington Post*, February 12, 2013.

2. See Honigsberg, *Our Nation Unhinged.*

3. Honigsberg, *Our Nation Unhinged.*

CHAPTER 6: FAUX LAW

1. In 2009 President Obama abandoned the term "enemy combatant," substituting language more consistent with the Geneva Conventions. Nevertheless, "enemy combatant" is still in the legal lexicon.

2. Memorandum from President George W. Bush to Vice President, Secretary of State, et al., on Humane Treatment of al Qaeda and Taliban Detainees. See also

note 8 below on Col. Manuel Supervielle's invitation to the International Committee of the Red Cross/Red Crescent to visit the base.

3. Ex parte Quirin, 317 U.S. 1 (1942).

4. *NewsHour with Jim Lehrer*, March 21, 2002.

CHAPTER 10: FLIGHT (I)

1. Honigsberg, *Our Nation Unhinged*, 179–93.

2. Email to author, March 10, 2016.

3. Associated Press, "US Army Sergeant Jailed for Life over Iraq Killings," *Guardian*, May 17, 2013.

CHAPTER 12: FROM PRIDE TO SHAME

1. Colonel Brittain Mallow, commander, Criminal Investigation Task Force, US Army. Mallow died in 2017.

2. Mallow.

3. Reprieve, *Briefing: Bagram Airbase Prison*, https://reprieve.org.uk/wp-content /uploads/2014/10/2009_08_14_Briefing_Bagram_conditions.doc, accessed May 21, 2019.

4. Reprieve, *Briefing: Bagram Airbase Prison*, 6–7.

5. Exceptions include Department of Defense, Naval Criminal Investigative Service, and the Office of Special Investigations of the Department of Justice.

6. Jim Clemente, FBI agent.

7. Mark Fallon, deputy commander of the Criminal Investigation Task Force; Clemente. Similar phrases, such as "fear up/down" and "pride/ego up/down," as well as information on developing rapport, appear in the 1992 US Army field manual and the 2006 manual, Department of the Army, Field Manual 34–52, Intelligence Interrogation (1992) at 3–12, 3–16, 3–18. Torin Nelson, a Guantánamo interrogator from fall 2002 to February 2003, explained in an article that these and other interview techniques were adopted by the military. Pratrap Chatterjee, *An Interrogator Speaks Out*, AlterNet, March 6, 2005. Nelson noted that Army manual FM 34–52 listed seventeen methods of interrogation, including "direct approach," "silence," "rapid fire," "pride and ego up," "pride and ego down," "fear up mild," and "fear up harsh."

8. Manuel Supervielle, US Army general counsel. Supervielle was the Southern Command Judge Advocate from 2000 to 2003. In early January 2002, Supervielle—believing in the importance of the rule of law and transparency—invited the International Committee of the Red Cross/Red Crescent (ICRC) to visit the base. The ICRC arrived a few days after the first group of detainees was transported to Guantánamo, on January 11, 2002. The ICRC visit did not go over well with administration officials. Less than one month later, on February 7, 2002, President Bush issued a memorandum declaring that the Geneva Conventions did not apply to al Qaeda and Taliban captives held in Guantánamo. The ICRC is the protector of the Geneva Conventions.

9. Inquiry into the Treatment of Detainees in US Custody, Report of the Committee on Armed Services, US Senate, November 20, 2008, 113.

10. Mark Fallon, deputy commander of the Criminal Investigation Task Force, confirmed: "At the time of 9/11, the number of people who you would consider al Qaeda probably range between two and four hundred."

11. General Court-Martial Order, 25 July 2006, Number 20.

12. General Court-Martial Order.

13. Ahmed al Darbi, deposition at Guantánamo Bay, Cuba, March 8, 2006.

14. Investigating Officer's Report of testimony of Jennifer N. Higginbotham, Appendix A, Charge 1, Specification 2, December 7, 2005, 21.

15. Higginbotham, 6.

16. Jamie Sterling, "Military Interrogator Pleads Guilty to Afghan Detainee Assault," JURIST, August 23, 2005; Holly Manges Jones, "US Interrogator Demoted for Assaulting Afghan Prisoner," JURIST, August 4, 2005; Tom Henry, "US Soldier Sentenced to 3 Months, Demoted in Afghan Assault," JURIST, May 23, 2005.

17. Tim Golden, "In U.S. Report, Brutal Details of 2 Afghan Inmates' Deaths," *New York Times*, May 20, 2005. Dilawar's murder was memorialized in the Academy Award-winning film *Taxi to the Dark Side*. Corsetti was not involved in the death of either man.

18. Golden, "In U.S. Report, Brutal Details of 2 Afghan Inmates' Deaths."

CHAPTER 13: PAYING RESPECT

1. Marion (Spike) Bowman, FBI senior executive service position.

2. Jim Clemente was one of countless Americans who placed our country ahead of their own lives. He was teaching a class at the FBI training center in Quantico, Virginia, when the towers fell. He immediately drove up to Ground Zero and spent five days digging for survivors. Later, he rejoined his unit working at the site where the Pentagon was hit, "digging and recovering body parts." Clemente was subsequently diagnosed with non-Hodgkin lymphoma. When the chemo treatment was not effective, he had an autologous stem cell/bone marrow transplant. "I'm still standing," he told us. Clemente has been certified as a World Trade Center victim in the World Trade Center Health Fund.

CHAPTER 14: FOR HIS SON

1. Steven Erlanger, "Terror Convictions Overturned in France," *New York Times*, February 24, 2009.

2. Mourad Benchellali, *Voyage vers l'enfer* (Paris: Editions Robert Laffont, 2006).

3. Erlanger, "Terror Convictions Overturned in France."

4. Perrine Mouterde, "Après Guantanamo, le combat de Mourad Benchellali pour faire entendre ses mots," *Le Monde*, February 27, 2016, updated March 16, 2016.

5. Action Resilience, "Our Charter," https://www.actionresilience.fr/en/our-charter, 2018.

6. Hénin told us that ISIS wanted to "mirror" Guantánamo. Their captors told them that they were living in a "model prison" and were "high-value detainees." Hénin was released April 2014. He did not know the terms of his release. Foley was murdered August 2014. US policy was to not negotiate with terrorists.

CHAPTER 15: GUANTÁNAMO SAVED MY LIFE

1. With the assistance of Julia Hall, Human Rights Watch senior legal counsel and later Amnesty International's expert on counterterrorism, Swedish human rights lawyer Sten de Geer, and American lawyer Sabin Willett.

2. Julia Hall.

CHAPTER 16: TIMMY
    1. The Guantanamo Docket, *New York Times*.

CHAPTER 17: HALF-FULL
    1. Abdul Aziz al-Swidi, brief phone interview, March 22, 2016.

CHAPTER 18: BEING UP CLOSE TO TORTURE
    1. Bryan Stevenson, *Just Mercy: A Story of Justice and Redemption* (New York: Spiegel & Grau, 2014), 288–89.
    2. Pardiss Kebriaei, email to author, December 4, 2017.

CHAPTER 19: THE EMPTY CHAIR
    1. Kuwaiti Fayez al Kandari was transferred home January 2016.
    2. Terry Hicks, email to author, February 8, 2016.
    3. Matt Apuzzo, "Guantánamo Conviction of Australian Is Overturned," *New York Times*, February 18, 2015.
    4. See Peter Jan Honigsberg, "In Search of a Forum for the Families of the Guantánamo Disappeared," *Denver University Law Review* 90 (2012): 433.
    5. United Nations, *International Convention for the Protection of All Persons from Enforced Disappearance*, December 20, 2006, part I, article 2, https://www.ohchr.org/Documents/ProfessionalInterest/disappearance-convention.pdf .
    6. Hamdan v. Rumsfeld, 548 U.S. 557 (2006).
    7. International Committee of the Red Cross, *Protocol Additional to the Geneva Conventions of 12 August 1949, and Relating to the Protection of Victims of International Armed Conflicts (Protocol I), of 8 June 1977*, https://www.icrc.org/en/doc/assets/files/other/icrc_002_0321.pdf.
    8. See Honigsberg, "In Search of a Forum."

CHAPTER 20: BLINDSIDED
    1. In his interview, Alberto Mora passionately commented, "If we can't lead on human rights, then we become another country."

CHAPTER 21: THE PAIN INSIDE
    1. Major General Michael Dunlavey, commander of US Army, Joint Task Force 170 (JTF 170) at Guantánamo February to November 2002, created the BSCT team. JTF 170 was the military interrogation unit at the camp. Dunlavey wanted the BSCT team of clinical and mental health professionals to assist in interrogations and torture of detainees. Mark Fallon, deputy commander of the Criminal Investigation Task Force, created a separate BSCT team of career behavioral scientists, medical specialists, and operational psychologist. Fallon's team did not participate in torture of prisoners. They consulted and assisted in rapport-based interrogations. Mark Fallon, email to author, January 2, 2018.
    2. Fallon.
    3. Neil Lewis, "Charges Dropped Against Chaplain," *New York Times*, March 20, 2004.
    4. Mohamedou Ould Slahi, *Guantánamo Diary* (New York: Little, Brown, 2015), 252–63.

5. Slahi, *Guantánamo Diary*, 254; US Department of Justice, Office of the Inspector General, *A Review of the FBI's Involvement in and Observations of Detainee Interrogations in Guantánamo Bay, Afghanistan, and Iraq*, May 2008, 122–23.

6. Ayub Mohammed, Abubakir Qasem, Rafiq Al Hami, and others. Qasem and Mohammed both interviewed in Tirana, Albania; Qasem, August 4, 2009; Mohammed, August 5, 2009. Al Hami interviewed in Tunis, Tunisia, July 18, 2012. Common Article 3(1)(c) of the Geneva Conventions. As noted later in this book, the Supreme Court held in *Hamdan v. Rumsfeld* that Common Article 3 of the Geneva Conventions applies to al Qaeda detainees in Guantánamo.

7. Confirmed in Slahi, *Guantánamo Diary*, 248–49. See also US Senate Committee on Armed Services, *Inquiry into the Treatment of Detainees in U.S. Custody*.

8. Jess Bravin, "'Imagine the Worst Possible Scenario': Why a Guantánamo Prosecutor Withdrew from the Case," *Atlantic*, February 11, 2013.

9. Damien Corsetti, Bagram interrogator.

10. The Supreme Court of Israel and the European Court of Human Rights (ECHR) found sleep deprivation constitutes torture or cruel, inhuman, or degrading treatment. HCJ 5100/94, The Public Committee against Torture in Israel v. The State of Israel, 53(4) PD 817, 845 (English translation provided by the Israel Ministry of Foreign Affairs beginning at p. 25 of *Judgements of the Israel Supreme Court: Fighting Terrorism within the Law*, available at https://perma.cc/MMD3-3XRB); ECHR, Case of Ireland v. the United Kingdom, Judgement of 18 January 1978 (No. 91), available at https://perma.cc/5DEU-3P4W.

11. Honigsberg, *Our Nation Unhinged*.

12. See Church Report (2005)—Review of DOD Detention Operation and Detainee Interrogation Techniques. Sleep deprivation appears under "prohibited techniques"; Schmidt-Furlow Report (2005)—Army investigation into allegations of abuse, including sleep deprivation. Sleep deprivation was approved December 2, 2002–January 15, 2003, and again after April 16, 2003; DOJ OIG Report (2008)—Sleep deprivation or disruption was the "single most reported interrogation technique."

13. Ben Fox, "Prisoner Tells of 'Mental Torture' in Secret Guantánamo Camp," *Washington Post*, June 3, 2016.

14. Adam Zagorin and Michael Duffy, "Inside the Interrogation of Detainee 063," *Time*, June 12, 2005; "Secret Orcon, Interrogation Log, Detainee 063," *Time*, June 20, 2005, www.time.com/time/2006/log/log.pdf.

15. Honigsberg, *Our Nation Unhinged*, 1.

16. Honigsberg, *Our Nation Unhinged*, 2–3.

17. Honigsberg, *Our Nation Unhinged*, 3.

18. Carol Rosenberg, "Guantánamo Prison: A Primer," *Miami Herald*, October 26, 2016.

19. Rosenberg, "Guantánamo Prison."

20. Pardiss Kebriaei, "Life After Guantánamo: A Father and Son's Story," *Harper's*, April 2015.

21. Examples: Michelle Shephard, *Guantanamo's Child: The Untold Story of Omar Khadr* (John Wiley & Sons Canada, 2008); Patrick Reed et al., *Guantanamo's Child: Omar Khadr*, White Pine Pictures (2015).

22. See Honigsberg, *Our Nation Unhinged*, 162.

23. Honigsberg, *Our Nation Unhinged*, 165.

24. Celia Perry, "Guantánamo's Dirty Secrets," *Mother Jones*, February 12, 2008.

25. Joseph Hickman, *Murder at Camp Delta: A Staff Sergeant's Pursuit of the Truth About Guantánamo Bay* (New York: Simon & Schuster, 2016); "The Guantánamo 'Suicides,'" *Harper's*, March 2010.

26. An example is described in chapter 16, "Timmy."

CHAPTER 22: ALONE

1. United Nations, *Interim Report of the Special Rapporteur of the Human Rights Council on Torture and Other Cruel, Inhuman or Degrading Treatment or Punishment*, G.A., U.N. Doc. A/66/268, ¶ 70 (2011). The report asserts that social isolation is contrary to article 10, paragraph 3, of the International Covenant on Civil and Political Rights, ¶ 76.

2. United Nations, *Interim Report*.

3. Transcript of Hearing, United States v. Jawad (Military Comm'n Guantanamo Bay, Cuba, August 13–14 (2008), available at https://archive.org/details/Jawad Transcript1314August.

4. See, e.g., Ayub Mohammed in Albania and Murat Kurnaz in Germany. Both learned English in Guantánamo.

5. Linguistic isolation is not limited to Guantánamo or to prisons. Refugees and immigrants held in detention centers may suffer linguistic isolation, although likely not for as long as Sunnat did.

6. See Peter Jan Honigsberg, "Linguistic Isolation: A Human Rights Violation Constituting Torture, and Cruel, Inhuman or Degrading Treatment," *Northwestern University Journal of International Human Rights* 12 (2014): 22.

7. Juan Mendez, United Nations special rapporteur on torture and other cruel, inhuman, or degrading treatment or punishment.

8. US Department of Justice, Federal Bureau of Prisons, *Program Statement: Special Housing Units*, no. 5270.11 (November 23, 2016).

9. Stuart Grassian, "Psychiatric Effects of Solitary Confinement," *Washington University Journal of Law and Policy* 22 (2006): 325, 328. See also Peter Scharff Smith, "The Effects of Solitary Confinement on Prison Inmates: A Brief History and Review of the Literature," *Crime and Justice* 34 (2006): 441, 456–57.

10. Grassian, "Psychiatric Effects of Solitary Confinement," 325, 328.

11. Hope Metcalf et al., "Administrative Segregation, Degrees of Isolation, and Incarceration: A National Overview of State and Federal Correction Policies," Yale Law School, Public Law Working Paper No. 301 (June 1, 2013), 1–2.

12. *The Istanbul Statement on the Use and Effects of Solitary Confinement*, International Psychological Trauma Symposium, Istanbul, December 9, 2007.

13. United Nations, *Interim Report*.

14. Candace Gorman, in Honigsberg, *Our Nation Unhinged*, 239.

15. See also United Nations, *Interim Report*, *supra* note 119 at ¶ 70, 76 [social isolation is contrary to article 10, paragraph 3, of the International Covenant on Civil and Political Rights].

16. The thirty-day period is a federal guideline. States have different reevaluation cycles. US Department of Justice, Federal Bureau of Prisons; Cal. Code Regs. tit. 15, § 3341.5(c)(2)(A)(1).

CHAPTER 23: WE TORTURED HIM

1. Roberta Rampton and Steve Holland, "Obama Says That After 9/11, 'We Tortured Some Folks,'" Reuters, August 1, 2014.

2. Honigsberg, *Our Nation Unhinged*, 179–93.

3. Dana Priest and Scott Higham, "At Guantánamo, a Prison Within a Prison," *Washington Post*, December 17, 2004.

4. Zagorin and Duffy, "Inside the Interrogation of Detainee 063."

5. Bob Woodward, "Guantánamo Detainee Was Tortured, Says Official Overseeing Military Trials," *Washington Post*, January 14, 2009.

6. Iacopino is author of the UN Istanbul Protocol, which sets out norms for investigation, documentation, and evaluation of physical and psychological evidence of torture.

7. See Honigsberg, *Our Nation Unhinged*, 25–29. Jamil Dakwar, Staff Attorney for the American Civil Liberties Union—who was born and raised in Israel and practiced as a human rights lawyer in Israel on behalf of Palestinian communities before coming to the US—noted that the US government also looked at the practices and legal arguments that Israel used to support torture and enhanced interrogation techniques, such as sleep deprivation and stress positions, and those used to support targeted killings.

8. Scott Shane, "2 U.S. Architects of Harsh Tactics in 9/11's Wake," *New York Times*, August 11, 2009; "Tortured by Psychologists and Doctors," editorial, *New York Times*, December 16, 2014.

9. Dana Priest, "CIA Holds Terror Suspects in Secret Prisons," *Washington Post*, November 2, 2005.

10. Carol Rosenberg, *Miami Herald*.

11. Adam Zagorin, "At Guantánamo, Dying Is Not Permitted," *Time*, June 30, 2006.

12. SOP for Medical Management of Detainees on Hunger Strike at Guantanamo, pg. 2; Jason Leopold, "Revised Guantanamo Force-Feed Exposed," Al Jazeera, May 13, 2013, https://www.aljazeera.com/humanrights/2013/05/201358152317954140.html.

13. Interviewee wishes to remain anonymous.

14. Albert Shimkus, naval hospital commanding officer until August 2003.

15. Dhiab v. Obama, 70 F. Supp. 3d 486 (D.C. Cir. 2014).

16. World Medical Association, World Medical Assembly Declaration of Malta on Hunger Strikers, originally November 1991; updated through October 2017.

17. Ron Meister, attorney.

18. Carol Rosenberg, "Navy Nurse Who Refused to Force-Feed at Guantánamo Keeps His Job," *Miami Herald*, May 13, 2015.

19. Defense Health Board, *Ethical Guidelines and Practices for U.S. Military Medical Professionals* (Falls Church, VA: Office of the Assistant Secretary of Defense, Health Affairs, 2015), https://apps.dtic.mil/dtic/tr/fulltext/u2/1027321.pdf.

20. Scott Allen et al., *Aiding Torture: Health Professionals' Ethics and Human Rights Violations Revealed in the May 2004 CIA Inspector General's Report* (Physicians for Human Rights, 2009).

21. Scott Roehm, John Bradshaw, Sarah Dougherty, Phyllis Kaufman, and Michael Payne, *Deprivation and Despair: The Crisis of Medical Care at Guantánamo*

(St. Paul, MN: Center for Victims of Torture/Physicians for Human Rights, 2019), https://www.cvt.org/DeprivationandDespair.

22. Algerian Djamel Ameziane to lawyer J. Wells Dixon, August 31, 2017.

23. Brahim Benchakroun of Morocco and Nizar Sassi of France both told us this.

24. Djamel Ameziane, email to author, September 5, 2017.

CHAPTER 24: CASTAWAYS

1. Claire Ward, "Former Guantánamo Detainee Dies in Kazakhstan," Vice News, May 21, 2015.

2. Connie Bruck, "Why Obama Has Failed to Close Guantánamo," *New Yorker*, August 1, 2016. Al Sawah told us further details about his situation in Camp Echo but asked that we turn off the camera.

3. Colonel Morris Davis, chief prosecutor.

4. See, e.g., Somini Sengupta, "Yemen Mediator Optimistic as Humanitarian Crisis Worsens," *New York Times*, June 19, 2015.

5. Mark Mazzetti and William Glaberson, "Obama Issues Directive to Shut Down Guantánamo," *New York Times*, January 21, 2009.

6. Daniel Fried, special envoy for Guantánamo closure, Department of State, Washington, DC, April 16, 2013.

7. Fried.

8. Fried.

9. Clint Williamson, ambassador-at-large for war crimes.

10. Marian Blasberg, "New Lives in Uruguay: Freedom Elusive After 12 Years at Guantánamo," *Der Spiegel* online, May 21, 2015, https://www.spiegel.de/international/world/former-detainees-discover-life-after-guantanamo-in-uruguay-a -1033992.html.

11. Paul Lewis.

12. Communication from anonymous source to author.

13. See, e.g., Ward, "Former Guantánamo Detainee Dies in Kazakhstan."

14. Ward, "Former Guantánamo Detainee Dies in Kazakhstan."

15. Paul Lewis.

16. Polly Rossdale, director, Reprieve—Life After Guantánamo Project.

17. Carol Rosenberg, "The U.S. Lost Track of Some Freed Gitmo Inmates," *Miami Herald*, November 13, 2018.

18. Ward, "Former Guantánamo Detainee Dies in Kazakhstan."

19. Columbia Law School Human Rights Institute, *Promises to Keep: Diplomatic Assurances Against Torture in US Terrorism Transfers* (December 2010).

20. Tim Johnson, "2 Former Guantánamo Detainees Have Left El Salvador," McClatchyDC.com, September 26, 2013, https://www.mcclatchydc.com/news /nation-world/world/article24756010.html. Clint Williamson interview was July 29, 2013, in Brussels.

21. Lee Wolosky, US special envoy for Guantánamo closure.

22. Katherine Taylor, coordinator, Reprieve—Life After Guantánamo Project.

23. See, e.g., Uighur Abdul Ghappar Abdul Rahman.

24. See, e.g., Uighur Abubakir Qasem.

25. Sangeeta Dhami and Aziz Sheikh, "The Muslim Family: Predicament and Promise," *Western Journal of Medicine* 173 (2000): 352, 356.

26. Taylor.

27. Katherine Taylor, telephone call, June 2, 2015.

28. Carol Rosenberg, "Captive Who Wouldn't Leave Guantánamo Decided at Door to Europe-Bound Plane," *Miami Herald*, February 11, 2016.

29. Carol Rosenberg, "Saudi Arabia Accepts 4 Guantánamo Captives; Prison Now Holds 55," *Miami Herald*, January 5, 2017.

30. Maria Abi-Habib, "After Guantánamo, Freed Detainees Returned to Violence in Syria Battlefields," *Wall Street Journal*, June 3, 2014; Moroccan detainees Souleimane Laalami Mohamed and Brahim Benchakroun.

31. "Counseling Helps 2,950 Extremists Mend Ways," Arab News, February 28, 2015, http://www.arabnews.com/saudi-arabia/news/711386.

32. Taylor Luck, "Returning Jihadis: At Luxurious Rehab Center, a Saudi Cure for Extremism," *Christian Science Monitor*, May 17, 2015.

33. Christopher Beam, "Jihadis Anonymous," *Slate*, January 23, 2009, https://slate.com/news-and-politics/2009/01/what-happens-in-terrorist-rehab.html.

34. Beam, "Jihadis Anonymous."

35. Luck, "Returning Jihadis."

36. "David Hicks: Former Guantánamo Bay Detainee, Foreign Fighter, Author," ABC News, January 22, 2015.

37. Jenifer Fenton, "Gitmo Military Court Conviction Reversed for Australian National," Al Jazeera America, February 18, 2015.

38. Interview with Manfred Nowak, UN Special Rapporteur on Torture.

39. Vandeveld added that, although he believes the story, he has no independent verification.

40. Boumediene v. Bush, 555 US 723 (2008).

41. "2 Guantánamo Detainees Send [*sic*] Home to Algeria Despite Resistance," *Washington Post*, December 5, 2013.

42. J. Wells Dixon, email to author, May 29, 2018.

43. Mark Denbeaux confirmed.

CHAPTER 25: DRONES

1. New York Times Co. v. U.S. Dept. of Justice, Appellants Motion Seeking Documents under FOIA, 0:2013cv00422, ECF No. 229; available on PACER and at https://perma.cc/BAK6-TEMV.

2. *New York Times Co. v. U.S. Dept. of Justice*. See also "Lawfulness of a Lethal Operation Directed Against a U.S. Citizen Who Is a Senior Operational Leader of Al-Qa'ida or an Associated Force," Department of Justice White Paper, February 5, 2013, https://archive.org/details/566484-020413-doj-white-paper.

CHAPTER 26: RISING ABOVE

1. Special FBI agent Ali Soufan said similar words to us: "Even in our darkest moments we have people in the United States who believe in what America is all about, stood up for the right thing, did the right thing, and did not care about the consequences. And America is a better place because of the actions of these individuals."

2. Memorandum from President George W. Bush to Vice President, Secretary of State, et al., on Humane Treatment of al Qaeda and Taliban Detainees.

3. The Military Commissions Act (MCA) was prompted by the 2006 Supreme Court *Hamdan* decision. The case held that the Geneva Conventions applied to Guantánamo and that the military commissions created by President Bush in November 2001 were unconstitutional. Congress created new military commissions under the MCA. See Appendix I.

4. Military Commissions Act of 2006, 28 U.S.C. § 2241 (e)(2), (the MCA), Sec 7(a).

5. 18 USC Sec. 2441, amended 2006.

6. Torture Victim Protection Act of 1991, 102 Pub.L. No. 256, §2(a) 106 Stat. 73, (1992).

7. Harbury v. Hayden, 444 F. Supp. 2d 19, 41 (D.D.C. 2006).

8. See Jawad v. Gates, 113 F. Supp. 3d 251 (D.D.C. 2015); affirmed, 832 F.3d 364 (D.C. Cir. 2016).

9. Jay Bybee, memorandum for Alberto R. Gonzales, *Re: Standards of Conduct for Interrogation under 18 U.S. C. Secs. 2340–2340A* (Aug. 1, 2002); John Yoo, memorandum for William J. Haynes II, *Re: Military Interrogation of Alien Unlawful Combatants Held Outside The United States* (March 14, 2003).

10. Yoo, memorandum for William J. Haynes II.

11. Padilla v. Yoo, 678 F.3d 748 (9th Cir. 2012).

12. *Rasul v. Myers*; in accord Al Bahlul v. United States, 767 F.3d 1 (D.C. Cir. 2014); Ali v. Rumsfeld 649 F.3d 762 (D.C. Cir. 2011).

13. Bivens v. Six Unknown Named Agents, 456 F.2d 1339 (1972).

14. See Ziglar v. Abbasi, 137 S. Ct. 1843, 1860 (2017).

15. Esmail v. Obama, 639 F.3d 1075 (2011).

16. See, e.g., *Rasul v. Myers*; in accord *Al Bahlul*.

17. Priscilla B. Hayner, *Unspeakable Truths: Transitional Justice and the Challenge of Truth Commissions* (New York: Routledge, 2001), 21.

18. See, e.g., Ta-Nehisi Coates, "The Case for Reparations," *Atlantic*, June 2004.

19. Justice John Paul Stevens, *Reflections About The Sovereign's Duty to Compensate Victims Harmed by Constitutional Violations*, Lawyers for Civil Justice Membership Meeting, May 4, 2015.

20. Nick Assinder, "Gitmo Inmates Settlement: Why Britain Decided to Pay," *Time*, November 18, 2010.

21. Honigsberg, *Our Nation Unhinged*, 188–90.

22. "Europe Court Award for Rendition Victim Khaled al-Masri," BBC News, December 13, 2012.

APPENDIX I: TIMELINE

1. Siobhán O'Grady, "State Department Offers $1 Million for Information on Osama bin Laden's Son," *Washington Post*, March 1, 2019.

2. Martin Chulov, "Hamza bin Laden Has Married Daughter of Lead 9/11 Hijacker, Say Family," *Guardian*, August 5, 2018.

3. "Guantánamo Periodic Review Guide," *Miami Herald*, updated March 23, 2018, https://www.miamiherald.com/news/nation-world/world/americas /guantanamo/article68333292.html; Miami Herald Staff, "Who's Still Held at Guantánamo," Miami Herald, August 24, 2016, https://www.miamiherald.com /news/nation-world/world/americas/guantanamo/article2203501.html.

4. Carol Rosenberg, "Congress Weighs Whether to Allow Guantánamo Prisoners to Travel to the U.S. for Medical Care," *New York Times*, May 31, 2019.

5. Charlie Savage and Carol Rosenberg, "Justice Breyer Raises the Specter of Perpetual Detention Without Trial at Guantánamo," *New York Times*, June 9, 2019.

APPENDIX II: REFLECTIONS AND EVOLUTION OF WITNESS TO GUANTÁNAMO

1. In his interview, Wilkerson also said that "the greatest crime that [Secretary of Defense] Donald Rumsfeld and [Vice President] Dick Cheney and their minions performed during the first Bush administration . . . [was] blessing those who participated [in the abuse and torture] and cursing those who stood up against it."

2. Email to author August 9, 2010.

INDEX

ABOUT THE AUTHOR

Peter Jan Honigsberg is a professor at the University of San Francisco School of Law and the founder and director of Witness to Guantánamo. His research and teaching focuses on the rule of law and human rights violations that occurred in the detention center at Guantánamo, as well as on the study of terrorism, national security, and post-9/11 issues. His work has been reviewed in the *New Yorker* and the *Economist*. Honigsberg's pieces have appeared in the *Washington Post* and the *Huffington Post*, and he has given presentations to the United Nations Human Rights Council in Geneva, Switzerland. His books include *Our Nation Unhinged: The Human Consequences of the War on Terror* and *Crossing Border Street: A Civil Rights Memoir*. He lives in Berkeley, California.